Exploring Individual and Organizational Boundaries

WILEY SERIES ON
INDIVIDUALS, GROUPS AND ORGANIZATIONS

Series Editor
Cary Cooper,
Department of Management Sciences,
University of Manchester Institute of
  Science & Technology,
Manchester

Associate Editor
Eric J. Miller,

Tavistock Institute of
  Human Relations,
London

Exploring Individual and Organizational Boundaries

A Tavistock Open Systems Approach

Edited by

W. Gordon Lawrence

Tavistock Institute of Human Relations
Tavistock Centre, London, England

JOHN WILEY & SONS

Chichester · New York · Brisbane · Toronto

Library of Congress Cataloging in Publication Data:
Main entry under title:

Exploring individual and organizational boundaries.

   (Wiley series on individuals, groups, and organiza-
tions)
   Bibliography: p.
   Includes index.
   1. Group relations training.   2. Small groups.
3. Organizational behavior.   I. Lawrence, W. Gordon.
II. Tavistock Institute of Human Relations, London.
HM134.E97   301.18'5   78–8603

ISBN 0 471 99679 3

Photosetting by Thomson Press (India) Limited, New Delhi
and printed in Great Britain at the Pitman Press, Bath

Acknowledgements

James P. Gustafson
'The pseudomutual small group or institution' first appeared in *Human Relations*, **29**, No. 10, 1976. It is reproduced by permission of the Tavistock Institute of Human Relations and Plenum Press.

Edward B. Klein
A shorter version of 'Manifestations of transference in small training groups' entitled 'Transference in training groups' appeared in, and is reproduced by permission of, *Journal of Personality and Social Systems*, **1**, no. 1, 1977.

Margaret J. Rioch
'The A. K. Rice group relations conferences as a reflection of society' first appeared in, and is reproduced by special permission from, *The Journal of Personality and Social Systems*, **1**, no. 1, April 1977. Copyrighted by the A. K. Rice Institute.

David L. Singer, Boris M. Astrachan, Laurence J. Gould, Edward B. Klein
'Boundary management in psychological work with groups' first appeared in, *Journal of Applied Behavioral Science*, **11**, no. 2, 1975.

Contributors

W. GORDON LAWRENCE,
MA
Editor

Consultant, and Joint Director of The Group Relations Training Programme, Tavistock Institute of Human Relations.

BORIS M. ASTRACHAN,
MD

Professor of Clinical Psychiatry, Yale University School of Medicine; Director, Connecticut Mental Health Centre.

JOHN BROADBENT,
MA, PhD

Professor of English Literature, University of East Anglia.

ROBERT H. GOSLING, MD,
FRCPsych., DPM

Chairman, Professional Committee of the Tavistock Clinic; Consultant, Tavistock Institute of Human Relations.

LAURENCE J. GOULD,
PhD

Associate Professor and Director of the Clinical Psychology Doctoral Training Program, City College of the City University of New York; President, A. K. Rice Institute, Washington.

DENNIS GUERECA, BA

Industrial Relations Adviser, Central Personnel Department, Tube Investments Limited.

JAMES P. GUSTAFSON, MD

Assistant Professor of Psychiatry, University of Wisconsin.

EDWARD B. KLEIN, PhD

Professor of Psychology and Psychiatry; Director of Clinical Training, Department of Psychology, University of Cincinnati; Board Member, A. K. Rice Institute.

ROBERT H. KLEIN, PhD

Associate Professor of Clinical Psychiatry, University of Pittsburgh School of Medicine.

ERIC J. MILLER, MA, PhD

Consultant, and Joint Director of The Group Relations Training Programme, Tavistock Institute of Human Relations.

JAMES C. MILLER, PhD — *Professor and Director, Clinical Training Program, George Washington University.*

BARRY W. M. PALMER, MA — *Senior Consultant, Grubb Institute of Behavioural Studies.*

MARGARET J. RIOCH, PhD — *Professor Emeritus of Psychology, American University; Clinical Professor, Department of Psychiatry (Psychology), Georgetown University School of Medicine; Member, Executive Council, Washington School of Psychiatry; Board Member, A. K. Rice Institute.*

ROGER L. SHAPIRO, MD — *Professor, Department of Psychiatry and Behavioral Sciences, George Washington University School of Medicine.*

DAVID L. SINGER, PhD — *Chairperson, Department of Professional Psychology, Antioch/New England Graduate School; Board Member, A. K. Rice Institute.*

SUSAN TAYLOR, MARCIA BOGDANOFF, DANIELLE BROWN, LINDA HILLMAN, CHERYL KURASH, JULIE SPAN, BARBARA THACHER, LISSA WEINSTEIN — *Susan Taylor is a doctoral candidate in clinical psychology at the City University of New York, and a predoctoral psychology fellow in the Department of Psychiatry, Yale University School of Medicine. The other authors of 'By women, for women' are also advanced students in graduate and undergraduate programmes in psychology at the City University of New York.*

JOHN ZINNER, MD — *Section on Personality Development, Adult Psychiatry Branch, National Institute of Mental Health, Bethesda.*

Contents

Editorial Foreword to the Series

Over the last decade, there has been an enormous growth of interest in the social and psychological aspects of institutional and organizational life. This has been reflected in a substantial upsurge in research and training in the field of organizational behaviour particularly in Institutes of Higher Education and Research throughout the Western World. Attention in this development has focused on the interrelationship between the individual, the variety of groups to which he belongs and the organizational environment within which he and his group operate.

The purpose of this series is to examine the social and psychological processes of these interrelationships, that is the nexus of individual/personal development, group processes and organizational behaviour and change. Within this context, a wide range of topics will be covered. These will include: the individual, his role and the organization; multiple roles and role conflict; the impact of group processes on personal and organizational development; strategies for 'humanizing' the organizational environment to meet individual and group needs; and the influence of technical and economic factors on organizational life.

The series will attempt to draw together the main schools of organizational behaviour including, for example, the American behavioural science tradition as reflected by Harvard, UCLA and National Training Laboratories, and the British socio-technical and open systems approaches of the Tavistock Institute of Human Relations. It is hoped that this will add significantly to understanding the distinctive characteristics of the various approaches and also provide a link between them through which individual, group and organizational behaviour can be seen in fuller perspective.

CARY COOPER
ERIC MILLER

Preface

Pierre Maurice Turquet, MA, MRCS, LRCP, FRCPsych.
(1913–1975)

This volume is dedicated to the memory of Pierre Turquet, who was killed in a car accident in France on 27 December 1975, at the age of 62. In planning the volume, which subsequently has been a long time in the making, it was felt that the invited papers ought to report any new shifts in thinking about group relations training as developed and practised around the ideas of W. R. Bion by A. K. Rice and his colleagues at the Tavistock Institute of Human Relations. The wish of the editor was for a volume of papers that would be associative and reflective of experiences around group relations training, as opposed to a somewhat more didactic text.

The principal reason for this policy was inextricably bound up with the editor's experiences of Pierre Turquet in working with him in group relations training and as a member of the same unit within the Tavistock Institute. It has to be said that this relationship between the two was not always a calm one and could, at times, be very angry. But there was always a worked-through rapprochement. To work with Pierre Turquet was essentially to move into an educational adventure. It is the idea of adventure that needs to be held on to in retrospect. There might be discomfort, even pain, often amusement, but always learning.

When surrounded by a set of sympathetic colleagues on the staff of a group relations conference, Pierre Turquet would lead them into new problem areas. When colleagues were less sympathetic to the primary task he would somewhat more contumaciously attack what he thought were the problems. By doing this he stretched the capability of his colleagues to experience and interpret group and institutional phenomena and so, quite directly, enhanced their ability to take risks in leading themselves, in the roles of consultants, into the conscious and unconscious issues of group and institutional life. Thus members of working conferences were also led into issues so that they, too, could find their authority to explore and name phenomena for themselves.

Turquet's ability to ratiocinate about the larger issues of group relations training often was best demonstrated at the midday staff meetings during the working conferences of which he was director. Quite explicitly at times he would lead the staff outside the immediate 'skin' of the conference to consider particular institutions of which staff members had experience—universities and schools, the health services, prisons, the churches, for example. The boundary between a conference as a system and other institutions as systems he always saw as an open one. The relatedness between and among institutions would lead into a questioning of the state of contemporary societies in the world. At times he could be monstrously wrong in his judgements, but then that did not matter quite so much to him as the fact that he had led into a discussion by attempting to relate what might be happening within the boundary of a conference across that boundary into what might be happening in the environment of institutions and societies.

From these discussions psychoanalysis was never far absent but neither was classic literature, both English and European, nor the social sciences, nor contemporary politics. It was on such a large canvas that he worked. And art was one of his many interests. Those of his colleagues who could not engage on all these dimensions sometimes were left feeling angry or unwanted. But for others he pointed to new realms. He awakened in some the wish to come to grips with their cultural heritage and relate it to contemporary society in order to illuminate what C. Wright Mills (1970 edn) has called the 'private troubles and public issues' of our times.

An indication of the size of canvas Pierre Turquet could work on can be illustrated by an experience in Ireland. There he was acting as a consultant on a working conference on group behaviour in institutions, entitled 'Leadership and Authority', organized by the Grubb Institute and the Tavistock Institute of Human Relations. He was excited about the possibilities offered by this conference and he was committed to its success because representatives were present of various Irish political parties, the predominant religions, and various interest groups from the whole of Ireland. He suggested that the conference was timely because Ireland was being given the problems of the world to solve on its behalf. In his view, South Africa had failed to take the opportunity to make a creative purchase on the issues of intergroup relations, but now Ireland was being given the chance to interpret its experiences of the problems and to provide an innovative solution that might provide a tentative model for other countries experiencing intergroup problems. It became clear in subsequent conversations that he was viewing the world as a massive group and as such subject to irrational and unconscious social and psychological forces but, nevertheless, able, albeit unconsciously, to give authority to particular nations. To report his thought thus is, however, to oversimplify because clearly he was holding in his mind some conception of the world and its large-scale social phenomena that was beyond the ken of others.

Turquet wrote a great deal even though he published sparingly. He kept notes on all his work and reading. Now, after his death, it is possible to realize why he could bring such sustained enthusiasm to his work in the field of group relations training. In the background, he was continually adumbrating ideas, relating his experiences to his wide-ranging reading.

As is well enough known, it was the 'large group' that was Turquet's particular interest and his unique *metier* was as a consultant to large groups. He and the late A. K. Rice were the first consultants to take a large group which was introduced to a working conference at Leicester in 1964. His conceptualization of what were, at the time, incomprehensible forces present in large configurations of people, numbering between 40 and 80, are substantial. Turquet's two papers, 'Leadership: the individual and the group' and 'Threats to identity in the large group' (Turquet, 1974; 1975), are likely to stand the test of time.

What Pierre Turquet brought to bear on group relations training, then, was a passionate search for what might be the truth of phenomena and processes in the large group, the small group, between groups, and between institutions. To aid him in his chosen task he could call on a wide range of cultures with their literature and art, together with psychoanalytic thinking as well as other social sciences, but essentially it was his lived experience that enriched so much of his work in group relations training.

The writer only knew Turquet in the last few years of his life and so had to search out the facts from his wife and family and professional colleagues. Born in London in 1913, Turquet attended Westminster School from 1927 to 1932, and Trinity College, Cambridge, for the next four years. Although a College Prizeman in English and History, he graduated in the Natural Sciences. Immediately he followed this with attendance at the London Hospital Medical School and qualified as a medical practitioner in 1939. At one point earlier he considered entering the library service, but he opted for medicine. This choice may well have reflected his preoccupation with the human predicament. That he was able to hold the world of scholarship and the human predicament in some creative tension was evinced in the largeness of the view he brought to bear on his professional work.

Turquet first became interested in group phenomena while concerned with the selection of officers (War Office Selection Boards). He was a member of the original team which instituted this procedure and so would have had contact with those who subsequently were to found the Tavistock Institute of Human Relations in 1946. Later in the war he was seconded to special selection duties and work in the Psychological Warfare Section on enemy and allied morale. His career in the Royal Army Medical Corps ended in 1946, but for just over a year before that he had been seconded to the French War Office to help organize their Selection Services for the French Army, Navy, and Air Forces.

After the war, Turquet worked in the field of psychiatry. Subsequently he was employed in the Social Medicine Research Unit, the Medical Research Council, concentrating on the intrapersonal and interfamily relations of young people suffering with duodenal ulcers, until he joined the Tavistock Clinic in 1952 as a consultant psychiatrist.

Turquet's interest in group phenomena was, as his colleague Dr Robert Gosling pointed out in his memoir delivered at Turquet's memorial service, 'not however as an academic observer or participant, but always as a deeply committed participant, a stance that was further refined by his psycho-analytic training. In these matters he was chiefly influenced by Herbert Rosenfeld, Wilfred Bion, Melanie Klein, Michael and Enid Balint and A. K. Rice' (Gosling, 1976). His passion for understanding the overt and unconscious processes at work in groups meant that he deployed himself in a wide range of activities (in addition to his National Health Service work) to ensure that all kinds of colleagues in the helping professions became more familiar with group processes because he believed that such understanding would enrich people's experiences of themselves and their work.

Within the frame of the Tavistock Clinic he worked for the Adult Department and the School of Family and Community Psychiatry. In these departments he was engaged in psychotherapy and in the advanced training of general practitioners, probation officers, social workers, health visitors, and physiotherapists. With the Tavistock Institute he was among those who helped to establish the Institute of Marital Studies, which was formerly the Family Discussion Bureau. In 1962 he also became a part-time consultant in the then Centre for Applied Social Research of the institute. This seemed appropriate given his involvement in the Group Relations Training Programme of that unit since 1957. Here amply demonstrated was Turquet's capacity to work across institutional boundaries and he remains one of a very small band of people in the Tavistock Centre who have wanted and been able to do so.

To new ventures he would give his unstinting support. He had been a consultant for the Grubb Institute of Behavioural Studies since 1965, and he was the first consultant to the Chelmsford Cathedral Centre for Research and Training established in 1969 by Canon R. W. Herrick. For a number of years he annually travelled to America and Canada to take part as a staff member in the working conferences of the A. K. Rice Institute in Washington, DC, and the Rosehill Institute of Human Relations in Toronto.

It can be seen that publication was an activity on which Turquet placed little value. His thrust was always towards experiencing, discovering, and articulating his thoughts. In some ways we, his colleagues, are all the beneficiaries. If he had published more, much of our understanding of group phenomena might have been captured. As it is, he gave us his energy through talking and arguing, causing us to explore for ourselves—which is the greatest of gifts he could possibly give, and which he constantly offered to those who participated in any group, small or large, which he took as a consultant.

In the last two months or so of his life he was full of sadness* at the human condition. He was angry about the National Health Service, with which he was disillusioned. He felt passionately that the Tavistock Clinic, with which he had been associated for just under half his life, had failed to move psychoanalysis from its essentially dyadic preoccupations to become a cultural tool, which he, along with others, had tried to do within the frame of group relations training. And he, at times, would despair at the inability of men and women in contemporary society to question the authority structures and organizations of their institutions; to get behind the easily understood and taken-for-granted assumptions of group and institutional living. This had been his elected task which consumed much of his energy for much of his life.

*This is a personal observation of the editor based on his conversations with P.M.T.

In preparing this volume, which has been part of the process of mourning for Pierre Turquet, I am immensely thankful to the contributors who each have attempted to put into words experiences that are difficult to describe: the conscious and unconscious processes that take place in groups. To my colleague Eric Miller, who is joint director of the Group Relations Training Programme with me, I am indebted for his continuing professional support. It has been, however, on Rita Friend, another colleague, that much of the burden of getting this book ready has rested. To her I am grateful.

W. G. L.

References

Gosling, R. H. (1976) 'A memoir presented at a service of thanksgiving for the life of Pierre Turquet'. Hampstead Parish Church, 4 February 1976.

Mills, C. Wright (1970 edn) *The Sociological Imagination*. Harmondsworth. Penguin Books.

Turquet, P. M. (1974) 'Leadership: The individual and the group'. In G. S. Gibbard, J. J. Hartman, and R. D. Mann (eds) *Analysis of Groups*. San Francisco: Jossey-Bass.

Turquet, P. M. (1975) 'Threats to identity in the large group'. In L. Kreeger (ed.) *The Large Group: Therapy and Dynamics*. London: Constable.

Chapter 1

Introductory Essay: Exploring Boundaries

W. Gordon Lawrence

A Tavistock Model of group relations training

This collection of papers has been brought together to convey some of the current thinking of those involved in the kind of group relations training which was developed within the Tavistock Institute of Human Relations and is now conducted by its Group Relations Training Programme. Since the beginnings in 1957 when the first conference was held in conjunction with Leicester University, and which is described by E. L. Trist and C. Sofer in *Exploration in Group Relations* (1959), there have been a number of institutional developments. Within the Tavistock Institute a group of people led by the late Dr A. K. Rice, and principally supported by Mrs I. E. P. Menzies Lyth together with Drs P. M. Turquet, R. H. Gosling, and E. J. Miller, pressed forward the particular version of group relations training with which this volume is concerned.

Between the first conference and those under the directorship of A. K. Rice there occurred a critical division among those scientific workers of the Tavistock involved in group relations training. At the first conference the events were Study Groups and Application Groups. The former were designed to give participants experiences of the dynamics of small groups and the latter to explore how the learning could be applied in real-life situations. It was realized that while this design gave participants opportunities to become intensely aware of the destructive and creative processes of the unconscious in Study Groups there was a gap between such experiences and the world of work. Hence, H. Bridger introduced the Inter-Group Exercise at the second conference which was held at Buxton in 1959 (Higgin and Bridger, 1965). Bridger's version of the Inter-Group Exercise provide participants with opportunities to form their own groups for the purpose of deciding on a programme of special interest sessions which would occupy the second half of the timetable for the conference. This event had a *double* task: the study of group processes in relation to a particular project. A. K. Rice and his colleagues, however, believed that the educational objectives of conference would be better realized if events had a *single* task, i.e. if the task of the event was framed in such a way that the existential nature of the event was preeminently available for study by all the participants. To have a double task for an event would mean that the exploration of the 'here and now' processes, which undoubtedly

1

raise anxieties, could be defended against by participants. Thus the phenomenal stuff of unconscious group phenomena would be lost.

Since the time of Rice's directorship (from 1962 till his death in 1969) of this programme in the Tavistock, the conferences have had the title 'Authority, Leadership, and Organization', or some variation on that. The focus of these conferences is on the exercise of responsibility and authority, and therefore of leadership and followership, in interpersonal and intergroup settings. This is a minimal statement because these concepts relate to others such as management and organization. Because the word 'authority' occurs in the title, there is often the fantasy that they are 'authoritarian'. Be that as it may, what needs to be stated at the outset is that the concern of these Tavistock conferences is about the political relatedness of the individual through his roles to his groups, institutions, and the larger society.

Other institutions have been founded to develop not only this version of group relations training but also related consultancy and action research activities. Because of the institutional seeding it has been convenient to refer to this version of group relations training as the Tavistock Model. It has, however, been taken on and developed by people who have founded institutions and is now, therefore, not just located in the Tavistock. In America there is the A. K. Rice Institute in Washington, DC, with six regional centres and affiliated institutions such as GREX in San Francisco and the Institute of Applied Study of Social Systems in New York. In Canada, the Rosehill Institute of Human Relations also mounts working conferences and continues to develop as an institution for consultancy. In Britain there are the Grubb Institute; the Scottish Institute of Human Relations; the Chelmsford Cathedral Centre for Research and Training; and the Centre for the Study of Group and Institutional Relations based in Bristol University. In addition, there have been a number of individuals who have introduced this version of group relations training into business and educational institutions.

The term 'Tavistock Model' refers to a heuristic framework for identifying and understanding what conscious and unconscious processes take place within and between groups of people. Its use, however, is both accurate and misleading. It is accurate in the sense that it has its beginnings in the Tavistock Institute and is still being developed there. It is misleading in two senses. First, the tradition is now located in a number of institutions and so 'Tavistock' becomes a common identifying tag. Second, the tradition is a living one and is continually being reinterpreted by institutions in the light of changing circumstances in the environment; so the term 'model' needs to be explored. The notion of a 'model' can imply some 'thing'—a reification—which is fixed and stable. Here the usage of the word 'model' implies a tradition with identifiable, experiential, and intellectual roots that is being reinterpreted and reworked by representatives of different institutions. These differences are not to be obliterated but celebrated; one institution's thinking can inform other institutions. Predictably, technical leadership will move among the different institutions depending on how well their representatives are experiencing and interpreting across the boundary of their institutions. Somewhat ambivalently, therefore, I propose to refer to the version of group relations training which this book explores as the Tavistock Model. The reluctance, I hope, is understandable. Nevertheless I believe that the heuristic concepts used by the institutions to which I have referred above are identifiable and their shared usage ought to be acknowledged.

All these institutions are not founded merely for the task of providing group relations training. As in the Tavistock, the training has to be seen as complementary to other action research and consultancy projects. Hence, there is a good deal of interpenetration of ideas, values, and concepts from the research field to conferences and vice versa. Working conferences use such concepts as open-systems thinking about the organization of enterprises. The first text in this area was Rice's *Productivity and Social Organization* (1958). Other books have taken this idea, among others, about organizations further. There is *Systems of Organization* by Miller and Rice (1967) and, as a companion volume in this series of John Wiley & Sons, Miller's *Task and Organization* (1976). Action research studies which have taken such thinking further, and which rely on the heuristic concepts of the model, have been Richardson's (1973) *The Teacher, the School and the task of Management*; Miller and Gwynne's (1972) *A Life Apart*; and an earlier text by Rice (1970), *The Modern University*.

The editorial policy for this volume has been to try to open up thinking about the Tavistock Model rather than to see it as a closed system of ideas which need only to be elaborated. Although it is a somewhat extravagant notion, the volume with its papers can be seen as a metaphor of the working conferences it explores. The papers, which are interpretive, are akin to the contribution of a staff in a working conference. The role of the editor, like a director of a conference, has been to set these alongside each other holding in mind their relevance for environmental issues and problems.

This volume also has to be situated in relation to other books and pamphlets which have set out this Tavistock Model of group relations training. Of these W. R. Bion's *Experiences in Groups* (1961) stands preeminent because it elaborates the working hypotheses and methodology on which this model is founded. To radically alter this method would be to establish a different model. Subsequently, in 1965, A. K. Rice published his *Learning for Leadership* in which he meticulously described the working conferences in interpersonal and intergroup relations that had developed from Bion's ideas. Having set out the basic concepts and described the structure, culture, and activities of the conferences by using an open-systems analysis, Rice pulled together much of the key thinking about working conferences. There have been no major radical shifts since then. The most recent text is the *Group Relations Reader* (1975) edited by Arthur D. Colman and W. Harold Bexton. The merit of this last text is that it makes available the best of the published material up to that date on the theory, method, and application of the Tavistock Model of group relations training. The important point, in respect of this volume, is that because others have done the basic work of explicating the conceptual, methodological, and central values of the model as exemplified through working conferences, writers for this volume have been freed to be associative and to take thinking further. Nevertheless, I want to describe aspects of this training in order to provide a context for the contributions that follow.

Aspects of working conferences

Working conferences for group relations training are usually residential and can last from a weekend to a fortnight. They are temporary education institutions and can be seen as open systems taking in members who have an interest in understanding issues of authority. The staff of a conference have two subroles: that of collective management and that of consultants. As management they provide conditions for members to learn, and in their consultant role they interpret what is taking place from this role perspective. Essentially, they manage a process which is to study group behaviour. This process is the transforming of feelings and ideas about authority into new ones. Hopefully, members will export themselves back into their institutions with fresh insights. The conference process is open-ended in the sense that the staff do not determine what members and they will learn. Experiences are provided through activities and consultants attempt to interpret the experiences of these events as they occur. Hence, it does happen that some insight will emerge in a conference of which neither staff nor members were aware before.

Working conferences have a primary task. Among the most recent statements of task for these has been the following: 'To provide members with opportunities to find sanction within themselves to experience and interpret the nature of authority and the interpersonal, intergroup and institutional problems encountered in its exercise within the Conference Institution.' The primary task is determined by the dominant import–transformation–export process which is to study group behaviour. It is upon this task that the design of the conference and the role of staff is based. What members choose to do is on their authority.

'Living methodology'

The more I think about conferences the more I am inclined to say that they are designed to provide opportunities for members to internalize and make for themselves a 'living methodology' for inspecting the conscious and unconscious realities of groups and institutions and the political relatedness (authority, management, and organization) of individuals in roles within these configurations. 'Living methodology' is a cumbersome term but it carries the idea of the individual using his subjectivity and sensibility to explore realities, forming working hypotheses about the realities as he construes them, and testing the hypotheses with others as a way of arriving at some externalized, objective statement about the truth of the social situation as it is perceived from the role of member.

If we accept that what Kant called the *noumenon*, the thing in itself, is only known through phenomena and that we are only in a position to guess 'that corresponding to these phenomena, which are something that we know about because they are us, is the thing itself, the *noumenon*' (Bion, 1974), notions about an education in a living methodology may become somewhat clearer. It is living in the sense that it is based on the individual testing his changing constructions and perceptions of his social world as an ongoing process. The method uses subjectivity but in the process takes into account the state of the person as an instrument. So it is just not a matter of perceiving but also of personally inquiring into how one arrived at a particular perception. Something of what is involved has been captured by one writer:

In a paradoxical way, then, objectivity requires the cultivation of specific subjective states, the disciplining of attention and selected habits of thought, the screening out of other sources of consciousness, control over emotions, and a commitment to private and public honesty, to care and precision, to technical statement and social cooperation. Objectivity is a highly selective, highly developed subjective state. (Novak, 1971)

What all this points to is that reality is not something exclusively 'out there', that there is not a domain of order outside of the individual which merely has to be discovered, but that the individual is a bearer of that reality. Reality is both inside and outside of him. Furthermore, it is his construction of the phenomena of reality that is to be investigated. Ultimate reality, which can be referred to by such terms as 'absolute truth, the god-head, the infinite, the thing in itself' (Bion, 1974), does not fall into the domain of knowledge. Ultimate reality can only be in a state of 'becoming'; it cannot be known. And it is this idea of 'becoming' that is to be held on to when thinking about modes of inquiring into social processes in groups and institutions. The 'becoming' enables us not to fall into the traps of either solipsism or positivism but to engage with the creative tensions among what people believe to be realities and fantasies.

The role of the consultant

The pressing forward of this methodology is initially in the hands of the consultants. What follows is certainly not a prescription but my thoughts around this role. First, the relatedness between the consultant and a group is one focus of study. The consultant interprets from his role perspective. Whether that is perceived and experienced as having more power than that of the members is open to examination. He interprets and formulates working hypotheses about the social processes, conscious and otherwise, that he understands to be present in the group. Transference phenomena are part of the data. But he is part of that configuration in the room even though he is not in the group and is not in the role of a member. If he becomes a member, his function is lost which is sedulously to pursue the primary task. Yet the data from which the interpretation is derived are his experience of being pulled into membership on the one hand and extruded into limbo on the other.

Second, I sometimes explain to myself that the task of a consultant is a maieutic one in that he is helping members to realize their interpretations of the situation; in short, to exercise their authority to test realities. Clearly, the role is not didactic in the conventional sense but is to puzzle out from a role perspective what social phenomena are present in the situation, to form hypotheses, and to further learning. It is fashionable in educational settings to talk about raising the level of consciousness. This educational context includes just that, but it also provides a model, through behaviour, of how one gets in touch with unconsciousness. This is part of the conditions that the consultant provides to enable members to undertake these tasks for themselves. Just as for the work group leader who is in touch with the primary task, there will be continual attempts to seduce the consultant into a membership role and preferably one which satisfies the primitive wishes of the members. But if this happens transference and countertransference feelings will be removed from the situation and the aim of understanding the nature of authority will disappear.

There is, third, a necessity that the consultant leads the group in a work fashion into problem areas for himself in his role in relation to the members with whom he is working. At the same time he needs to understand for himself the experience of containment, the ability to allow the members to 'be' in their terms. The boundary between these two is always puzzling, just as are the limits of certainty and uncertainty, chaos and order, which are all personally defined.

Fourth, the consultant is working with his subjectivity and attempting to use himself as an instrument in the situation. The internal disentangling of what is being projected into the consultant and what is already there, having been introjected from his own past experiences, is a continual private task for the consultant. He needs to be able to work out, for example, how much uncertainty he owns and how much he is projecting on to the group when he leads into new areas of exploration by offering hypotheses. It is for this reason among others that those who have directed the Group Relations Training Programme in the Tavistock have always undergone a personal psychoanalysis at least, and attempt to recruit staffs for working conferences who will have psychoanalytic skills in their midst. To do otherwise is, to my mind, irresponsible.

Fifth, the consultant frames working hypotheses and interpretations on the basis of his experience in the role. These two terms are used interchangeably though it would be better if only the former was used. A working hypothesis is the social science equivalent of an interpretation which I tend to see as being a more appropriate tool for explicating interpersonal relationships.

The working hypothesis is a sketch of the reality of a situation to be either elaborated or erased and replaced by another sketch. The working hypothesis is always an approximation; valid and reliable at a particular point in time of the relationship between members of a grouping in a conference and the consultant or consultants. Reality, as I have said earlier, is construed subjectively. In the course of his personal development the individual has established a set of assumptions as to what constitutes reality and has organized his behaviour in relation to collective definitions of that reality. These assumptions and recipes for conduct give meaning to the individual's life. As important, they give some protection from fear and uncertainty and so 'even personal attempts to recognise and reconsider such deeply-rooted assumptions arouse anxiety and resistance' (Wilson, 1951). A working hypothesis, therefore, must always be directed at the space between the members and the consultant, not directed at a particular member. If it is in the space between, so to speak, the member's freedom to work or not with the hypothesis is preserved. Then he knows that what he decides is on his authority.

Dr Pierre Turquet in his lectures has a particularly useful passage on what he refers to as the interpretation. (Here let me acknowledge my gratitude to Dr Gustav Schulman for letting me see his notes on Pierre Turquet's lectures to the Advanced Training Group held in the Tavistock.)

The Interpretation
It creates usually a healthy pause where thinking and examining takes place. The interpretation has put people in touch with the here and now and releases certain phenomena that happen in the pause. Often members speak individually and closer to the task after an interpretation.

The interpretation has a certain content. So has the pause. It is important to observe closely the fact of the content of the interpretation. This gives usually clear information to the leader of what forces are in operation in the group and in the members. In the work group situation the content of the interpretation is clearly used for further efforts to tackle the task. The content of the pause that emerges after the interpretation should show this.

Turquet also pointed to the necessity for providing evidence for an interpretation; what he called the 'because clause'.

The 'because clause' in the interpretation is very important because it is (a) 'out of time' and emphasises a long span of time of the group life, and (b) it gets at the repetition compulsions of the members of the group since it reveals the past and the motives operating which were, before the interpretation, out of touch with the here and now. The past, so to say, has to be differentiated from the here and now so that unrealistic historical motives can be given up. It is also the way and method whereby the interpreter is exposing his own sense of reality and his understanding of what is going on at any moment. Thus he also, as it were, tests his own sense of reality. Often new ideas flow into the here and now after the 'because clause' has been mentioned. The 'because clause' in the interpretation differentiates the past motives from the present and thus, as it were, cuts off the repetition compulsion where the individual tries to repeat past history. When the leader takes this historical motive into the current reality he exposes it and can release the group to work more accurately on the actual task without the past interfering.

Ideally, members can internalize this mode of working and exercise their authority to interpret on the basis of their experience.

Events of a conference

These experiences are possible through participation in a range of activities each of which will have a primary task. Usually there are two events which are concerned with the study of experience in the 'here and now' within different sizes of groups. There is the *small (or study) group* which has nine to twelve members with one consultant, and the *large group* which is composed of the total membership, which may number between 35 and 40 upwards, with three or four consultants. Both these events are designed to enable authority and relationships to be studied and they focus on intragroup relations.

It is around the small group that the thinking that has now come to be associated with the Tavistock Model was first developed by Wilfred Bion. Apart from his own writings (1961), and the account of his thought by Greenberg and others (1975), there are numerous other accounts of which the most useful is that of Rioch (1970). Wilfred Bion was an early worker at the Tavistock and he not only emphasized the notion of groups being seen as wholes but detected other dimensions: the unconscious processes.

His hypotheses about small groups have provided a set of heuristic notions for understanding what takes place in groups. Bion was able to see that in any one group there are simultaneously present two groups; the *work group* and the *basic assumption group*. The former functions like a mature ego does. Its members operate by testing out realities through making hypotheses and exploring them. Such a group tries to discover and work on increased understanding of external realities in relation to the internal world of the group. Its members have the ability to stop and think, question the life of the group, make suggestions, allow free association and make hypotheses. Such a group nurtures the skills of its members and recognizes their differences in a realistic fashion. It is a group which is not fixed to roles or to a structure or to past history or to an exclusive future orientation. Such a group can change according to the changing circumstances of the environment.

The work group has to be contrasted with the basic assumption group which is the unconscious group; the group which operates on certain unspoken assumptions. Bion identified the *basic assumption dependency group* (BaD), the *basic assumption pairing group* (BaP), and the *basic assumption fight/flight group* (BaF/F). None of these groups exist in a pure form as does the Work Group but Bion's descriptions provide us with benchmarks to understand the unconscious reality of groups. A BaD group operates on the assumption that, or 'as if', it is met to be dependent on one leader who is experienced as omnipotent and omniscient in contrast to other participants who feel the opposite. The leader is made into a kind of god. A BaF group is one of action and the role of the leader is to mobilize fight or flight in order to preserve the group. The mood is one of paranoia and all such feelings have to be projected out of the group. The third kind of basic assumption group, BaP, is one in which the mood is that of expectancy and hopefulness and so two members will be paired, irrespective of gender, to bring forth a Saviour or Messiah.

This can be a leader, an idea, or some version of utopia. Predictably, the messianic wish must never be fulfilled otherwise the feeling of hope is lost.

Any group of up to twelve participants, Bion hypothesized, will oscillate among these various kinds of groups (Work, BaD, BaF and BaP). A mature group will be able to mobilize and use these group cultures for the pursuance of work. Indeed one set of basic assumptions keeps at bay the feelings associated with the other two. Whether the goals and activities of the work group are being modified negatively or not by the basic group is always an open question.

This thinking around the small group has had the qualities of an architectonic paradigm for considering other group activities. The tendency very often is, however, to utilize Bion's thinking about small groups in relation to other group events which is to press interpretations of their unique phenomena back into a small group mould of thinking.

One proposition can help us do this: Bion's hypotheses are essentially about the myths on which groups of people operate. There is always in any group a conflict between the individual and the group. If we allow notions about individuals and groups being open systems, this conflict can become a positive way of testing realities in a changing environment. It is, however, not experienced as this very often. Rather the individual is seen to be a closed system and the group is felt to be a closed system. In such situations the fear of the individual is of being lost in the group. This can be described as the conflict between narcissism and socialism. As an attempt to solve this experienced problem, myths are created. The purpose of the myth seems to be to unite the aim of the individual with that of the group so as to bind them together in such a way that what is understood to be destructive conflict will be prevented. In small groups of up to twelve people the typical myths are the basic assumption myths. In larger groups different myths will be present. In general, the cultural language of myths is expressions of the forces which unite the group and contribute to the feeling of oneness between the individual and the group—a systemless world with no boundaries. In such a culture there will be resistance against naming the myth because the fear is that the unity of the group, with its attendant feelings of closeness and intimacy, will be destroyed. The fear is that if the myth is elucidated it will take away the basic security of the group.

It is the shared myth, usually unspoken, which binds the group members together. This is, of course, an illusory togetherness which can be seen when the myth is interpreted. This creates a feeling of disillusionment and the individuals never like it. The elucidation of the myth is difficult because it is usually unconscious and strongly clung to as common property. The elucidation causes a feeling of loss but frees the individual from illusory togetherness. This is the reason why an accurate interpretation of the myth can create a situation where members begin to speak individually. The basic assumption group tries to create myths and gather around these, in contrast to the work group which tries to find unity around the task definition. The basic assumption group has a myth-producing atmosphere. There is the myth of Oedipus, myth of rumour, myth of sacrifice, myth of blissfulness and oneness, myth of marriage, myth of Robinson Crusoe, just to mention some of the usual ones. The Robinson Crusoe myth is about omnipotency where the members feel that they are in control and command of the whole environment and nature. Usually there is an atmosphere of exploitation and control where everything is done for the members' own benefit or the group's own benefit without thinking about the others. It is some sort of group selfishness where the outside bodies, or even members in the group, can be treated like things or possessions. (To my mind this is the counterpart of narcissism in groups, group narcissism or group self-centredness. There is no sense of concern or ability to feel depression. Even apparently loving and good comments or deeds are done because of a selfish motive.)

Myths are created due to the basic assumption wishes for altogetherness and easy life. They are kept away by accurate task definition, developing skills, reality testing, realistic notions of time boundary, realistic perception of external reality; in short by vigorous and vigilant work group leadership. When these fail, myths are generated to focus on the internal life of the group, as a flight from the outside reality which demands work and faces the individual with pain. The harder or the more frustrating the outside reality or the task, the greater is the need to turn exclusively into the internal life.

I think, also, that group life, irrespective of the size of the grouping, is organized around defences against the anxieties of uncertainty and chaos which, in turn, produces myths. When an individual member joins a group for the first time it triggers off in his memory models of his own past behaviour patterns and experiences in similar situations. There is a search for familiar models and familiar situations. There is, therefore, always a possibility that the here and now experience will be determined by past experience. The past represents something familiar, tangible, controllable, and secure. It provides a good opportunity to escape from the uncertainties of the moment. In basic assumption groups this happens especially.

I think that this is one of the essential elements of the mythologies of groups. An individual who is in touch with, or holds inside himself, a conception of primary task will be very much involved in the here and now, but will be trying to relate it realistically to the past and the future as he experiences it. He will start from the experience of the moment in its terms, and work at its relatedness to the past and the future as opposed to construing the moment, in the here and now, in their terms.

The large group

Myths are preeminently available for study in the large group. Until fairly recently the primary experience in a working conference has been felt to be that of the small, or study, group. This is, I think, because Bion's hypotheses best fit that situation. Increasingly, however, there has been a shift towards making the large group the primary experience by, for example, giving it first place on the programme each day. This is for two reasons. First that the large group, and its immediate related activity, the median group, are recent, post-Bion discoveries. A. K. Rice and P. M. Turquet were the first to consult to a large group. Subsequently, Turquet developed what thinking there has been around this complex event. His two papers, 'Leadership: The individual and the group' (1974) and 'Threats to identity in the large group' (1975), stand alone as the only sustained efforts to explore and explicate the phenomena of large groups.

The second reason why the large group experience is being made more salient is that it is an event which provides members with opportunities to study what I have called the crowd that lies behind the organization of every large-scale system or enterprise. I am becoming increasingly preoccupied with large group phenomena because it is possible to hear, with the 'third ear', what is taking place in the wider society. The large group is a frame for catching what is unconsciously taking place in the society at large even though that is not the stated preoccupation nor is life in society the topic of discussion. It is here that we see the narcissism of individuals struggling with a phenomenon which is experienced as being akin to 'society'. It is here, for example, that we experience the two related myths that society is unknowable and that only the individual is knowable.

The large group is usually the total membership working with three or four consultants. It is, at times, 'hell' realized, be it of total order or buzzing chaos or nothingness. It is the situation which can be seen as somewhere between that of the small group with its inevitable emphasis on interpersonal relationships—no matter how hard the consultant attempts to focus on role relationships and authority—and other events which can more readily be conceptualized in political terms.

There are two experiential events which focus on intergroup relations: the intergroup event and the institutional event.

The intergroup event

In a working conference the composition of small groups and large groups is determined by the staff in their management subrole. In the intergroup event representatives of the staff meet with the membership in a plenary session to outline the task, time, and territorial boundaries of the event. The aim is to provide opportunities for members to experience the forming of groups of their own choice and exercising authority on behalf of others through re-presentative roles. The primary task is to study relationships between groups as they occur. Consultants are available to help the groups in their task.

It is this event which sharpens up the focus on political relationships both within and between groups of members. In particular this is because staff are not present only in their consultant subrole and not as management. To emphasize the absence of management usually the director of the conference opens the event and then withdraws. Members can then project into the situation their internal conceptualizations of management. It is a situation in which the member in order to manage has to call entirely upon his own inner objectifications of what he believes is the process of management. This is termed 'management in the mind'. How the members manage the process of studying relationships between groups will be a function of this 'management in the mind'. There is no external object, no Other as management, on which to project. The consultants' task is to help explicate the different notions of 'management in the mind' as a way of pointing to what authority is being exercised by members. The intergroup event is often seen as a necessary preliminary to the major political event of the conference: the institutional event.

The institutional event

In this event there are two major groupings: staff and members. Members are free to form subgroups of their own choice. Management can either divide into a management subgroup and a consultant subgroup or stay as a staff group or management. Even if they stay as one group they carry the two subroles.

As in the intergroup event task, time, and territorial boundaries are specified. These, as in the former event, are for the convenience of staff; what members choose to do is on their authority. The focus is on the political relatedness of members and staff, and the task is to study what conscious and unconscious relationships are present or do not exist between them. It is in this context that the concept of 'institution in the mind' comes into play. Both members and staff are relating politically to their perceptions of and visions for the institution within whose frame the action is taking place.

All these events have a *single* task which is to study behaviour in the event as it happens in the here and now. A study group has the primary task of studying the relatedness in the group as it happens, the intergroup event has the task of studying relationships between groups as they occur. The group and intergroup behaviour is the focus of study. This has to be compared with events which have a *double* task, for example to form a group to make, say, a learning institution and then to study the group processes by which decisions were made. This Tavistock Model concerns itself exclusively with single-task events because group processes are then available for existential study without other factors being present which can be used as a defence against the anxieties of examining what processes take place at an unconscious level in group settings.

*Review and application groups, orientation groups,
and role analysis groups*

I describe these four together because they essentially serve the same functions: to enable a member to consider his role within the conference as an institution and to consider what learning is appropriate to his back-home situation. All these events can be seen as providing spaces in the time of the programme for the member to consider his relatedness to the conference as an institution, as a paradigm of his relatedness in outside systems.

The conference is an open system taking in members who wish to consider issues of authority in relation to their work and other organizations. In crossing the boundaries of the conference it is important that opportunities be provided for members to consider what is relevant in taking up the role of member as opposed to merely attending a conference. Similarly, as members move towards the output boundary, they ought to have an opportunity to reflect on what is involved in taking up their outside role again. All these events can be seen as being between the inner experiential skin of the conference and the outer organizational one. They are designed to enable members to consider what authority they have in relation to various internal and external realities.

Conference plenaries

There are normally at least two conference plenaries. They are events in themselves. The opening plenary sets the task and administrative boundaries of the conference and points the membership towards the experiential events that are being made available.

The final plenary (or plenaries) is designed to provide opportunities for ending work relationships between members and staff without applying closure to the learning of the conference. It is important to understand that the 'product' of a conference is a 'process'; what has been called a living methodology.

In this outline I have not attempted to describe in any detail what takes place in a conference and its events. Even if I had the ability, I would never capture their complexity of behaviour. A conference is there to be experienced and whatever I might say about experience would be mine and would not be the same as another person's. Nevertheless, there are some aims and principles which would be shared by those organizing and staffing these conferences.

Aims and principles

I can do no better in this introduction than selectively quote from what is usually stated in the brochures describing a conference. A working conference

is based on the belief that men and women can work more effectively, with greater satisfaction and, possibly, create organization of their choice if they come to understand in a direct and personal way the dynamics of groups and inter-group processes within social systems. The overall interest of the Conference Institution is in the functioning of groups as wholes and not in the personality factors of individual members: the latter are for the private scrutiny of each member. The processes, both manifest and covert, of groups and social systems can best be understood when they are seen in actual operation. The Conference, therefore, offers an opportunity to examine what happens within, among and between groups; to work in the 'here and now' of experience as it occurs.

Such aspects of organisational life as task, authority and role are examined in the

Conference Institution. There are opportunities to become aware of discrepancies between the stated primary task of a group and the task it actually appears to be pursuing; to discover what differences there may be in perceptions of authority and management and what are the conscious and unconscious sanctions for exercising responsible leadership and followership. Such roles and others may not always be officially designated but can be invoked by groups for quite other purposes than the pursuance of the primary task. But these are all open to examination.

In the work of the Institution the concept of boundary is important. Leadership (which may not always be invested in a designated leader) is conceived in terms of managing a boundary between what is inside and what is outside—for example, boundaries between group and organisation, organisation and environment. The Institution affords opportunities for examining the nature and meaning of such boundaries, including experience of the member–staff boundary in a variety of settings. Within this framework, members may also explore such related boundaries as those between the individual's inner and outer worlds, person and role, individual and group, leader and followers, group and institution, institution and environment. In this context authority is vested in and accepted by individuals and groups to manage transactions across these boundaries.

The Institution is open-ended in the sense that there is no attempt to prescribe what anyone will learn. This educational approach, therefore, with its focus on learning from the here and now of experience, implies that what each member learns is unique. It is on his or her own authority that each member accepts what is valid and rejects what is not. Through this process members may become better equipped to reconsider the exercise of their authority in institutions which exist in an uncertain environment.

The more I think about working conferences which use the Tavistock Model, the more I am convinced that they will lose their value if the focus shifts from authority and political relatedness. There is a continual pressure on staffs in their consultant roles to explore only interpersonal relationships. The concern has to continue to be the exploration and explication of the real and fantasied relatedness of the individual in his roles to his groups, institutions, and society: that is his political responsibility and authority.

Because this is an uncomfortable concern I suspect that a number of socially structured arrangements are established by people providing group relations training to defend themselves against the anxieties that such a concern arouses. These defences can resonate with the feelings held by participants who sometimes see themselves as consumers of experiences which must be 'good' and free of any psychic pain or anxiety. So all collude to avoid the challenges of the joint educational venture they could make.

The principal seduction I have already referred to: group relations training is reduced to interpersonal skill work as if the conscious and unconscious political processes and issues of contemporary institutions in societies could be smoothed away if people would meet people as people without any differences of sex, age, race, creed, political affiliations, and indeed authority and power.

Because industrial societies engender social passivity in their citizens by creating and fulfilling the wish for dependency on the State there are dangers that group relations training can resonate with the wish for basic assumption dependency. There can be a collusion on the part of consultants to bring about this dependency and create 'patients' of participants. This, in turn, unquestioningly defines the role of the consultant. Nothing is problematic. We can expect a mirroring of aspects of society in group situations, but if they are merely reinforced they cannot be interpreted. So such a group situation becomes a socialization exercise and does not allow for any internalization of a methodology for questioning the *status quo* of the group setting that, in turn, could provide a model of how the participants could start to question the *status quo* of their outside institutions. The other feature of the kind of group activity I am indicating is that social or public issues are neatly converted into individual or private troubles.

There is a good deal spoken about self-actualization in group relations training. The reason for the popularity of the notion of self-actualization is, I suspect, that its promise resonates with the narcissistic preoccupations with which so many people find themselves engaged. If self-actualization becomes an end in itself—a product—it is likely that the means employed to attain that end will bring about quite unintended outcomes. Such a self-ish search could be quite irresponsible in that it denies the freedom of others. Self-actualization can be understood as a process; a journey with no terminus. Victor Frankl starts from the idea of responsibility in relation to one's actual life situation, and maintains that 'man can only actualize himself to the extent to which he fulfils meaning. Then self-actualization occurs spontaneously; it is contravened when it is made an end in itself' (Frankl, 1964). In another context Frankl has stated his perception of the issues: 'By declaring that man is a responsible creature and must actualize the potential meaning of his life, I wish to stress that true meaning of life is to be found in the world rather than with man and his own psyche, as though it were a closed system' (Frankl, 1967).

The only gloss to be made to this formulation is to suggest that the individual is to be seen as an open system in various states of relatedness to other open systems in his social world. It is this notion of open systems interacting with open systems that needs to be held on to because it allows for the possibility of conflict as a social process. There is always a wish for some kind of homeostatic relationship—a perfect equilibrium between the individual and his society. This needs to be turned on its head, so to speak, and perhaps conflict—with both its destructive and constructive aspects—could be mobilized as a social process to forge new meanings as a basis for cooperation between the individual and his groupings.

To tie all this somewhat more together. My postulate is that group relations training is about exploring the responsibility and authority of the individual in relation to his social environments: the choices the individual has to face if he wants to feel in, of, with, for, or against his social groups and the institutions of his society. I think this comes down to the meaning he places on his relatedness to institutions. It is a matter of inspecting the taken-for-granted connection between the individual and society. Increasingly, it seems to me that the inspection of the subjective apperceptions of groups and institutions— distinguishing what is believed to be knowable from the unknowable; the naming of the experience of the society 'in the mind', as a way of externalizing, objectifying, the meaning the individual puts upon himself, his social world and its relationships—is the proper preoccupation of group relations training.

Exploring boundaries

The theme of the volume is boundaries and their exploration. As Kurt Back has demonstrated in his account of sensitivity training and the encounter movement, *Beyond Words*, such versions of group relations training have de-emphasized boundaries and as such have reflected a trend in American society which has been apparent in other industrial societies. In particular, this trend 'has been to decrease the importance of certain social categories, such as race, social status, class background, and more recently even the biologically determined categories of sex and age' (Back, 1973). Furthermore, he rightly points out that such a trend coupled with the high valuation placed on the individual and his relationships is characteristic of millenarian movements in societies. Millenarian movements have wish-fulfilment as their underlying psychological mechanism and are created 'to deal with unsatisfying reality' (Toch, 1966). That people in societies through their social institutions and other social arrangements experience unsatisfying realities has been documented at least from the beginnings of sociology as a discipline of thought. That, therefore, people have a wish to be reborn in another reality is understandable. Since industrial societies are characterized by impersonality in social relations, by the experience of alienation at work and even in the family, for example, it is quite comprehensible that there will be an unconscious, and often quite conscious, wish to create new social groupings that will be satisfying and transcend all other groupings. The point is that such millenarian movements have to offer 'extreme hope for a quick solution of all problems' (Back, 1973).

By contrast the Tavistock Model has always recognized that boundaries are necessary, but must be always open to inspection. Boundaries are necessary in order for human beings to relate not only to each other but through their institutions. If there are no boundaries, relatedness and relationships are impossible because we become one; lost in each other, lost in institutions, lost in societies. At the same time it is readily recognized that boundaries can be used and experienced as impregnable barriers. Both the wish for no boundaries and the desire to remain totally imprisoned within a boundary are expressions of 'madness' in that there is no desire to distinguish between fantasy and reality; to take authority for what one perceives, how one sees, and why one understands.

In editing the volume I have decided not to make the usual division into parts—this is because such boundaries would have been imposed but also because each paper could stand in its own right as a bounded piece of writing. In other words, each paper is a system of ideas and collectively they show a kind of complementarity.

All the papers have the theme of boundaries. David Singer and his colleagues' paper, 'Boundary management in psychological work with groups', adumbrates a typology of group events which enables the model to be set in a wider context. Margaret Rioch's paper relates the content of working conferences to the wider issues of society, i.e. works across the boundary of conferences as institutions.

James Gustafson's contribution, 'The pseudomutual small group or institution', has been set alongside Robert Gosling's 'Another source of conservatism in groups' because they both explore defensive systems in groups. They take us up against the boundaries of anxiety, which are less tangible boundaries than the ones that have been described in the earlier papers.

Similarly, Edward Klein's 'Manifestations of transference in small training groups' explores a little-known set of boundaries, those between the members of a small group and the consultant. He also makes comparisons with other training events and thus elucidates something of the boundary around the Tavistock Model.

As has been said, within conferences there are small groups, large groups (cf. Turquet, 1974, 1975), intergroup events (see Rioch in this volume; Astrachan and Flynn, 1976) and an institutional event. Little has been written about this last event and so it is with some interest that Dannis Guereca's paper, 'A manager's view of the institutional event', is included. He writes from his experience both as a consultant on group relations training conferences and as a practising businessman who has a management role in a large enterprise.

One recent development in group relations training has been the conferences on male and female relations in working groups. The boundary between male and female is often obliterated, and certainly authority is often based on and used through sexuality by individuals and groups. A contribution by Laurence Gould, 'Men and women at work: A group relations conference in person and role', explores this area of boundary management. Another paper, 'By women, for women', is a description of a group relations conference which was totally female. This has been written by Susan Taylor and her colleagues.

The boundaries between different kinds of group exploration are written about by Robert Klein in his essay, 'A model for distinguishing supportive from insight-oriented psychotherapy groups'. Since the Tavistock Model has one of its roots embedded in psychoanalysis, what he has to say may help to clarify the boundaries within which version of group relations training is contained.

Another set of boundaries are between different open systems such as the individual, the family, and wider groupings in society. Roger Shapiro and John Zinner in their paper, 'The adolescent, the family, and the group: boundary considerations', deal with aspects of this. It is also to be set alongside, and be seen as complementary in some measure, with Robert Klein's contribution.

The papers that follow shift our perspective. Barry Palmer's essay, 'Learning and the group experience' sets the tone because he takes us into a range of ideas and conceptual systems that hitherto have tended to be outside the boundary of the Tavistock Model or, at least, have not been so carefully articulated.

'Darkness' by John Broadbent again causes another shift in perspective. He takes us into Conrad and reveals the richness of that text in relation to this version of group relations training. It is also illustrative of the kind of associative thinking that one would want to have within the frame of a working conference on authority.

Two contributions take us firmly across the boundary of group relations training into the outside world. James Miller explores the psychology of innovation in an industrial setting. Eric Miller similarly is exploring innovation, and in his 'Open systems revisited: a proposition about development and change' causes us to look at the political complications of open-systems thinking based on his consultancy work in rural development.

The final paper is by no means a summary, but attempts to think through some implications of the version of group relations training that can be called the Tavistock Model. Its title, 'A concept for today: the management of oneself in role', states its thrust: that group relations training is valueless unless it provides people with opportunities to explore and clarify boundaries as a means to establishing their authority for their being.

References

Astrachan, B. M., and Flynn, H. R. (1976) 'The intergroup exercise: A paradigm for learning about the development of organizational structure'. In E. J. Miller, (ed.) *Task and Organization*. London: John Wiley.
Back, K. (1973) *Beyond Words*. Harmondsworth: Pelican Books.
Bion, W. R. (1961) *Experiences in Groups*. London: Tavistock Publications.
Bion, W. R. (1970) *Attention and Interpretation*. London: Tavistock Publications.
Bion, W. R. (1974) *Bion's Brazilian Lectures*. Rio de Janeiro: Imago Editora Ltd.
Colman, A. D., and Bexton, W. H. (eds) (1975) *Group Relations Reader*. Washington: A. K. Rice Institute.
Frankl, V. E. (1964) *Man's Search for Meaning*. London: Hodder and Stoughton.
Frankl, V. E. (1967) *Psychotherapy and Existentialism: Selected Papers on Logotherapy*. New York: Pelican.
Greenberg, L., *et al.* (1975) *Introduction to the Work of Bion*. Strathtay: Clunie Press.
Higgin, G. and Bridger, H. (1965) *The Psychodynamics of an Inter-group Exercise*. Tavistock Pamphlet No. 10.
Miller, E. J. (ed.) (1976) *Task and Organization*. London: John Wiley.
Miller, E. J., and Gwynne, G. V. (1972) *A Life Apart*. London: Tavistock Publications.
Miller, E. J., and Rice, A. K. (1967) *Systems of Organization*. London: Tavistock Publications.
Novak, M. (1971) *The Experience of Nothingness*. New York: Harper Colophon.
Rice, A. K. (1958) *Productivity and Social Organization: the Ahmedabad Experiment*. London: Tavistock Publication.
Rice, A. K. (1965) *Learning for Leadership*. London: Tavistock Publications.
Rice, A. K. (1970) *The Modern University: A Model Organization*. London: Tavistock Publications.
Richardson, E. (1973) *The Teacher, the School and the Task of Management*. London: Heinemann.

Rioch, M. J. (1970) 'The work of Wilfred Bion'. *Psychiatry*, **33**, 56–66.

Toch, H. (1966) *The Social Psychology of Social Movements*. London: Methuen.

Trist, E. L., and Sofer, C. (1959) *Exploration in Group Relations*.

Turquet, P. M. (1974) 'The individual and the group'. In G. S. Gibbard, J. J. Hartman, and R. D. Mann (eds) *Analysis of Groups*. San Francisco: Jossey-Bass.

Turquet, P. M. (1975) 'Threats to identity in the large group'. In L. Kreeger (ed.) *The Large Group: Therapy and Dynamics*. London: Constable.

Wilson, A. T. M. (1951) 'Some aspects of social process'. *Journal of Social Issues*. Supplementary Series No. 5.

Chapter 2

Boundary Management in Psychological Work with Groups

David L. Singer, Boris M. Astrachan, Laurence J. Gould and Edward B. Klein

We have found the social systems based organizational concepts developed by the late A. K. Rice and his colleagues (e.g. Rice, 1963, 1969; Miller and Rice, 1967; and Turquet, 1974) of the Tavistock Institute, London, useful in thinking through a variety of issues in therapeutic, educational, and group training enterprises. For example, we have applied these concepts to analysis of group psychotherapy (Astrachan, 1970), a comparison of group training models (Klein and Astrachan, 1971), the intake process in mental health centres (Levinson and Astrachan, 1974), the role of psychologists in schools (Singer, Whiton, and Fried, 1970), the dilemmas of a group of nonprofessional T-group trainers in a school district (Bunker and Singer, 1974), and a compensatory education programme (Klein and Gould, 1973). In this paper we examine some management aspects of leading small group events in which the feelings and behaviour of the participants—in the here and now or in their outside lives—are central to the group's work. This would include 'psychotherapeutic', 'encounter', 'training', 'sensitivity', 'Gestalt', 'T-A', 'marathon', 'personal growth', and 'human relations' groups, among others. In particular, we shall focus on issues of task, role, structure, contract, and accountability.

We view group leaders (including group therapists) as inevitably involved in the managerial processes (even though they are by no means 'managers' in the traditional sense of that term) of task definition, contract setting, definition of leader and member roles, as well as monitoring task and role boundaries during the course of the event. These, together with the issues of responsibility and accountability for what occurs, are crucial, and particularly thorny, problems. Unfortunately, there is little systematic consideration of these issues in the group literature—perhaps because most group leaders tend to see themselves as teachers or therapists rather than as administrators, and because they prefer to deal with human interaction processes rather than management decisions. None the less, since we believe that the organizational and managerial aspects of a group event profoundly affect its dynamics and

21

hence its success or failure, we consider clarity about these matters to be crucial for the effective conduct of any group event.

A social systems organizational perspective on small group events

Group events can be viewed as temporary institutions whose manifest goal or task is to provide some psychological benefit (e.g. reduction in suffering, increased awareness of interpersonal phenomena, awareness of one's body, etc.) to their clients: the group members. Their 'structure' encompasses all arrangements for utilizing time, space, material, and human resources; but task specification and role definition are primary aspects of any group's structure. Another key aspect of a group's structure is its boundaries: those dividing lines, sometimes abstract and sometimes concrete, which define what is 'in' and what is 'out'. Group events have time boundaries, membership boundaries, role boundaries, and task boundaries. Nevertheless, any particular arrangement (e.g. a male *v.* a female leader, rigidly defined and limited roles for members *v.* greater member freedom to define individual roles) invariably has psychodynamic as well as practical implications for persons and subgroups, and will thus influence task performance.

The task as well as the major structures of group events are contractually derived. The sponsoring organization, if any, or the prospective leader(s) offers a group event with potential benefits of one sort or another under certain conditions. In return, they typically receive some combination of fees, research opportunities, and training opportunities. In practice, the explicitness, clarity, and specificity of the task, the contract, and the real and perceived power of the various parties to influence them vary widely, with consequences we shall discuss below.

Boundary management and the group leader

Ideally, the major purpose of structure is to facilitate task accomplishment. Achieving the benefits offered prospective members should therefore be the primary criterion used in group planning and composition; screening procedures for applicants; number, duration, and frequency of meetings; the leader's role; and the myriad choices the leader makes from moment to moment in the ongoing group event.

The major leadership function of a small group event, as in any organization, institution, or enterprise, is management of its boundaries—both internal and external. Management of external boundaries is concerned with relating the enterprise to the outside world; that is, deciding which population shall be recruited, who actually comes in, and what is promised. Management of the internal boundaries involves monitoring the relationship between the task of the enterprise and its structures, so as to assure that form is appropriate to function, and monitoring the relationship between the task of the enterprise and the personal and emotional needs of the individuals and subgroups within it. In sum, the management function involves regulating who comes in, what is done, and in what format.

In reality, however, in group events, as in any organization, many factors unrelated to task performance influence the development of structure. These include the personal needs that members and leaders bring with them; covert tasks, which may be subtly assigned to the group by some other group, by society at large, or by a superordinate sponsoring institution; and group needs that arise during the course of the group's life.

For example, a major need of any group or organization is to cope with the anxieties which inevitably arise (fear of losing one's individuality, fear of incompetence or failure, threat to self-esteem, etc.). Bion (1961) has described defensive manoeuvres, which he calls 'basic assumption', that he claims operate in all human systems, though he first identified them in self-study and therapeutic groups. Menzies (1960) and Jacques (1955) have described the development of structure as a defence against anxiety in a hospital and industrial setting, respectively. Appropriately harnessed, covert tasks and needs may enhance a group's capacity to work effectively and creatively by providing vitality as well as material which can be used in its work. When undetected or ignored, however, they may provide major constraints on task accomplishment.

The total process of offering and conducting a small group event can be conceived as a throughput operation (Miller and Rice, 1967). During the *import phase*, plans are made, policies formed, recruitment undertaken, and members and leader(s) are taken in across the external boundary under some sort of contract; during the *processing phase* the group event is conducted; during the *export phase*, the group, its roles, and its structures come to an end, and the various participants recross the boundary into the external environment. Though it is usually clear that the responsibility for boundary management during the processing phase rests with the group leader, it is often not clear where the boundary management function lies during the import and export phases. Problems inevitably arise when only some boundaries are managed, when those ultimately responsible are not aware of the consequences of letting others manage significant boundaries, or when boundary management is not attended to at all.

In what follows we shall examine some of these issues, beginning with those arising during the import phase and then moving on to issues of boundary management during the conduct of the event and the export phase.

The import phase: issues of task and contract

When group events are viewed as small, temporary institutions, their tasks and structures can be theoretically defined and made explicit with relative ease. Crucial early management responsibilities for those who initiate a group event include defining the task, defining the leader and member roles, recruiting the leader(s) and members, and developing a contract among them—though not necessarily in this sequence.

Defining small groups by task and level

The task of a group event is decided upon by some combination of representatives of the sponsoring institution (if any), the prospective leader, and, increasingly, prospective members. This process takes place either explicitly or implicitly, consciously or unconsciously, actively or by default. Sometimes a sponsoring institution or leader decides for some reason that it wishes to offer a particular type of group event. At other times, clients or an institution assess client needs either formally or informally and develop a group event to meet those perceived needs.

We propose that for a successful outcome of a group event, two conditions must be met: (1) the group's task and structure must fit member needs; (2) leader decisions and techniques must be geared to the group's overall task. All too often, however, group goals are vague: members and leaders tend to think of group events in terms of techniques (encountering, transactional analysis, interpersonal exercises) or theoretical orientations (psychoanalytic, humanistic-existential) rather than in terms of task. At worst, techniques and theories have become sacred rituals rather than tools for task performance (service delivery). Similarly, a variety of group events which emerged to serve specialized purposes are often seen as competing ventures rather than different modes for achieving different ends.

We have therefore developed a heuristic 'cognitive map' of the group field which categorizes group events in terms of two basic parameters: (1) the *task system* of the group event, and (2) the *psychological level(s) or system(s)* involved in this task.

Group events have tasks which lie somewhere on a hypothetical continuum that has *learning* (in the sense of cognitive/perceptual change) at one end and *psychological change* (in the sense of altered coping capacity, personality structure, or response repertoire) at the other end. In between is the region of dual task systems, with coequal learning and change tasks located at the midpoint. Certainly, learning and change are not mutually exclusive; indeed they often mediate each other. Yet, in any reasonably conducted group event there is typically an explicit or implicit priority which determines which task shall be pursued at the expense of the other, given constraints of time and resources.* †

The relevant psychological levels are: *group processes, interpersonal processes,* and *intrapersonal processes.* Each is a system conceptually different from, but related to, the others. Since behaviour is multidetermined, any event occurring within a group can be understood as the product of processes

---

*Many writers and practitioners appear to hold the implicit belief that there can be no *learning* about human behaviour without corresponding emotional or personal *change* of a quasi-therapeutic nature. This leads to a fusion of the two concepts, exemplified by Lieberman *et al.* (1973) in their study of 'encounter group' outcomes. These authors speak of 'learning', are studying some group events which clearly employ learning-oriented techniques, yet use outcome measures which tap personal *change*.

†We shall argue below that without a task priority system or a clear agreement that there is no priority system, the end result may at best be chaos, and at worst, destructive consequences for members and/or leader.

occurring on *all* of these levels simultaneously. Consider the following example from an American group:

It is the second session of a group with a female leader. Early in the meeting a male member attacks one of the female members quite vigorously, accusing her of being a 'controlling bitch'. He is actively supported by several other men.

On the *group* level, this transaction may be viewed as partially determined by the dilemma facing a group working with any leader, but particularly a female leader, given the powerful sex-linked stereotypes which consciously or unconsciously persist in contemporary American culture. The attack may be a displacement of hostile feelings towards the leader, which the males in the group were finding difficult to acknowledge openly or express. The man resonating to the issue most strongly may simply be the first to put it out in the open, albeit in deflected form. On the *interpersonal* level, there may *also* be a history of miscommunication or resentment between the two persons directly involved, partially as a function of their history in the group, and partially based on their internalized representations of members of the opposite sex. And, on the *intrapersonal* level, like all of us, the two members in question have long-standing anxieties, conflicts, fantasies, defences, and compensations surrounding the selves which they brought with them. A full understanding of the attack would require data on all three levels. Only then would there be enough information to explain why this behaviour became salient in these members, in this group, at this time.

In relation to a *learning task*, the concept of levels refers to the processes or system which is the *object of study*. In the context of a *change task*, the concept of levels refers to those processes utilized as the *vehicle for intervention to produce change*. For example, peer group pressure (group level), a dyadic therapeutic relationship (interpersonal level), and interpretations of defensive structures (intrapersonal level) are all possible ways of altering a person's behaviour.

Most small group events offered to the public can be included within the following six categories: (1) interpersonal learning groups, (2) group process learning groups, (3) personal growth groups, (4) individually oriented change groups, (5) group process-oriented change groups, and (6) focused criterion change groups. These six types of groups are described below and are schematized in Figure 1. Although devised on the basis of our informal observations of task and structure in the group events with which we are familiar, our categories and 'cognitive map' are consonant with, but more articulated than, the empirical factor analytic results of Lomranz, Lakin, and Schiffman (1972). Of course there are many group events which defy categorization in this typology; we have simply tried to reflect modal features of current practice as systematically as possible.

Interpersonal learning groups are typified by the classical sensitivity training or T-group (Bradford, Gibb, and Benne, 1964; Shaffer and Galinsky, 1974)

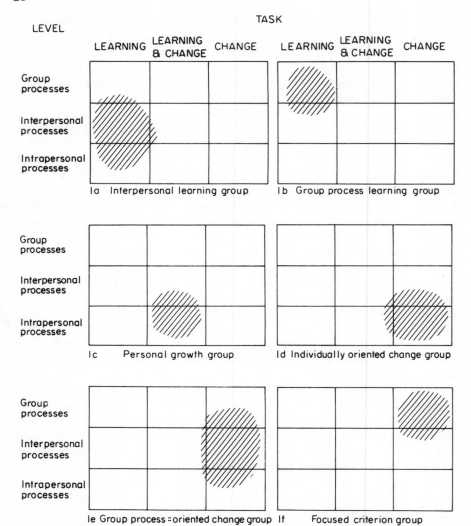

Figure 1. Task and level in the six types of small group events. This grid is modelled, in part, on a scheme for classifying laboratory goals devised by Schein and Bennis (1965, p. 58)

but are currently offered under a wide variety of labels. Their stated aim is to help members learn about the effects of their behaviour on others, others' behaviour on them, and the effects of feelings and motives on communication and behaviour. Thus, their primary learning task focuses on the interpersonal level (Figure 1a). Some variants utilize the behavioural unfreezing which often occurs to foster a subsidiary change task (e.g. Argyris, 1964). Techniques used include leader-modelling and confrontation, nonverbal exercises, role-playing, transactional analysis, and others.

Group process learning groups are best exemplified by the Tavistock-type 'small group' or 'study group' (Bion, 1961; Rice, 1965; Klein and Astrachan, 1971). Typically, but not always, these are one component of group relations conferences sponsored by the A. K. Rice Institute or its affiliates. Early 'sensitivity training' groups or 'T-groups', particularly those conducted in Bales's laboratory at Harvard, were often group process learning groups. Out of that tradition came the classic papers of Bennis and Shepard (1956) on developmental phases in groups, and Slater's work (1966) on symbolization, structure, and religious myth in small groups.

Group process learning events have a unitary learning task which focuses on group-level phenomena—particularly those surrounding authority issues and covert processes—and only secondarily (if at all) on interpersonal phenomena (Figure 1b). Interpretation of phenomena occurring within the group as a system and rigorous observation of time, role, and task boundaries are the prime leader techniques.

Personal growth groups include a wide variety of events offered under a wide range of labels. What they have in common are more or less coequal learning and change task systems. Often referred to as 'therapy for normals', they typically offer increased awareness and increased capacity for freer, creative, enriched experience in one domain or another (Schutz, 1967; Schloss, Siroka, and Siroka, 1971). These groups primarily focus upon and utilize intrapersonal phenomena; they involve interpersonal processes only secondarily (Figure 1c). Techniques include fantasy, sensory, and physical exercises; meditation; encountering; role playing. A personal growth event frequently restricts itself to one technique or one focus.

Individually oriented change groups have as their primary task member change: reduction in suffering, increased coping capacity, and increased capacity for freer, more creative functioning. While they reflect a wide array of technical and theoretical approaches to group therapy, including the classical psychoanalytic (e.g. Slavson, 1964); interpersonal/encounter (e.g. Burton, 1969); Gestalt (e.g. Perls, 1969); psychodramatic (e.g. Moreno, 1971); and bioenergetic (e.g. Lowen, 1969), the *vehicle* for change in all of them is intrapsychic or interpersonal (member–therapist dyad) intervention (Figure 1d). The group is regarded as an aggregate of individuals and the leader typically works with one at a time—doing 'psychotherapy in the round'—while the rest function variously as observers, contributors, 'alter-egos', and 'significant others'. Group processes, with the exception of 'peer support', 'supportive culture', or the provision of multiple 'transference figures', are usually viewed only as a distraction or a constraint upon treatment and are not actively utilized in the work.

Group process-oriented change groups, however, use group processes to bring about change (Figure 1e). The member is regarded both as an individual and as a member of the group *qua* system. Unfolding group processes and the role that each member plays within them are used as springboards for examining and intervening in roles and situations which are problematic in members' lives and in which they collude. This approach to group therapy includes the work of the English object theorists (e.g. Bion, 1961; Ezriel, 1950; Foulkes, 1961; and Sutherland, 1952), American psychoanalytic and eclectic workers (e.g. Astrachan, 1970; Burrows, 1927; Whitaker and Lieberman, 1964; and Yalom, 1970), as well as some practitioners of group transactional analysis (Berne, 1963, 1966).*

Focused criterion groups are specifically designed to change or eliminate one self-destructive or undesirable target behaviour shared by members, e.g. overeating, alcoholism, drug abuse, smoking, and illegal/antisocial activity. Though the confrontational, encountering style of many Focused criterion group leaders may make it appear that intrapersonal or interpersonal processes are key vehicles for change, closer inspection suggests to us that group processes —covertly utilized—are the primary change inducers (Figure 1f). All of the target behaviours are addictive in nature; each has become a way of avoiding anxiety, despair, depression, meaninglessness, or powerlessness, and each has been psychologically reinforcing in addition to any physical dependence. The programmes in which these events are nearly always embedded (e.g. Phoenix House, Weight Watchers) and their leaders first utilize rituals of entry, such as confession and humiliation, to promote a powerful identification with the programme and the group. This substitute dependency makes withdrawal from the target behaviour possible. Leader-fostered group pressure, support, and sanctions—not interpretation or dyadic transference†—help members stay abstinent after the initial withdrawal (see Kaufman, 1973).‡

In what follows we shall be using this typology in discussing the various issues to be addressed. We shall begin with an examination of some issues surrounding the development of a contract for a group event.

The contract and its boundary implications

The recruitment of members and leader(s) and the development of a contract among them to participate in an event of a given type are an early and crucial management function in the life of a group. It is through the contract-setting process that task definition is finalized and the roles of leader and member clarified. A contract is not necessarily a formal or written document to be adhered to legalistically, but rather, a mutual understanding of the common task and the conditions under which it will be pursued. We use the term in the

---

*Parloff (1967) and Astrachan (1970) identified three types of group therapeutic orientations, corresponding to an emphasis on each of our three levels (intrapersonal, interpersonal, and group processes). However, as we view contemporary practice, the crux of the issue appears to focus on the individual–group dichotomy.

†Many focused criterion groups have no regular leader. Rather, the leadership role is rotated among experienced members who keep group processes devoted towards achieving and maintaining abstinence.

‡The sponsoring institutions frequently make a clear distinction between this type of event and 'group therapy'. The latter is utilized to help already abstinent members develop alternative coping mechanisms and, later, to separate from the programme and reenter the outside world.

sense intended by psychotherapists when they speak of 'the therapeutic contract'.

It is through the contract that the leader derives his authority to work: to propose activities, to confront a member, to make interpretations. And it is by virtue of the contract that certain other activities can be declared 'out of bounds' by either leader or member. The contract thus defines the role of each party; that is, the boundaries of the obligations and rights of each. It provides the social reality, as it were, against which any demand, request, or proposal may be held up for scrutiny to determine whether or not it is 'appropriate'. In the view presented here, 'appropriate' may be translated as *task-relevant* under the terms of the contract. Which possible leader or member behaviours are task-relevant and which are task-irrelevant will vary as a function of the type of group. A clear contract provides valuable guidelines by which both leader and member can *legitimately* act or make demands in or on the group.

Will the real client please stand up? This often ignored question looms as a critical issue for group leaders who work with institutions and vice versa. A group leader may be called in to conduct a group event ostensibly for the benefit of the members but finds that there is overt or covert pressure to utilize the event for other purposes. Some examples follow.

Information gathering or 'spying' Managers have arranged 'sensitivity training' groups for employees and subsequently attempted to enlist the leader's help in using the resulting data to identify 'disloyal' individuals or potential 'trouble-makers' who threaten the current power structure or prevailing value system.

Screening Information gathered at group experiences for job applicants and trainees has been sought as a source of data for selection and deselection decisions, even though group members were told that the event was for training purposes.

Neutralizing conflict, 'cooling out' dissidents, and hiding institutional inadequacy Interpersonal learning and personal growth groups have frequently been introduced into business enterprises, communities, and university campuses at times of unrest and crisis. Forthright examination and confrontation of conflict that might legitimately be regarded as *political*, i.e. between groups, classes, or occupants of roles with differing interests, is thus avoided.

What does a group leader do when a conflict develops between the interests of the client institution and those of individual group members? With whom does the leader side? To whom is he or she responsible? Such dilemmas arise repeatedly in institutionally sponsored work. How is the practitioner to avoid or handle them? Walton and Warwick (1973) have raised many of these questions and discussed them from an ethical point of view. Though these issues are ethical in nature, organizational analysis and organizational competence on the part of group leaders can help in their resolution.

A clear contract between the leader and the client institution, fully shared with group members, is one solution to the problem of institutional 'spying' and the use of groups for selection purposes. If the contract guarantees confidentially, it protects both members and leader from subsequent demands for information based on claims that the institution which pays the bill has the right to a report of what occurs. Alternatively, a clear statement to potential members that a group event will be used as a selection vehicle would provide reasonable safeguards. Such work might not be pleasant or easy, and might indeed be distasteful to some. But it would be neither unethical nor duplicitous if members were fully aware of the boundaries of confidentiality and the purposes for which the group was being conducted.

The use of interpersonal learning or personal growth events to neutralize institutional conflict or 'cool out' dissidents is a more complex issue. Often those who call in a group leader for these purposes are not fully aware of the implications of what they are doing, and they may indeed be acting in good faith; at other times it is, premeditated with an ulterior motive. In any event, the effect is implicitly to define the organizational conflict in other than systemic terms. By conducting individually focused events—whether they be therapeutically geared to help dissidents 'better understand their authority problems', or personal growth groups to help managers 'fulfil their human potential'—the conflict has been defined as the result of psychological problems *within individuals*. Such groups can help neither the individuals in question to feel any better in their organizational roles, nor the organization as a whole to come to grips with the fundamental issues.

Similarly, by conducting interpersonal learning groups, the conflict is defined as the result of communication difficulty or personality clash *between individuals*. Here, typically, the stated goal is to 'open up communication' or 'let people get to know each other better'. But these efforts are also doomed to failure and are implicit 'cop-outs' or diversions.

In neither case do the dynamics, culture, and structure of the *social system* in question come under scrutiny. As we will discuss more fully below, to the extent that it focuses on relations between *persons* rather than on role-person constellations, role and power networks, and intergroup processes, any intervention—group event or otherwise—in a conflict-ridden organization is ill-fated. At best, such an intervention may be ineffectual. At worst, it may heighten distrust, disaffection, and despair (cf. Bowers, 1973).

To avoid being caught in this trap the practitioner needs a rather high level of organizational diagnostic skill. He must assess situations quickly enough to avoid becoming ensnared in an endeavour whose ulterior purpose becomes clear only too late. Moreover, he must be honest enough with himself to admit that a lucrative piece of work with interesting members would entail collusion with activities which he believes are ultimately destructive, and strong enough to resist the seduction. The desire for money, a lack of experience or sophistication in organizational politics, blended with genuine enthusiasm and joy in working with groups, often results in the use of group leaders for purposes they would not support, were they readily apparent. As a practical matter, involvement of potential members in negotiations for the group event or, if that is not possible, provision for a review of the contract with representatives of the sponsoring institution after the first session, can provide avenues for a leader either to prevent or stop his participation in a group event which is inappropriate for the organization, as he sees it.

Just as client institutions may pose problems for the practitioner, the enterprising group leader may present hidden problems for his client institution. Underlying both sets of problems is the fact that *conducting a group event within an institution is a system intervention*, particularly if the members are all from the same subunit or are involved in day-to-day work relationships. The nature and impact of that intervention will depend upon both the problems and dynamics of the institution and the type of group activity which is conducted. An interpersonal learning or group process learning event conducted within an organization for an intact group which has been binding and suppressing hostility and conflict is very likely to have explosive repercussions if the work is at all effective. Following a successful group process event, a heretofore depressed, fragmented group of individuals may band together and press for institutional change, having become aware of their common dilemma within the organization. Or, a personal growth group for ambitious, work-oriented executives who have previously ignored their spiritual and emotional development may lead to a rash of organizational dropouts by members who have come to realize that they are passing time in what has for them become a prison. Moreover, since organizations at least in part are open systems where changes in one sector affect other sectors, increased effectiveness, innovation, and personal satisfaction (or conversely, increased disaffection and flight from work) in one subunit may have repercussions in other subunits of the system (Klein and Gould, 1973).

Here again, accurate organizational diagnosis can help avoid potential difficulty. Negotiation of a clear contract laying out the potential difficulties, dangers, and remedies is necessary if the practitioner is to avoid being held responsible for negative consequences that do materialize. In a risky situation, the practitioner should be able both to spot the risk and to describe the various alternatives, so that the client system has the opportunity to consider whether or not the risk is one it wishes to assume.

Though we consider a clear contract a necessary condition for effective work in groups, we do not mean to advocate restricted contracts. There is no reason that the tasks or the roles of the members or leaders be narrow, unitary, or inflexible. Given adequate leader competence and sufficient member interest, highly complex group events can be arranged. One might contract to create, study, and influence a 'happening'. What we wish to highlight here is the importance to the outcome of a group event the development of a clear, mutual understanding—between leader and members—as to the *boundaries* of task and role prior to the first session.

Contract and casualties Members sometimes are solicited and enrolled in groups whose goals and methods are at best vaguely presented. If so, leader and members may all have different expectations of what will occur, what each is authorized to do, and for what each is responsible. In such a situation, the boundaries between task and unconscious dynamics can become very hazy, and unwitting manipulation or coercion can more easily occur, with moral imperatives used as façades for attempts to satisfy individual needs, maintain self-image, or reduce anxiety at others' expense. Leaders or members on 'id trips' or 'ego trips' are all too common phenomena.

Any leader has tremendous influence and power, whatever his contractual authority. He has: (1) expertise, either real or presumed; (2) the weight of his professional credentials and experience in the members' eyes; (3) the prestige or influence of the sponsoring institution, if any, and (4) the members' psychological investment in his position. These factors make it difficult for many members to resist leader instructions, to deny conscious and unconscious leader wishes, or to contradict leader judgements—especially in the early stages of group development. (See Bennis and Shepard, 1956; Bion, 1961; Slater, 1966; and Rioch, 1970.) It is thus relatively easy for the leader, acting either intentionally or inadvertently, to set the norms of the group or manipulate members.

In the extreme, vagueness of contract and the discrepancies between the resulting expectations of leader and member can facilitate the creation of 'casualties' and people who feel they have been subjected to 'man-handling' or 'psychic breaking and entering' in a group. Despite the relatively small numbers involved, Yalom and Lieberman's findings (1971) are quite suggestive. They studied casualties in a variety of group events which differed widely, though gathered under the rubric 'encounter'. A large percentage of participants who were rated subsequently as casualties were in groups whose leaders were rated high on a cluster of attributes defined by 'aggressive, intrusive stimulation; high charisma; high challenging and confrontation of each of the members; and authoritarian control', i.e. by leaders who acted as though *they* unilaterally had *the* answer for everyone's needs. The other side of this coin is that on measures taken before the groups were conducted, subsequent casualties showed lower self-esteem and self-concept, a higher 'growth orientation', and greater anticipation that groups would fulfil their needs. As Yalom and Lieberman put it, 'those individuals who came in believing in miracles were more likely to reap pain' (p. 28). Since the 'encounter groups' studied were not designed to alleviate deeply rooted, long standing difficulties, these individuals actually suffered, whereas they might have found what they needed in a differently structured type of group event which lasted longer.

The implications of these findings are quite clear. For effective work to occur—be it learning, change, or some combination of the two—there must be a fit between the needs and expectations of the group members and the group's task and structure. Which is to say that there must be a clear and appropriate contract between leader and members.*

Personal growth leaders especially need to be aware of these issues if they are to prevent situations where good intentions spawn tragic outcomes. The leader may be very clear that he wishes to help group members become more open, in touch with, and expressive of their feelings; more able to confront each other; and better able to surmount their difficulties with intimacy and physical contact. Indeed, he might be highly effective in accomplishing these goals with members who 'buy into' such a contract. But if participants arrive at the group event with little but a vague name to guide them and are carrying preconceptions of their own, problems are likely to arise.

A person arriving at a vaguely defined group process or interpersonal learning group expecting help with personal problems may at most be disappointed and infuriated. He may leave, but he will not be subjected to personal confrontation or attack by the leader for his wishes. However, the person expecting an educational venture who finds himself in a personal growth group and who is pressured to 'open up' or change will probably fare much worse. Well intentioned fellow members and a well-intentioned leader might unwittingly engage in destructive scapegoating or mystification (Laing, 1965) as a way of dealing with their own anxious annoyance or sense of impotence. It is a rare individual who has the strength and confidence to disregard the fear of shame and humiliation, to resist pressure from the group and/or leader, and to leave if necessary. If scapegoated for being 'closed', 'uptight', 'cold', and 'resistive', this member might experience considerable pain and disorientation. Were he not very well integrated to begin with, reactive symptoms might develop. The unclear task boundaries of the external situation could easily threaten and confuse a person with unclear internal (ego) boundaries, possibly even precipitating a psychotic episode.

Contract and expected stress Many, if not most, group events will at some time evoke considerable stress or anxiety in members. Some—particularly group process learning groups and personal growth groups—may generate more anxiety than can be comfortably handled by individuals going through periods of acute personal turmoil. Transient psychotic episodes are necessarily destructive; yet, in the long run, they may be highly productive, with the individual integrating at a higher level of functioning.

Left to their own devices and hearsay, some members will arrive at any group activity expecting gratification, warmth, and understanding; others, expecting conflict and confrontation. Active efforts to make sure prospective members understand the nature of the event in which they are being enrolled

---

*Egan (1970) has developed rather fully the notion that explicit contracts facilitate desirable behaviour, such as self-disclosure, in what we would term interpersonal learning groups. He cogently argues that clear contracts greatly enhance beneficial interaction in such groups and that such groups yield more favourable results than do traditional, non-contract groups, Ribner (1974) has recently reported research which tends to support this contention.

are thus necessary, both for the good of the client and the protection of the leader. Clients facing potential stress and possible exacerbation of charged conflict areas need to know what they are or may be in for, if they are to choose reasonably and responsibly whether the risk is worth taking.

Contract and leader values Value-free leaders do not exist, and in any group event there is danger of the leader's political and social values intruding as a 'hidden agenda'. It is often tempting for the leader consciously or unwittingly to use the charisma and 'transference potential' of his role or the powerful forces of the group to proselytize members into accepting a particular set of political, social, psychological, or sexual values. Bennis (1962), for example, noted the following values or metagoals which, though unannounced, are very much 'in the air' and permeate many sensitivity training groups: (1) expanded consciousness and recognition of choice, (2) a spirit of inquiry, (3) authenticity in interpersonal relations, (4) a collaborative conception of the authority relationship. Other meta-goals or hidden agendas may be prevalent in other types of events. However, these may run counter to the values of the members or institutions which sponsored their attendance. What happens when, having applied for membership in a learning experience in interpersonal relations or group processes, a member finds (or senses) that he is being indoctrinated? As Bennis notes, to the extent this has occurred, it is no accident that group events have been accused of being disguised forms of brainwashing by critics at both ends of the political spectrum.

In the long run, practices of this kind are bound to have unpleasant repercussions. Irate members may bolt during the group and make angry public denunciations. Others may make accusations of brainwashing at a later date. Or, 'converted' participants in groups with hidden metagoals may return home only to find that there is no place for their new values and philosophy in their family, home town, or workplace.

Of course, such events can never be fully avoided, even with the clearest of contracts. The capacity of powerful emotional dynamics to render even the most intelligent group members unable to read, assimilate, and believe what is clearly presented in a prospectus or brochure is sometimes staggering. But efforts at avoiding such a situation can be made. In particular, a leader might (1) openly state what philosophical, moral, social, or political values will be an underpinning of his work or affect the goals he had for members, and suggest that members consider this in choosing whether to join the group; or (2) accept these values as his own, but renounce any attempt to proselytize them and put forth disciplined efforts not to infuse the work of the group with them.

The processing stage

For effective work in groups, the leader's role, requisite skills, and behaviour should be determined by: (1) the task of the group event, (2) the level at which the work is pursued, and (3) the leader's own theoretical and personal orientation. Consequently, the same individual leading two different types of groups might behave quite differently in each.

Leader role

'Role' refers to the task-related functions a leader serves in trying to help members accomplish the work of a group event. We will begin an examination of leader role by comparing two events—the personal growth and group process learning groups—since they provide an illuminating contrast.

In the typical personal growth group, with its dual tasks of change and learning and its focus on the intrapersonal (the inner self) and the interpersonal levels, the role of the leader is varied and complex. He or she needs to be both teacher and model, guru and significant other, for the members. Typically, the personal growth leader fills these roles by adopting a very personal stance with members: open, accepting, and direct (see Horwitz, 1964). Confronting at times and supportive at other times, the leader will relate to members as individuals, and will often be a directive teacher, suggesting specific nonverbal exercises or other activities for the members.

This role would indeed seem to facilitate both the learning and change tasks of the personal growth event. For example, Culbert's (1968) findings suggest that early leader self-disclosure can facilitate member openness and member growth in this type of group. Similarly, improvement in counselling and psychotherapy tends to occur where the change agent (here, the leader) can establish a relationship offering 'high levels of accurate empathy, non-possessive warmth, and genuineness' (Truax and Carkhuff, 1967, Truax and Mitchell, 1971), and where the client feels that he is liked (Seeman, 1954; Parloff, 1961). Given the typically limited time in which to accomplish the change task, the personal growth leader must attempt to set up such relationships with members as quickly as possible. In addition, leader suggestions that members engage in specific activities or exercises as a way of eliciting new responses would appear congruent with both the change and the learning tasks—the relevant learning here being of the 'internal awareness' variety. Bernstein, Fisch, Pollack, and Singer (1971) suggest that such 'induced behaviours' may: (1) help members overcome inhibitions when behaviour is not frozen by intense conflict; (2) generate new behavioural and emotional responses to old dilemmas; and (3) open up new avenues of inner experience.*

The group process leader adopts a vastly different role and stance. Since the task is to study processes occurring on the group level, he relates to the group as a system, entity, or organism—not to the individual members. He comments upon what is happening within the group and among its subgroupings; not about what is happening within any individual. And, since the task is in part to study how primitive and covert fantasies about persons

---

*The role of the personal growth leader would not be unique in this regard. Induced behaviours are frequently utilized in interpersonal learning groups and more recently have been introduced by leaders of change (psychotherapy) groups.

in positions of authority affect the behaviour of groups, the distance and lack of personal input on the part of the leader are designed to facilitate the emergence of projective fantasies by the group as a whole, and by individual members, which are then available as material for study.

The 'blank screen' technique may or may not be what promotes cure on the part of psychoanalytic patients (cure may occur for other reasons). None the less, this technique can be quite valuable for nontherapeutic, educational purposes in which there is need for primitive and symbolic data, as in the group process event. The leader's frustration of the group's nontask-relevant dependency wishes may produce unpleasant feelings and lead the group into hostility, bickering, competitiveness, and fractionation. But the task is not to *reduce* anxiety about competence and success; it is to provide a place for members to *study* these phenomena. The silence of the group process leader in the face of a question he perceives as designed to manipulate or coerce him into responding, or his unwillingness to reply to a question whose answer is known by members of the group, can similarly be seen as task-relevant. To answer such questions would be to deprive the group of an opportunity to study (1) its use of dependency manoeuvres as an effort to reduce anxiety; and (2) the ways in which authority figures and leaders are invested with special meaning and power in the fantasy lives of those upon whom they exercise authority. Without frustration there would be no opportunity to study the ambivalence.

Any given leader role may have side effects which are potential constraints on task accomplishment. For the active and directive personal growth leader there is the danger that members will become overly dependent (Lundgren, 1971) and that when this powerful leader is absent they may fail to internalize or take away with them changes produced during the life of the group. Or, early and intense leader self-disclosure may frighten and inhibit a group. On the other hand, the impersonal, highly task-oriented stance of the group process leader may so frustrate, frighten, and enrage a group that unless there are enough active, counter dependent members, the group may have only the opportunity to learn about the dynamics of paralysis caused by flight from impotent, primitive rage. Here again, no prescriptions can be set forth. But given a clearly defined task or goal, various role possibilities for a leader may be thought through and tested.

Personal growth and group process leaders tend to agree among themselves as to the most effective role for their type of work. Leaders of change (psychotherapeutic) groups, however, differ markedly among themselves. Conceptions of appropriate leader role range from that of the classical psychoanalyst to that of Fritz Perls, the prototypical direct, confronting, 'no-nonsense' therapist. For whatever reason, ritual orthodoxy seems to have prevailed over pragmatic approaches to techniques within the area of psychotherapy in general—at least until recently (Parloff, 1967; Astrachan, 1970). Recent efforts at reassessment of technique in the light of research are a hopeful sign. Systematic attempts to match leader role with clearly defined therapeutic goals are still needed.

Role, person, and 'authenticity' Though we share the value configuration of authenticity, we believe that the current rhetoric surrounding the use of this term obscures many of the most significant issues in working with groups. One frequently hears from both practitioners and members that a group leader should be 'authentic', that he should be his 'real self' rather than 'hiding behind a role'. But what does it mean to be authentic? And how does this apply to leading a group?

In one widely used sense, authenticity appears to mean that one's experience must be made totally available to others. The corollary of this view is that learning or change can only occur (or at least are best facilitated) within the context of a totally revelatory 'I–Thou' relationship. But are learning and change, or all kinds of learning and change, necessarily facilitated by a relationship defined as 'authentic' in such terms? We think not. Moreover, the assumption underlying the definition of authenticity given above is that to take a role, i.e. to circumscribe or constrain one's behaviour, is to be, *ipso facto*, *non*authentic. In our view, authenticity thus defined is neither logical nor psychologically meaningful. In extreme form, it would mean that privacy and discretion are perforce inauthentic.

It can be argued, of course, that we have set up a 'straw definition'. However, we believe that authenticity is often defined in this way, and that it has become one of those indiscriminate catch-phrases that have little meaning beyond expressing the need for an alternative to the sham quality of many relationships.

By contrast, we suggest that authenticity can only be meaningfully defined within the context of role. Different roles demand the exercise of different skills and different types of personal output. The issue as we see it is how to be authentic-in-role. Under this view, the relevant question tends to be: what would be authentic within a given relationship, in given circumstances, with given commitments, as clearly or vaguely defined as they may be? Authentic behaviour would thus be quite different in the roles of lover, colleague, and group leader. The need is to be discriminating. That is, to be task-oriented and to apply oneself passionately to what one has contracted to do in relation to others—and, by implication, to 'keep out' of one's behaviour extraneous or gratuitous perceptions, expressions of feeling, and the satisfaction of one's personal needs to the extent that they will constrain task performance. (Even a love relationship has its 'tasks': e.g. providing gratification, security, and so on.)

From this point of view, authenticity in the role of group leader would consist of sharing with members one's thoughts, perceptions, and feelings within the boundaries of the contracted-for task. For example, in a personal growth, interpersonal learning, or focused criterion group, *selected* personal revelation of a leader's feelings about a member will be 'authentic'. However, such behaviour on the part of a group process learning event leader would *not* be authentic, and indeed would have overtones of manipulation. There, the leader has contracted to work with the group *qua* group and has foresworn interpreting or responding to the behaviour of individual members. Authenticity in such an event would consist of sharing his experience of the *group*.

Leader behaviour

The role a leader assumes provides a set of guidelines for his general stance and attitude towards the group, its members, and its work. How does this manifest itself in concrete terms? Let us take what is probably a fairly common situation and consider how a leader might deal with it in three different types of group events:

It is the first session. After a few moments of painful silence, the members exchange names. A male member then asks permission of the others to speak. He faces the leader, looks him in the eye, then looks down. Haltingly, he says he has something on his mind . . . a problem. He is having difficulty on the job, particularly with his boss, who accuses him of sabotaging the work of the office. The member claims not to understand the boss's complaints and feels misunderstood. As he tells his story he is questioned by other group members interestedly, albeit somewhat solicitously.

In an individually oriented change group the leader's response is rather predictable and familiar to both ourselves and most 'patients'. The leader will probably draw the member out and attempt to elicit further information about the office problem. Given the type of group, the members' behaviour is work-oriented (that is, in keeping with the primary task as set forth in the mutual contract) and would be treated as such by the leader.

One would expect the same behaviour to get a very different response in an interpersonal learning group. There, the primary task is not change or reduction in suffering but learning about interpersonal relations. Thus, on the surface, the member's behaviour is not task-relevant. Under their mutual contract, the leader would probably ask how the member was feeling in the here and now. He might wonder whether the member were using the job situation as a metaphor for expressing his anxiety and concern about his fate in the *present* group situation. And he might inquire how the rest of the group were reacting to his presentation-of-self-as-a-patient in this context, sharing with them his own reactions to this dilemma. Clearly the leader would not accept the role of patient as valid, nor would he accept the task of cure of neurosis as valid under this contract. If the member were so persistent that he could not learn about here-and-now events, or if he interfered with the learning of others, the leader might ask him to leave, with the recommendation that he find a psycho-therapy group.

In a Group process learning group, the leader would take yet a different tack. He would probably focus on the unwitting collusion between this particular member and the rest of the group, pointing out that the others were using this individual as a way of expressing their concern about their competence to learn and to function in the group. The leader might suggest that the others were putting forth a 'patient' in an effort to deny and protect themselves from their own feelings of helplessness and fright. That is, the individual seeking 'help', encouraged by the group, would be seen as a spokesman for commonly shared group concerns.

Another situation in which a clear notion of task can facilitate a difficult decision is the common request by several members that the leader 'become a member of the group and join in a trust exercise as a participant'. Such requests exert considerable pull on leaders with egalitarian leanings. The leader's decision is of crucial importance, since it involves what may be a shift in role. On the one hand, such requests are often the result of covertly held resentment towards the leader's seemingly higher status and importance in the group and reflect the wish to dissipate these distressing feelings by submerging role differences between leader and member. On the other hand, it is also true that strong negative feelings can often impede effective communication in a group.

The leader's decision should be made on the basis of task relevance rather than on the basis of his or members' needs—conscious or unconscious. Depending upon the contract, this demand may be congruent or incongruent with the group's task. In a group process learning event, the leader would probably realize that by joining the group he would lose the unique position on the psychological boundary of the group which enables him to work most effectively. The more he is 'in' the group, the more difficult it will be for him to see, understand, and comment on what occurs. To join the group would thus prevent examination of the covert issues motivating the request and would effectively subvert the group's work. Though gratifying for the members, and possibly enjoyable for the leader, acceding to the request would impede the group's work more than it might help it. Moreover, if the leader changed role without *total* group agreement, he would in effect be violating his obligation to any objecting member: he would be unilaterally refusing to follow through on his agreement to provide leadership in a group process group. In this context, the member demand can be seen as having the potential effect (however unintended) of imposing a tyranny upon dissenting members, depriving them of services for which they contracted and setting up a culture in which there is no responsibility to carry out commitments when they become painful or unpleasant.

In a group whose contract did not emphasize study of covert processes, quite a different approach might be appropriate. Some personal growth, focused citerion, and change group leaders might accede to such a request, understanding full well the dynamics behind it. They may decide to bypass opportunities for exploring authority relations in the interest of building a trusting relationship with members more quickly, thus demonstrating the possibility of collaborative effort.

In sum, we wish to emphasize that, depending upon the task of a group, the same occurrence will take on different meanings and might be responded to by the leader quite differently. Probably the most important aspect of leadership is identification of task-relevant issues for the group to work with at any moment in time, given its contracted-for task system. Techniques (e.g. nonverbal exercises, interpretations, and encouragement of extra-group data) are *tools for task performance*. We propose no one way to lead a group, save that *form follow function*. What is needed is an orientation which prompts the leader to ask, 'What is happening? What have I agreed to help these people accomplish? Given this situation, how can I best fulfil my part of the bargain (contract)?' There may never be one clearly correct choice, but there will be criteria terms of which options can be held up for evaluation.

Leader role in monitoring the task/sentience boundary

'Sentience' refers to the emotional bonds that develop between people. A 'sentient group' is a group to which people feel they belong, to which they feel committed, and from which they derive a sense of support. Each of us belongs to several sentient groups (e.g. family, friends, professional colleagues) which vary in their permanence and importance. We also relate to various fantasied sentient groups—families of origin, idealized models, and more.

In daily life, individuals move from place to place, working on various tasks with, and relating in various ways to, different people. One thus belongs simultaneously to many groups. These groups are infused with varying combinations, in both amount and type, of work tasks and sentience. A major phenomenon within group events is the tendency for intense ties to develop, probably because of the powerful emotions and the personal nature of the material which is expressed and exchanged. Since these experiences are not easily shared with, or communicated to, 'outsiders', there tends to be a sort of implosion. The persons one 'works' with thus become persons with whom one feels deeply involved. In organizational terms, the 'work group' becomes coincident with a 'sentient group'. This phenomenon will inevitably influence the contracted-for work. As Miller and Rice suggests, 'forms of organization in which task and sentient groups coincide may have relatively short-term effectiveness; in the longer term, such groups can inhibit change, and hence lead, eventually, to deterioration of performance and, in consequence, to social and psychological deprivation rather than satisfaction' (1967, p. 253).

An important aspect of any group leader's role is monitoring the boundary between task and sentience—maintaining awareness of how the group's sentient life is affecting its work. The nature—and some sources—of the sentient ties which develop in the different types of groups are thus worth examining. One dimension along which these groups tend to differ is the degree in which they are either time-bounded or open-ended. Typically, but not always, the two types of change groups and the focused criterion group have no fixed terminus and are spaced over time. By contrast, interpersonal learning, group process, and personal growth groups tend to be both time-bounded and massed—often in 'marathon' format. Consequently, differing *types* of sentience often develop in these two 'clusters'. In the time-bounded, massed events one sees group 'highs' and the emergence of highly charged, anxiety-laden material in a relatively short time. Since these groups are short-lived, typically composed of strangers, and conducted at a place removed from the members' everyday life, more risks can be taken; the likelihood of 'real' consequences is diminished. In a sense, these groups are bounded areas—one-night stands.

Focused criterion and the two change groups, by contrast, typically exhibit more initial caution and more dependency upon the leader. Yet a very strong commitment to the group, to the process, and to the individuals within it as a reference group in members' day-to-day lives also tends to develop. Several factors may underlie the character of these groups' sentience. First, they consist of people who feel the need for personal change and who in some way have labelled themselves as 'sick' or as 'patients'. The tendency for participants to feel stigmatized by the outside world and thus to huddle together for support and a sense of positive identity cannot be underestimated. Secondly, because of the hoped for 'cure', there may be more of a transference to the leader and his potential magic. Thus, psychodynamically, the group may be initially organized around a charismatic figure or institution and his or its special theory or technique.

Given the anxiety inherent in group life, let alone the tasks to which these groups address themselves, some sentience is necessary for task performance, if not for the very continuity of the group. But heightened sentience presents dangers as well. In the interpersonal learning or personal growth group there is the danger that the culture of instant intimacy and openness which develops will be misperceived. Members may assume that such phenomena can be recreated in the outside world and they may attempt to do so as soon as they return home. Unfortunately, however, the conditions prevailing in the laboratory that foster intimacy and openness do not often exist in the outside world; such members are in for postgroup disappointment and depression.

There is also the opposite danger—that the group event will become 'split off' from the outside world. If group events provide opportunities for saner, more open communication, intimacy, involvement, and more 'highs' than found in the outside world—and do so without also teaching members how to develop interpersonal skills, grapple with real risks, dilemmas, and uncertainties 'back home'—they run the risk of becoming *primary* sources of satisfaction and dependency rather than *temporary* vehicles for helping individuals improve their lives. In organizational terms, when this occurs the group event has not adequately prepared the client for the 'export' phase of the throughput process. It has been rendered ineffective by failing to develop linkages between the group experience and the outside world.

Clients and leaders face this danger at close range in the focused criterion group. Here, as a substitute for the self-destructive target behaviour, there is a short-run need for a powerful dependence upon or 'addiction' to the programme, the leader, the group, and their norms. It may thus be necessary at the outset to foster highly regressive dependent behaviour in members. The issue then becomes whether the group or sponsoring institution is strong enough to wean the individual and prepare him for export once the 'withdrawal' task has been accomplished.

One aspect of the leader role in monitoring the task/sentience boundary, then, is not to collude with members' tendency to (1) become the primary objects in each other's lives, and (2) treat the group as a cosy and protected substitute for other relationships and involvements. In his role, with its 'transference potential', the leader can help the group monitor the boundary between unrealistic fusion and realistic cohesiveness, between indiscriminate acceptance or homogenization and tolerant acceptance of real individuals with real differences.

In summary, all of the group events we have been discussing have overlapping task and sentient boundaries. And relatively high sentience is needed in each for task performance. The differences between them lie in how sentience can be effectively utilized in accomplishing the specific group task.

(1) In the interpersonal learning group, the need is to develop both quantitatively and qualitatively more satisfying sentience, thus making it more likely that members will apply their newly acquired interpersonal learning and skills by reassessing old relationships and developing discriminating, realistic sentient relations in the outside world.

(2) In the group process event, the study of how the group's task affects its sentience and how sentience affects task performance within a given structure is *the work* of the group.

(3) In the personal growth group, the focus of the sentience is not as important as the speed of its development and its intensity. If personal change is to take place in a relatively short time, members must open up, reveal themselves on a deep level, and unfreeze personality structures.

(4) In the individually oriented change group, the goal is to develop sentient ties which are primarily dyadic—between leader and individual members. It may even be necessary at times to discourage member–member sentience from becoming too intense in this type of group, since it is the leader–member relationship that forms the primary change vehicle and is central to the major task.

(5) In the group process-oriented change group, the issues are much the same as in a group process learning event. Here, however, the sentience is used not for the study of group processes but as a vehicle through which members may reexamine and readjust their roles and behaviour in life settings.

(6) In the focused criterion group, strong sentient ties to the group, to the programme, and the technique are developed and used as a vehicle for implementing specific behavioural change. Sentience is neither to be explored (as in the study group) nor experienced (as in the interpersonal learning group or personal growth group). It is to facilitate behavioural adaptation to some specified, and hopefully contracted-for, norm.

The export phase

The goals of export are to help members make a successful transition back into their environment, to preserve the work of the group, and to allow whatever learning or change has been accomplished to be meaningfully implemented within the members' back-home world. Most group enterprises have little in the way of structures specifically designed to achieve these aims. Certainly the latter phases of the group events we have been discussing are usually concerned with termination, and separate exercises may be designed to assist that process. In addition, leaders frequently encourage members to bring in material from the environment during the group's terminal phase. Yet conceptualization of, and structures for, the export subtask are typically rudimentary.

Member transition

The management task with regard to the individual member is to ensure that he (or she) leaves the group event in an appropriate condition and with appropriate opportunity for follow-up. What this means in practice varies with the type of group. One set of dilemmas typically attends both kinds of change and focused criterion groups, while a different set of dilemmas is typically germane for the interpersonal learning, group process learning, and personal growth events. This difference reflects the nature of the task and the formers typically used in the various events.

For both types of change and the focused criterion groups, the problem is how to help the member function without the group. In part, this issue was addressed in the section on sentience, where we tried to show how preparation for and consideration of the export phase is necessary at all stages of the group's life. As compared with learning-oriented events, change-oriented groups typically tend to be conducted in open-ended format—precisely to allow the greatest possible flexibility around this issue. The group does not die, but changed (cured) members are individually exported. With no arbitrary endpoint, the leader (or sponsoring institution) and member ideally can work together towards a separation as soon as the member is ready to leave, but not before reentry issues have been adequately addressed. Given the longer time span typically involved, it is easier for the leader and member to plan for possible follow-up experiences. The greater danger in change and focused criterion groups is the member who is allowed to become overly dependent upon the group and/or leader.

By contrast, in the interpersonal learning, group process learning, and personal growth events, with their typical 'marathon' format, separation has to be worked out within a predetermined time structure. Consequently, the need is to help members 'shift gears' adequately, realistically assess what they have achieved, and follow up the experience if they want to (or recover from it if they need to). In general, this involves: (1) adequately managing how material within the group is handled during the late phases of the group so that members are conscious of impending termination and separation issues are adequately surfaced and expressed; (2) seeing that members in whom conflictual material has been surfaced or exacerbated are helped to identify and accept this fact; and (3) assuring that such members are aided in identifying appropriate therapeutic help if needed.

Within large laboratories or conferences which have other events (e.g.

application groups, discussion groups) and additional staff, it is relatively easy to attend to the needs of a 'shaken-up' member outside of the group; but within the isolated group event it becomes more problematic. The leader somehow should attend to distressed individuals if he is to function responsibly, yet frequently there is little or no time set aside for this, nor is it within the boundaries of the group's task during sessions. Contracting for one or two postgroup, follow-up (decompression) sessions is one possible structure for dealing with this aspect of export in a way which minimally compromises the contracted-for work.

Separation is most problematic to manage in the personal growth event. There, a task system with a large change component is attempted in a compacted, time-bounded marathon format and with a membership which, more than any other, is likely to arrive with unrealistic fantasies about a changed life or a changed world. The dilemma is how to manage, within the available time boundaries, the unfreezing intensity that has been attained. One alternative is to attempt pregroup assessment of individual members' needs and negotiations around specific issues or problems to be worked on. Time within the group event can thus be saved, with correspondingly more time available for work on separation and reentry. However, this approach would be antithetical to the spontaneous, here-and-now, exploratory nature of many personal growth events. Yet in such a minimally structured group, it is even more important not to allow the fantasy of endlessness of opportunity for infinite change to be abruptly aborted at the very last moment. Either despair or reactive hyperdependency on similar group events is likely to result; one is reminded of the 'group junkies' of the 1960s. Perhaps planned follow-up sessions to help members decompress and to provide opportunities for them to assess and integrate the events of the group might be a useful vehicle for effective member transition in this type of event.

Preservation of the work

Once the 'person' has survived the transition, the leader needs to make sure that the work survives as well. In part this is a question of making follow-up opportunities possible, but the more important question is the fit between the 'graduating' member and the system to which he is returning. Will there be any support for newly acquired diagnostic/perceptual skills? For new behaviours? For new modes of experiencing? Or will there be a 'regressive pull' from other individuals or from a system whose equilibrium would be threatened by the learning change? At the very least, members need to be made aware of the issues involved. At best, specific structures may be devised to meet this problem.

Here again, effective management requires preplanning. In interpersonal and group process learning events this can be handled by encouraging attendance at such an event by more than one member of an organization. In this way there will be others in the back-home setting who are available for support and who share a common reference frame. In the isolated change or focused criterion group, what is usually done is to work intensively with members around this issue. Where change or focused criterion groups are institutionally embedded, however, other parts of the treatment programme are frequently delegated responsibility for working with family members and significant others to prepare them for the member's reentry.

As with the issue of member transition, our experience is that preservation of the work is likely to receive the least attention in personal growth groups, and perhaps for similar reasons. But a supportive, or at least benign, external environment, or adequate preparation for the discontinuity to be expected as one leaves the event, is just as necessary for the preservation of personal growth work as any other—if not more so. If members are indeed to be exported rather than remaining bound to the leader, group, or technique for support and confirmation, or if personal growth events are to be other than transitory 'highs', some structures for dealing with this issue must be developed.

Implementation in the back-home environment

Implementation involves more than preservation of learning or change; it implies the extension of its scope or its transfer to new domains. At this juncture, however, it is crucial to ask: what kind of implementation is sought? Where is implementation sought? In the individual member's person or life? In his work role? In the systems (e.g. family, work organization) of which he is a member?

It seems fair to put forth the following somewhat sweeping generalizations: (1) A variety of group events are capable of engendering a variety of learning and change outcomes in *persons*, which sometimes are integrated into their lives (Bednar and Lawlis, 1971; Gibb, 1971; Lieberman *et al.*, 1973). (2) To some extent, group events are capable of producing learning, attitude change, and behavioural change in members' *work roles* (Campbell and Dunnette, 1968; Friedlander and Brown, 1974). (3) Group events alone, however, are relatively ineffectual in producing changes in the climates, structures, and processes of *organizations* (Bowers, 1973; Friedlander and Brown, 1974). Although we are aware of no comparative data, it would seem likely that though a clearly contracted-for and well-conducted event of any type should be capable of producing effects in persons, only the group process and inter-personal learning events are likely to produce effects which reach work roles.

Unfortunately, however, because small group events can effect learning or change in persons and thus can affect the ways in which they function in their work roles, there is still a prevalent assumption that enough group-changed individuals—a 'critical mass', so to speak—will perforce effect a change in an organization or system. Occasionally something like this may happen, as when a huge percentage of an institution whose top management is committed to organizational growth and change attends residential group relations conferences that focus primarily on a here-and-now study of organizational processes (Menninger, 1972). But this is to be regarded as the exception rather than the rule, and it should be noted that such conferences are comprised of much more than small group events.

If organizational change is the desired outcome, then as Davis argued quite a while ago (1967) and as recent research has tended to confirm (Friedlander and Brown, 1974), there is no substitute for planned system intervention (OD)—with adequate diagnosis, planning, and conduct of a differentiated intervention designed to meet specific organizational needs in carefully thought through ways. Changing persons will *not* change systems in a positive direction; indeed, as Bowers's data (1973) suggest, such efforts may even have negative effects. For effective system change one needs to intervene in person/role constellations, role and power networks, structure/ process interfaces, intragroup and intergroup processes, and the organization's psychodynamics.

At this point we have come full circle. Export in a group event cannot succeed without help from the import system. Task, contract, and outcome are all interrelated and must be integrated by those responsible for management if there is to be a fully successful group event.

Accountability, responsibility, and competence

Who should be responsible—that is, accountable—for the outcome (positive or negative) of a group event? Who should be accountable to whom for the way in which a group's resources of time, money, emotional involvement, and skills have been used? Who is responsible for seeing that the structure and conduct of a group event are appropriate to the real needs of the members or client institution? What type of competence is needed by a group leader? Who is responsible for assuring that group leaders are adequately trained?

At present there are three parties involved in the question of responsibility for group events: the leader; the sponsoring institution, if any; and the individual member. For each the issues are somewhat different.

The group leader

We have already put forth our view that the leader bears significant (if only partial) responsibility for the success or failure of a group event in accomplishing its stated tasks. This is a corollary to our conception of the leader role as one encompassing significant managerial authority and responsibility. Without this, the leader cannot be held accountable—which may be why the managerial aspects of the leader role are often ignored.

Criticism in both professional journals and the general press, prompted by the 'group craze' of the late 1960s (e.g. Birnbaum, 1969; Gottschalk and Pattison, 1969; Lakin, 1969), led to increased awareness and concern about and among group leaders. The issues raised included: (1) criteria for and assessment of competency for group leadership; (2) criteria for adequate supervision and training; (3) client and peer evaluation of group leaders; and (4) protecting the public against malpractice.

In particular, our analysis leads us to several recommendations with regard to group leader competency. Some skills are required for leadership of *all* six types of groups we have considered; the need for other skills varies from type to type.

We suggested earlier that the leader of any group event needs organizational diagnostic skills if he deals with sponsoring institutions or works with institutional clients. Some individual diagnostic skills for screening members and composing the group are also necessary. Beyond this, we propose basic understanding of covert group-level processes as a fundamental skill for group leaders, whether or not such skills are ever explicitly incorporated into leader interventions. Within any group, strong feelings and fantasies about the leader will be active; competitiveness, rivalry, and attractions along a variety of dimensions will be operant; there will be a tendency for the group to act, albeit unwittingly, so as to maintain a minimum of experienced anxiety, and a tendency to punish any who threaten to raise the anxiety level of the group. A competent leader must be able to recognize such processes and take them into account when deciding how best at any given moment to help the group in accomplishing its primary task. Understanding of covert tendencies to scapegoat individuals and to 'split off' unacceptable aspects of the group and 'locate' them in one deviant member is also needed if undue distress and production of 'casualties' are to be minimized. Unfortunately, at present such understanding and skill are not always found among those working with groups. The increasing use of 'nonprofessional' group leaders—individuals trained to lead one type of group without broad-based behavioural science background—makes attention to the need for basic group process awareness particularly urgent (Bunker and Singer, 1974).

As we also noted above, group events generate anxiety, and there is always the possibility that some members may experience beginnings of acute panic, depression, or psychotic disorganization. Any leader, then, should be able to recognize the early signs of impending distress or disorganization and take preventative action—either within the group or by providing appropriate outside help. How this is handled should vary with the task of the group, specific conditions in the group, the availability of back-up resources, and the degree to which the leader has clinical training.

Lastly, and perhaps most important, the leader of any group event must have the personal competence to differentiate his own needs from those of the group and its members. Only then can he (or she) thoughtfully attend to client needs in designing and planning a group event.

Differing types of groups also pose clearly differing demands for skill and competence upon the leader. Leadership of personal growth and both types of change groups requires a mastery of the principles and techniques of behavioural and personality change as well as an understanding of human functioning at the levels relevant to the specific type of group. Group process leaders need a deep understanding of group and interpersonal dynamics and the subtleties of defence against anxiety in learning situations; they also need skill in communicating their perceptions effectively. Interpersonal learning group leaders, given the breadth of both the task system and the levels at which it can be pursued, appear to need a wide range of skills as well as the capacity to shift appropriately from task to task and from level to level in the pursuit of overall group aims.

Diverse client populations and the recent trend to use specially composed groups as a means of achieving highly specific goals also call for specific leader skills because of the special issues which may emerge. Thus, for example, the leader of an adult-youth interpersonal learning group needs an understanding of the dilemmas of adolescence and the nature of intergenerational sexual attraction (Bunker and Singer, 1974). Similar considerations would obtain for interracial events (Klein, Thomas, and Bellis, 1971) and groups composed of underachieving children (Singer, Whiton, and Fried, 1970), to name but a few.

Ideals for the future are: (1) to match leader competence and skill more adequately to the contracted-for task of the group event and the needs of the particular member or group, and (2) to encourage preparation of group leaders who have a wide variety of tools at their disposal and a willingness to use them creatively as task and context require.

Another facet of leader responsibility involves attending to aspects of the group which he himself cannot personally manage. Frequently, functions such as screening, selection of co-leaders, supervision of inexperienced leaders, and management of acute psychological disturbances either cannot be handled by the leader or cannot be attended to within the boundaries of the group event. Follow-up or 'application' work often cannot be performed by the individual who has agreed to conduct a group. If these functions are indeed necessary for task accomplishment, it is the leader's responsibility either to make arrangements himself or to arrange explicitly with the sponsoring institution for these tasks to be carried out. Based on his experience with the group, the leader can also suggest follow-up procedures to further member learning and/or change, if they have not been planned.*

The sponsoring institution

Here lies the responsibility—both to itself and to prospective individual members on whose behalf it negotiates—for obtaining the services of a competent leader who knows his area theoretically as well as technically. Here also lies the responsibility for providing the prospective leader with enough information to recommend a type of group experience appropriate to

---

*The International Association of Applied Social Scientists (IAASS), which evaluates and accredits leaders of laboratory education groups (interpersonal learning and group process learning groups in our scheme), and is considering accrediting personal growth leaders, has adopted many of the same principles proposed in this section.

the needs of the particular membership. In the very process of negotiating a contract with a leader, representatives of the sponsoring institution will be able to test the leader's interpersonal competency and organizational acumen. A review of the situation, contract negotiations, and recommendations from the potential leader should provide a client institution with a sophisticated view of the services it will be obtaining. Hopefully this process may also help client institutions to become more independent of professionals in this area, as well as more realistically critical of 'export judgement' in general.

The individual client: the group member

For the individual member, it is simply more difficult to fulfil his responsibility to himself. Prospective members may indeed have the opportunity to investigate the leader's credentials as best they can, read announcements describing the group event and any suggested literature, and then compare what actually occurs with the announced purpose. But even with all of these potentially protective factors, the individual member experiences himself as, and may indeed be, in a relatively powerless position. There is often the fear—groundless or otherwise—that there will be retaliation from the sponsoring institution for questioning of method or for noncompliance. With regard to the leader, there are all of the latent and primitive reactions to those in positions of authority—whether addressed as 'Doctor' or by first name. Until some form of effective consumerism develops, the major responsibility for the competent design and conduct of group events must be borne by group leaders and sponsoring institutions. The responsibility for competent *membership* once the group has begun, however, must inevitably lie with the individual member.

State government intervention

Since it sees itself on the boundary between the professions and the general public, a fourth party—state government—may soon enter the arena of responsibility for the conduct and outcome of group events. Most likely this intervention will take the form of licensure for group leaders. Who shall be licensed to conduct which types of groups? Who shall be excluded? The matter is certain to be hotly contested, raising once again the issues of interdisciplinary competition involving psychologists, psychiatrists, behavioural scientists, and social workers (among others), and precipitating heretofore relatively low-keyed conflict between 'professionals' and 'nonprofessionals' in group work. Hopefully, those who apply behavioural science theory to group work will be clear enough about the issues when that time comes to provide useful data, advice, and position papers so that those authorized to make the ultimate decision—the legislators—may act wisely.

Conclusion

In this paper we have tried to address several neglected boundary management aspects of the leader's role in group work—using a social systems based organizational perspective. Aside from the intellectual fascination which this topic holds for us, we have been disturbed by the vagueness and diffuseness of the goals held by many who conduct group events, their lack of clarity about the relationship between goals and technique, and the unpleasant consequences that sometimes result.

Though no group leader should have to conduct a group event which does not interest him, nor conduct one in a manner not in keeping with his predilections, it is really irresponsible to conduct a group event whose design grows out of staff needs without adequate consideration of member needs. Accurate *diagnosis* of the prospective clients' and/or client institution's needs is necessary for proper design of a group event; a clear *contract* between group leader and clients is needed to assure its optimal conduct; and adequate planning with the event's task system kept in mind is required if realistic expectations about, and implementation of *transfer* to, the back-home setting are to occur.

References

Argyris, C. (1964) 'T-group for organizational effectiveness'. *Harvard Business Review*, March-April, 60–74.

Astrachan, B. M. (1970) 'Towards a social systems model of therapeutic groups'. *Social Psychiatry*, **5**, 2, 110–119.

Bednar, R. L., and Lawlis, F. G. (1971) 'Empirical research in group psychotherapy'. In A. Bergin and S. Garfield (eds) *Handbook of Psychotherapy and Behavior Change*. New York: Wiley, 812–838.

Bennis, W. G. (1962) 'Goals and meta-goals of laboratory training'. *Human Relations Training News*, **6**, 1–4. Reprinted in R. Golembiewski and A. Blumberg (eds) *Sensitivity Training and the Laboratory Approach*. Itasca, Ill.: Peacock Publishers, 1970, 18–24.

Bennis, W. G., and Shepard, H. A. (1956) 'A theory of group development'. *Human Relations*, **4**, 415–437. Reprinted in W. Bennis, K. Benne, and R. Chin (eds) *The planning of change*. New York: Holt, Rinehart & Winston, 1961 (1st ed.), 321–340.

Berne, E. (1963) *The Structure and Dynamics of Organizations and Groups*. New York: Grove Press.

Berne, E. (1966) *Principles of Group Treatment*. New York: Oxford University Press.

Bernstein, A., Fisch, E., Pollack, K., and Singer, D. (1971) ' "T" stands for training'. Paper presented at the meetings of the New York Psychological Association, New York City.

Bion, W. R. (1961) *Experiences in Groups*. New York: Basic Books.

Birnbaum, M. (1969) 'Sense and nonsense in sensitivity training'. *Saturday Review*, **52**, 82–83. Reprinted in R. Siroka, E. Siroka, and G. Schloss (eds) *Sensitivity Training and Group Encounter*. New York: Grossett & Dunlap, 1971, 181–191.

Bowers, D. G. (1973) 'OD techniques and their results in 23 organizations: The Michigan ICL study'. *Journal of Applied Behavioral Science*, **9**, 21–43.

Bradford, L. P., Gibb, J. R., and Benne, K. D. (1964) *T-Group Theory and Laboratory Method*. New York: Wiley.

Bunker, B. B., and Singer, D. L. (1974) 'The "independent non-professional" dilemma: case history analysis of a human relations training program'. Paper presented at the meetings of the American Orthopsychiatric Association digested in *American Journal of Orthopsychiatry*, 1974, **44**, 273.

Burrows, T. (1927) 'The group method of analysis'. *Psychoanalytic Review*, **19**, 268–280.

Burton, A. (1969) *Encounter: The Theory and Practice of Encounter Groups*. San Francisco: Jossey-Bass.

Campbell, J. P., and Dunnette, M. D. (1968) 'Effectiveness of t-group experiences in managerial training and development'. *Psychological Bulletin*, **70**, 73–104.

Culbert, S. A. (1968) 'Trainer self-disclosure and member growth in two t groups'. *Journal of Applied Behavioral Science*, **4**, 47–73.

Davis, S. (1967) 'An organic problem solving method of organizational change'. *Journal of Applied Behavioral Science*, **3**, 3–21.

Egan, G. (1970) *Encounter: Group Processes for Interpersonal Growth*. Belmont, Calif: Wadsworth.

Ezriel, H. A. (1950) 'A psychoanalytic approach to group treatment'. *British Journal of Medical Psychology*, **23**, 59–74.

Foulkes, S. H. (1961) 'Group process and the dynamics of the individual in the therapeutic group'. *British Journal of Medical Psychology*, **34**, 23–31.

Friedlander, F., and Brown, L. D. (1974) 'Organization development'. *Annual Review of Psychology*, **25**, 313–341.

Gibb, J. R. (1971) 'The effects of human relations training'. In A. Bergin and S. Garfield (eds) *Handbook of Psychotherapy and Behavior Change*. New York: Wiley, 839–862.

Gottschalk, L. A., and Pattison, E. M. (1969) 'Psychiatric perspectives on t-groups and the laboratory movement: An overview'. *American Journal of Psychiatry*, **126**, 823–840.

Horwitz, L. (1964) 'Transference in training groups and therapy groups'. *International Journal of Group Psychotherapy*, **14**, 202–213.

Jaques, E. (1955) 'Social systems as a defense against persecutory and depressive anxiety'. In M. Klein (ed.) *New Direction in Psychoanalysis*. New York: Basic Books.

Kaufman, E. (1973) 'Group therapy techniques used by the ex-addict therapist'. *Group Process*, **5**, 3–19.

Klein, E. B., and Astrachan, B. M. (1971) 'Learning in groups: A comparison of study groups and t groups'. *Journal of Applied Behavioral Science*, **7**, 659–683.

Klein, E. B., and Could, L. (1973) 'Boundary issues and organizational dynamics: A case study'. *Social Psychiatry*, **8**, 4, 204–211.

Klein, E. B., Thomas, C. S., and Bellis, E. (1971) 'When warring groups meet: The use of a group approach in police–black community relations'. *Social Psychiatry*, **6**, 93–99.

Laing, E. D. (1965) 'Mystification, conflict and confusion'. In I. Boszormenyi-Nagy and J. Framo (eds) *Intensive Family Therapy*. New York: Harper & Row, 343–363.

Lakin, M. (1969) 'Some ethical issues in sensitivity training'. *American Psychologist*, **24**, 923–928.

Levinson, D. J., and Astrachan, B. (1974) 'Organizational boundaries: Entry into the mental health center'. *Administration in Mental Health*, Summer, 3–12.

Lieberman, M., Yalom, I., and Miles, M. (1973) *Encounter Groups: First Facts*. New York: Basic Books.

Lomranz, J., Lakin, M., and Schifiman, H. (1972) 'Variants of sensitivity training and encounter: diversity or fragmentation? *Journal of Applied Behavioral Science*, **8**, 399–420.

Lowen, A. (1969) 'Bio-energetic group therapy'. In Hendrik Rouitenbeek (ed.) *Group Therapy Today*. New York: Atherton, 279–290.

Lundgren, D. C. (1971) 'Trainer style and pattern of group development'. *Journal of Applied Behavioral Science*, **7**, 689–709.

Menninger, R. (1972) 'The impact of group relations training conferences on organizational growth'. *International Journal of Group Psychotherapy*, **22**, 415–432.

Menzies, I. E. P. (1960) 'A case study in the functioning of social systems as a defense against anxiety'. *Human Relations*, **13**, 95–121.

Miller, E. J., and Rice, A. K. (1967) *Systems of Organization: The Control of Task and Sentient Boundaries*. London: Tavistock Publications.

Moreno, J. L. (1971) 'Psychodrama'. In Harold Kaplan and Benjamin Sadock (eds) *Comprehensive Group Psychotherapy*. Baltimore: Williams & Wilkins.

Parloff, M. B. (1961) 'Therapist-client relationships and outcome of psychotherapy'. *Journal of Consulting Psychology*, **25**, 29–38.

Parloff, M. B. (1967) 'Advances in analytic group psychotherapy'. In J. Marmor (ed.) *Frontiers of Psychoanalysis*. New York: Basic Books.

Perls, F. (1969) *Gesalt Therapy Verbatim*. Lafayette, Calif.: Real People Press.

Rinber, N. G. (1974) 'Effects of an explicit group contract on self-disclosure and group cohesiveness'. *Journal of Counseling Psychology*, **21**, 116–120.

Rice, A. K. (1963) *The Enterprise and its Environment*. London: Tavistock Publications.

Rice, A. K. (1965) *Learning for Leadership*. London: Tavistock Publications.

Rice, A. K. (1969) 'Individual, group and intergroup processes'. *Human Relations*, **22**, 564–584.

Rioch, M. J. (1970) 'The work of Wilfred Bion on groups'. *Psychiatry*, **33**, 56–66.

Schein, E. H., and Bennis, W. G. (1965) *Personal and Organizational Change Through Group Methods*. New York: Wiley.

Schloss, G. A., Siroka, R. W., and Siroka, E. K. (1971) 'Some contemporary origins of the personal growth group'. In R. Siroka, E. Siroka, and G. Schloss (eds) *Sensitivity Training and Group Encounter*. New York: Grossett & Dunlap, 3–9.

Schutz, W. (1967) *Joy: Expanding Human Awareness*. New York: Grove Press.

Seeman, J. (1954) 'Counselor judgments of therapeutic process and outcome'. In C. Rogers and R. Dymond (eds) *Psychotherapy and Personality Change*. University of Chicago Press.

Shaffer, J., and Galinsky, M. D. (1974) *Models of Group Therapy and Sensitivity Training*. Englewood Cliffs, NJ: Prentice-Hall.

Singer, D., Whiton, M. B., and Fried, M. (1970) 'An alternative to traditional mental health services and consultation in schools: A social systems and group process approach'. *Journal of School Psychology*, **8**, 172–179.

Slater, P. E. (1966) *Microcosm: Structural, Psychological and Religious Evolution in Groups*. New York: Wiley.

Slavson, S. R. (1964) *A Textbook in Analytic Group Psychotherapy*. New York: International University Press.

Sutherland, J. D. (1952) 'Notes on psychoanalytic group therapy: 1. Therapy and training'. *Psychiatry*, **15**, 111–117.

Traux, C. B., and Carkhuff, R. R. (1967) *Toward Effective Counseling and Psychotherapy: Training and Practice*. Chicago: Aldine.

Traux, C. B., and Mitchell, K. M. (1971) 'Research on certain therapist interpersonal skills in relation to process and outcome'. In A. Bergin and S. Garfield. (eds) *Handbook of Psychotherapy and Behavior Change*. New York: Wiley.

Turquet, P. M. (1974) 'Leadership—the individual in the group'. In G. S. Gibbard, J. J. Hartman, and R. D. Mann (eds) *Analysis of Groups*. San Francisco: Jossey-Bass, 348–371.

Walton, R. E., and Warwick, D. P. (1973) 'The ethics of organization development'. *Journal of Applied Behavioral Science*, **9**, 681–698.

Whitaker, D. S., and Lieberman, M. A. (1964) *Psychotherapy Through the Group Process*. New York: Atherton Press.

Yalom, I. D. (1970) *The Theory and Practice of Group Psychotherapy*. New York: Basic Books.

Yalom, I. D., and Lieberman, M. A. (1971) 'A study of encounter group casualties. *Archives of General Psychiatry*, **25**, 16–30.

Chapter 3

The A. K. Rice Group Relations Conferences as a Reflection of Society*

Margaret J. Rioch

The A. K. Rice Institute, a national organization constituted at present by seven local centres in the United States, is concerned with the study of groups and institutions conceptualized as open systems. The work, which includes education, consultation and research, is based on a tradition which was developed in the Centre for Applied Social Research of the Tavistock Institute of Human Relations of London under the leadership of the late Dr A. Kenneth Rice. A major part of the educational work of the A. K. Rice Institute is done through group relations conferences, which provide opportunities for the study of intragroup and intergroup processes in the 'here and now' as they occur. The emphasis is on the nature of authority and the problems encountered in its exercise.

The concepts underlying the conferences stem from three major sources: psychoanalysis, the social sciences and practical experience. The psychoanalytic concepts are primarily those of Melanie Klein and Wilfred Bion. From the social sciences the concepts from field theory and systems are the most significant. The practical experience of Dr A. K. Rice in government and commerce led to the development of fruitful ways of thinking about any enterprise, whether it be commercial, educational, religious or any other kind, as an open system. The conferences have learning as their primary task and the level of focus is on the group as a system. One of the most important exercises in the conferences as they have developed is called the 'intergroup event' or the 'intergroup exercise'. It was developed by A. K. Rice and has served for over ten years to illuminate the problems, tribulations, joys, and vicissitudes of life among groups. Its purpose is to provide opportunities for the study of intergroup relations as they happen.

The exercise begins with members of the conference (usually about 50–70 people) meeting all together with the director and sometimes the total staff. The director announces what the primary task is. He tells the members what space and times are available and how the staff will be deployed. He does not indicate where the members should go. Sometimes consultants are assigned to specific rooms. Sometimes they are available on request only. As soon as the director has finished his opening remarks, the members begin the process of forming

*This work was supported in part by Grant 5T03MH 12060–04 from the Center for Crime and Delinquency of the NIMH.

groups. It would be possible for the whole membership to stay together and to organize themselves as a total group without breaking up, but this never happens in the beginning of the event. They always divide up. The director's mention of rooms available for small sectors is apparently sufficient indication that they should do this, although no one says that they must. The interesting thing is how and on what basis they break up.

Some things have remained fairly constant over the past ten years. The breaking up of the total membership into small sectors has almost always been a pretty chaotic affair. Some members get up and start for the door as soon as the director stops speaking. They have either preplanned a course of action or they want to get away from the uncomfortably large, unstructured mass of people into what they think will be a safer or more comfortable situation. People feel that if they do not go quickly they may be left out. Others linger on, wondering what to do or where to go, trying to find some congenial person or persons with whom they can join. Sometimes someone comes up with an idea for forming a group and tries to recruit adherents. For example, someone says he would like to get people together who want to see what it is like to be in a group in which there is no leader. (The fact that he is at the moment exercising leadership is not noticed, but no matter.) A few people join him. A woman wants to form a group to study the problems of men and women. A few join her. Someone wants to study black–white problems. People follow him. Someone wants to form a group to oppose the staff, either in general or on some specific policy. He can be sure of followers.

Somehow groups are formed. They look for a consultant they like if there are some available. Or they look for the room with the most comfortable chairs, or the coolest room in summer and the warmest in winter. And so one could not really expect that these groups would have a great deal of cohesion or coherence since they usually form in a rather stupid and thoughtless way. But in this respect things have not remained constant over the past ten years. In the 1960s the groups usually found an identity in spite of their chaotic beginnings. In the early 1970s this has not been nearly so much the case. In many conferences in 1970–1976 it has scarcely been possible to distinguish one group from another. Groups have been able to merge and individuals have moved from one to another without noting much difference. The staff has found it difficult to distinguish one sector from another, just as it is difficult to tell one super-market or one international airport from another.

Although there is no clear line of demarcation between the earlier decade and the beginning of this one, the trend in the 1960s was towards the formation of more distinguishable and more cohesive groups.

It might be that an event occurring in the history of a particular group helped its members to create an image of themselves as the refugees or the predators or the peaceful ones or the rebels. Often a strong sense of loyalty and cohesion emerged. Usually the rebel group had the most cohesion: but others too developed a remarkable sense of belonging together, a wish to show the other groups that 'ours' is the best. This was not always a wonderful thing. It was often associated with a good deal of paranoia about other groups and what they were up to with respect to 'our' group. An incident that occurred in 1963, in the first conference in which I was a member, illustrates some of these tendencies. Before the group in which I found myself was in any way properly organized, one of our members decided he would go out and visit the other groups. We were in no condition either to stop him or to authorize him and so he simply went. In fact we scarcely paid any attention to his leaving. When he returned he reported that the people in Room A (which he had visited first) were very hostile, disagreeable people, indeed quite warlike, to put it mildly; in Room B they were somewhat indifferent; in Room C the group was delightful, they might soon come to visit us to exchange views, and we should be prepared, he said, to welcome them warmly. Only later did it emerge that he had gone to Room A really quite frightened by his own initiative in leaving our group, but putting up a bold front. He had barged into the room without even a 'by your leave', interrupted their proceedings, and announced that he was sent from our group. Not surprisingly he had been brusquely told to get out. In the next room, B, he behaved in a more neutral manner. And in Room C, feeling somewhat less nervous as he became more experienced, he knocked on the door, requested permission to speak and was received in a correspondingly affable manner. Not long after, a delegate marched into our room from Room A, demanding to know what our plot was against them and demanding an apology for the insulting behaviour of our ambassador. We were all overwhelmed, first with laughter at the idea that our disorganized group would be capable of a 'plot', and then with horror that out of stupid negligence in letting one of our members go out quite ill-prepared to represent us properly, so much real enmity had arisen. It seemed to all of us that we were witnessing in microcosm a phenomenon which must have occurred many times in the world. To be sure, it would be oversimplifying to say that we witnessed the beginning of a war. But we did realize how much damage can be done in foreign affairs and in interorganizational, interinstitutional affairs when a group is too badly organized or too preoccupied with internal matters to think about what its representatives may be doing in its name outside. This episode is a good example, both because it really happened and because it is simple enough to recount. But innumerable episodes occurred which illuminated problems among groups.

During the 1960s it was possible to experience vividly one of the most important aspects of intergroup life—namely, the pull of loyalties between one group and another when one is a member of both. A participant might be designated by his group as its representative to an intergroup meeting. Once there, he found himself a member of a new group, that of the representatives, a more prestigious and often more interesting group, more international, so to speak, than the local club. But still he felt a strong loyalty to the local club. The experience of the tugs and pulls upon him in this situation often brought home to him the conflicts in which he himself or his representatives are caught in the intergroup situations in and among organizations. There was often quite a bit of exhilaration and fun associated with all this. The competition among groups was challenging even when one was not entirely sure what one was competing about.

In the years of militant protest and student revolt, protest and revolt against authority was reflected unmistakably in the conferences. The members were quite articulate in wanting a part in designing the conference, not for next year, but right now. In 1969 the black people demanded that a black consultant be placed on the staff. There were acts of overt violence during which nobody got hurt, but territory was occupied and doors locked so that the staff could either not get in or not get out as the case might be. The room which had been designated as the place where the staff would meet was occupied in advance of the exercise by militant groups so that the staff was forced to meet in the hall or in some other place. Doorknobs were removed and radios played so loudly that no one could be heard speaking. Not all of the subgroups were involved in the militancy, but it was the dominant theme at that time. One conference began the day after the assassination of Robert Kennedy. The conference as a whole was pervaded by fantasies of violence and death which found their symbolic representation in the intolerance of groups for each other.

Although the formation of groups has usually been chaotic, twice during this period of the 1960s members have stopped to plan what they agreed was an intelligent way to subdivide. Both times this happened through the intervention of a strong leader or leader pair who forcefully urged members to wait and work out a manifestly sensible system. Both of these interventions occurred seven or more years ago. In 1969, one other event occurred that is unusual in residential conferences. In that year the total membership got together and chose a leader who would be a spokesman for all of them in negotiating with the staff. He was a very effective spokesman, articulate and well-balanced, and he put forth the point of view of his constituents very ably. These examples of leadership were made possible because each group member was willing to give over some of his own autonomy to the leadership. Few, if any, members regretted this since the leaders who emerged really represented their interests in a competent way. The function of these leaders clearly was to serve the members.

As the protest movements subsided, both the violent revolt and the emergence of effective leadership of the whole receded from the conferences. Of course, both may begin again tomorrow. But the parallel is obvious and very striking.

It is now expected not only that local issues that affect the institutional affiliations of members will show up in the conferences, but often, even more strongly, that the tone or the preoccupation of the nation will appear. In one conference in 1973 the dominant theme in the intergroup event seemed to stem from concentration camps: not to let oneself be noticed. Fascism and terror, familiar from the days of Joe McCarthy, were casting a dark shadow, as if the membership were already responding with a concentration camp mentality to such things as the use of the Internal Revenue Service as a weapon against political enemies. In such an atmosphere it seems better to be as unobtrusive as possible and make no enemies at all. In the first half of 1974 corruption, deception and lack of trust in management were important themes.

In the early 1970s members do not attach themselves with any great zest to their sectors. One has to dig to find the competition. Rebellion is there, to be sure. One can almost count on at least one rebellious group being formed. But there is a relatively lackadaisical quality which pervades the formation and the life of the sectors, even of the rebellious group. It seems not to matter whether one belongs to this group or that. Nobody finds much of anything worth standing for or fighting for. People may be interested enough in huddling together in small groups, and in continuing the study of the intra-small-group dynamics, which is a separate exercise in the conference. But it is difficult to get real participation in intergroup life. This would necessitate the giving up of some autonomy on the part of each member so that some person or persons could be authorized to represent and speak for the group. It would mean allowing effective leadership to emerge. The individual would have to be a little bit submerged in the whole.

This goes hand in hand with a relative reluctance on the part of many members to assume positions of leadership and authority. Leadership is not so much to be coveted as it is to be avoided. And, as I shall amplify later, this is not exactly surprising.

In 1963, in the conference to which I alluded earlier, I was sent as a representative of my group to the director of the exercise, who was ensconced with several other staff members in a large room at the end of a long hallway. He was not sitting behind a large desk, but in my memory he always seems to be. In fact he seems to be sitting in something like an oval office. I was sent upon some relatively harmless errand, which I have now forgotten, but what I remember was the sudden impulse, which surprised me and which seemed to come unexpectedly from unconscious depths, to push him out of his place at the end of that 'oval office' and take it myself. The idea was, of course, impractical and quite ludicrous. What did occur, however, was a mild battle of words in which we each defended, I think, relatively indefensible positions. On looking back, I am impressed by the essentially political significance of what I experienced. The director had not really done anything against me or my group. My impulse to unseat him had to do with his position at the end of the long hall and in the centre of the 'oval office'. The impulse was there quite apart from how well or how badly he was doing his job as director. Since then, in many similar conferences I have been sitting essentially in his chair as director of the exercise and of the conference as a whole. Behind the loyal words and deeds of my staff and the polite gestures of the members which my grey hair seems to inspire, it is not difficult to sense the same ruthless wish to overthrow that I had discovered in myself. There is some irrational part of me that learns slowly or not at all, which is over and over again outraged at this, though I know each time that it is to be expected. 'What, me?' it says. 'When I am doing nothing but acting in their interest? What do they want?' The answer is, of course, 'They want my head.' And it is not too difficult for them to find reasons, since people are very clever at finding reasons for what they want to do.

Whereas throughout the past ten years, and probably before that, one could always find evidence in every conference of a strong wish to 'get the leader', it is becoming more difficult in the early 1970s for leaders to maintain themselves in the face of this wish and its various expressions. It is becoming more and more difficult for leaders to function intelligently and effectively; and this is true both for leadership on the staff and among the members.

Another development has gone hand in hand with the decreasing zest and loyalty which members have brought to group formation and with the increasing difficulty in finding and supporting intelligent and effective leadership. It occurs in the exercise known as Intergroup II, used frequently nowadays, in which consultants are not assigned to specific rooms but are available to member groups on request. In the 1960s, if a representative came to the staff from a group requesting a consultant, the request was practically always granted. The more recent trend on the part of the staff is to question the emissary closely about what the nature of the contract is which the group proposes to make with a consultant. Only if this seems reasonably and consonant with the purpose of the exercise is a consultant sent. He stays only so long as his contract warrants. This procedure is meant to convey to the membership the importance of a contact—i.e. a clear understanding by representatives of groups of their mutual obligations and their respective rights. This is all well and good, and theoretically should result in additional learning. It is noticeable, however, that the staff's demands for rationality in the members in producing a well-thought-out task the consultant can contract to perform, are becoming greater and greater. In other words, the standards for what is required before a staff member will go out as a consultant are becoming higher and higher. And the members' rationality seems to be developing inversely. The higher the standards set by the staff for the groups' rationality, the less meaningful and the more nonsensical the groups' behaviour, and the less likely it is that a consultant, even if he goes out, will find he has a significant task to perform when he gets there.

Outside the conference in the 'real world' similar shifts seem to have taken place in the last few years. The three shifts which have been discussed are: (a) the decreasing zest and zeal for forming cohesive groups; (2) the decrease in the emergence of intelligent leadership and the concomitant less effective functioning of such leadership; (3) the higher standards required for performance of tasks, and an accompanying lowered creative output.

With regard to the first point, many people currently lack interest in becoming part of meaningful groups. This is particularly noticeable among students, who sometimes say that they do not belong to any groups—in fact, they avoid belonging to any. Even classes of the size of a small or medium group are sometimes avoided in favour of either enormous lecture courses in which the individual is anonymous, or individual self-paced courses or independent study. This may correspond to a tapering off of interest in the group scene generally; or it may be the other side of the coin of the popularity of encounter groups, marathons, etc., which so often try to provide a significant group experience for those who do not find it in their daily lives. In any case, loyal, *working* groups which require members to abdicate some autonomy to the leadership for the sake of effective functioning are not easy to find either outside or inside a group relations conference.

With regard to the second point, it is not easy to find the appropriate people who want to be leaders, both outside and inside the conferences. The following account illustrates some of the forces that seem to be at work. In a university class of about 20 recently, students were asked to take the following roles. One was to be director of a mental hospital. He had an assistant director and a receptionist-secretary. A few students were to constitute the board of the hospital, which had a chairman and several members. The rest of the class was divided up into ward personnel and patients. The suggestion was made that the nursing personnel might feel overworked and that the patients might feel neglected, but the script from then on was left to the class. There were just 15 minutes left in the period to take these roles and a rather chaotic situation ensued in which the 'patients' occupied the place where the board wanted to meet and the ward personnel besieged the director. The role play began again in the next period. The man who had taken the role of director became ill and the assistant director moved into his place. Since the new director had known about the absence, he had prepared himself in advance for this role and he wrote on the blackboard a carefully thought-out schedule of events for the class period.

A deluge of protests descended upon his head. The board had not been properly consulted. The head of the ward staff had been bypassed. The patients were not being given their cocoa and cookies.

In the discussion after the role playing was over, the students were very impressed by the immediate impulse they had experienced to 'get the director', each group finding its own seemingly cogent reason for doing this. The people who enjoyed the exercise most were the 'patients'. The ward personnel, torn between some semblance of responsibility for the care of the patients, and the wish to beleaguer the director, were in conflict. The director was torn apart by the conflicting demands of the board, the staff and the patients. But the patients were enjoying the discomfiture of all those who were above them hierarchically; and they settled in to unregenerate happy irresponsibility, adding to the chaos and to the threat to leadership. The 'director' left the class shaking his head and commenting that he did not want a job as director of anything.

In the larger world as well, people tend to shy away from leadership positions, or to dilute them by appointing committees to do the work or by passing the buck to some other part of the organization, from congress to president, from dean to vice-president, or vice versa. Titles and prestige are pleasant, authority and responsibility are not. It is not easy to find appropriate people to serve as heads of anything. People who become leaders in many fields are often the eager beavers, those who might be called the over-achievers, who by dint of tremendous effort and industry are awarded posts above their capacities. Or they may be people eager for personal gain, in terms of money, personal power or renown, with little thought for the followers whom they are supposed to serve.

A column in the *Washington Post* by Joseph Kraft once pointed out

(25 December 1973) that the recurring American national 'crisis in leadership' was not the only crisis, that in Europe, in governments quite untouched by any breadth of scandal, there was also at that time 'general decline of public faith in leadership'. Kraft proposed the explanation that 'governments are not up to the responsibilities which have been thrust upon them. They lack the tools, the brains, and the moral fibre to manage modern economic life in a fair and effective way. They cannot play Santa but they do not admit it.'

It is hard to believe that tools and brains and moral fibre have all rotted away so quickly in the last few years. Perhaps it is that the issues have become so serious, so much a matter of life and death, that no one dares to experiment with them any more, no one, that is, who might be capable of experimenting responsibly.

With regard to the third point, there is a phenomenon in the world outside which corresponds to the higher standards required of the members by the conference staff in defining contracts and tasks in intergroup life, and the increasingly nonsensical but compliant and smoulderingly resentful responses of the members. The parallel lies in the increasingly difficult problems set; first, impersonally by the facts of pollution, overcrowding, and shortages, to which no really effective response is made; and second, in the field of education, by the tremendous demands put upon students who wish to enter medical school or graduate departments such as psychology. Everyone is familiar with the proportion of only about one in 100 to be accepted into graduate pro-grammes. This should mean a higher standard; and indeed high grades, excellent recommendations and consistently good records are required. But it is far from certain that the actual performance of students in response to these requirements is truly better. The response, to be sure, is overtly compliant. When on occasion these young people reveal themselves honestly it becomes clear that smouldering resentment underlies the compliance. The dissertations which they write in conformance with the requirements are often in their own eyes trivial nonsense. They give their professors what they think the professors want, in order to get the necessary grades and recommendations. They work hard but the work rarely results in a production which is truly meaningful to them. It is rare to find in their dissertations any evidence of the play of creative imagination. And indeed how could there be, since their preoccupation is with conformity whether it is meaningful or not?

I have attempted to make the point that three significant shifts which have occurred in society at large are reflected clearly in the group relations confe-rences, especially in the intergroup event. The term 'reflected' implies that the intergroup event functions as a kind of mirror which can be held up to society as a whole. While maintaining that this is essentially true, I would say that in one respect it is a questionable assumption, in that the segment of the population which attends the conferences is very small and highly selected. Many segments of society (e.g. the very poor, the very young, big business, high government officialdom) are rarely represented. By and large the conferences are populated by very serious, intelligent, moderately to very well-educated people, who want to learn about how groups function. The reflection which occurs is that of an important but limited aspect of society. I have in fact drawn my analogies from the field of formal education, which is in itself a limited aspect of our lives.

Another implication of the word 'reflection' is that a conference is a passive recipient of whatever society, or an important segment of it, offers, just as a mirror gives back whatever object appears before it, but has no active image of its own. This again is not an entirely correct assumption. A conference has a life of its own. Like all educational institutions, it attempts to influence; not towards a specific course of action, but towards greater awareness, psychological understanding and sense of responsibility with regard to the groups of which the members are a part. In this respect it is allied to all individuals and institutions which are attempting to influence society in this same direction. It finds itself in a paradoxical adversary position over against tendencies to shirk social responsibility, to avoid arduous leadership positions, and to conform or rebel mindlessly. This is paradoxical since the conference leadership takes the position that the task is simply to study, that whatever happens is grist for the mill, that consultants are simply interpreting in their comments what the processes are which they see occurring. They are presumably not saying what should or what should not go on. They point out repeatedly that the initiative for action belongs to the membership, who, by virtue of their sheer numbers, have the power to do whatever they like in any and all of the conference exercises.

But the 'pure' position of an objective observer who simply interprets or mirrors what he sees and hears without exerting any influence on his hearers is really impossible to maintain. The parallel to psychoanalytically oriented psychotherapy and to psychoanalysis itself is very close. As many observers have pointed out, and most cogently perhaps Perry London in his *Modes and Morals of Psychotherapy*, the neutral position is a self-contradictory and impossible one. Not only do conference consultants have values of their own but some of their values are readily observable. The conference leadership does indeed exert influence.

When people are attempting to exert influence in one direction, they necessarily become highly aware of the counter forces which impede their work. Thus the 'reflection' of society which is observed in the intergroup event is not a pure mirror, any more than the conference consultant is a pure mirror of the processes he perceives in the groups before him. Tendencies which run counter to the thrust of the conference are in general felt more strongly than those which are irrelevant to or even allied to the direction in which the institution wants to go. Consultants become acutely aware of changes in the strength of the opposition to their thrust. The tendencies and shifts pointed out in this paper represent increases in strength of oppositional forces.

My hypothesis is that all these tendencies, in and out of the conferences, have to do with our decreased ability to play. We either work or 'kill time' in some way which anaesthetizes us and makes us forget our anxieties. This is not anything very new, but the phenomenon is on the increase. Everyone seems to be working harder and longer than he used to. The original sense of recreation as re-creation has been forgotten. Who are the great creative players in their 20s, 30s, and even 40s who will take the places of Picasso, Auden, and Casals, to mention only a few of the giants who have died in the very recent past?

So that the introduction of the concept of play shall not seem frivolous, a quotation from the eighteenth-century German philosopher and poet, Friedrich Schiller may be in order. 'Man only plays', he said, 'when, in the full meaning of the word, he is a man, and he is only completely a man when he plays.' And the extraordinary South African writer, Laurens van der Post, agrees 'that a culture expresses itself most creatively by stimulating in men the instinct to play'.

The essential aspect of play is that it is accompanied by a *relative* lack of attachment to results even though it may be performed with great interest, energy, seriousness, and intensity. The playful activity is performed more for its own sake than for what will come of it. The lack of attachment to results, along with the high degree of interest in the activity, gives to play that extraordinary quality which Schiller ascribes to it when he says that man is only completely a man when he plays.

Some of the great players of the world are the artists. Van Gogh would surely have liked to sell his paintings, but he continued to paint in spite of never selling one. Some writers are said not to want to see their works again once they are finished. However this may be in the case of the individual artist, the non-attachment aspect of play gives it the sense of being at one and the same time most delightful, precious, and unimportant. 'It's only a game, and therefore of no consequence,' we say; and at the same time it is in the creative play of the imagination that our most beautiful and treasured objects are created.

To return to the field of education and to the conferences, it is as if in the late 1960s the issues had begun to be so serious that no one dared to play with them either in the conferences or in the world. Dr A. K. Rice was moved to say in 1969 that some of the issues which arose in a conference that year could no longer be used for a learning experience. They dealt too much with life and death and were therefore not appropriate for experimentation in an educational institution. It is as if, having reached a peak of grim seriousness, the issues have become senseless. The middle ground of creative play is lacking.

When we set out to educate people, we are engaged in a gamelike or playful situation. To be sure, one learns from very unplayful and ungamelike situations, such as severe illness, of one's relatives or oneself. People also learn by accident; if, for example, they stumble on some yellow sand which indicates there is gold in the nearby hills. But these are situations which are not planned. To set up a learning situation one must plan. And what we plan is something more or less set apart from the 'real' world.

Even vocational schools and 'work programmes' in colleges are often more like rehearsals than like the real performance. To be sure, many students, as well as teachers, have become impatient with too much rehearsing and have wanted to be involved in the real world. And so political science students come to Washington to take part in the running of government. Psychology students have field experiences. Everyone wants a job of some kind to taste this marvellous thing called reality. But in our natural and understandable impatience with conventional, traditional ivory tower learning, we may overlook the assets of the 'unreal' situation.

It is in the nature of a game to be time and space limited. Of course there are serious games and professional games like major league baseball, professional boxing, Davis Cup tennis, or international chess which continue over a long time. When we empathize with the participants in such events we understand that success or failure is as important in these games as it is in someone's professional career. It is like winning or losing an election for the US Senate, like performing a difficult successful or unsuccessful operation as a surgeon, like winning or losing a complicated case as a lawyer. But there may well be a game-like quality in these things too. When there is, it has to do with the sportsmanlike way in which one competes, in an election, for example, as opposed to a fanatical life or death way, as in a war. If we kill off our opponent he will not be there to play with us tomorrow. It has been claimed that in a recent election the aim was not to beat the opposing party, but to kill it dead, so that it would be wiped off the map. Then no more elections would be necessary. The games would be finished and reality, for which in this case we may read 'dictatorship', would begin.

One of the major differences between a game which resembles work and one which is *just* for fun has to do with how much attachment the players feel to the weight of the consequences. This varies from one extreme of making or breaking a person's career, let us say in professional baseball, to a casual summer afternoon's game of croquet with friends whose relationships are grounded elsewhere and who will forget the game before sundown. Since everything in the world supposedly has consequences, it is not that the game of croquet has none, but that they weigh very light in the scales. We may say that they are at one end of a continuum at the other end of which might be either disaster or great good fortune in career or marriage or health. Education lies, or should lie, somewhere in the middle of the continuum. Rehearsals of all kinds lie in the middle and education is one kind of rehearsal. If we want to carry the point further we might say that all of life is education, or some might prefer to call it a rehearsal.

Unhappily for our formal educational process, whether a student receives an A or a B or a D in a course is likely to have rather large and incalculable consequences for his future career. Whether or not he will get into college from high school and whether or not he will get into graduate school from college and thus become a member of one of our supposedly desirable professional guilds depends to a large extent upon his scholastic record. And so, alas, he cannot afford to play. Playing is not the equivalent of 'goofing off'. A student who plays tries out new strokes, rehearses parts in various ways until he finds his own way. He experiments with different roles to see which suits him best. If failure in these tryouts were not so important, he would be able to play freely and vigorously, making use of his imagination, developing his talents, casting aside some choices and following up on others. Paradoxically, the more serious education has become in terms of its consequences, the less significant it is for the students' development.

In this context, the policy of the group relations conferences that no reports are made on the behaviour of members to their supervisors, teachers, employers, is extremely significant. The intention is to minimize the consequences in the external world of the participants' behaviour in the conferences so that they may have maximum freedom. The phrase used is 'freedom to experiment' and that sounds serious and scientific. But with a slight shift in terminology, though not in meaning, one might say 'freedom to play'. Or if that is unacceptable, one could say 'freedom to rehearse'.

But actually the policy of no reports turns out to be not a sufficient guarantee of freedom to play. There are apparently plums to be had, prizes to be won, within the conferences themselves, without any reports. First of all it happens that people's employers or supervisors are sometimes staff members or fellow participants who are thought to be carefully watching and judging the members' performance in order to give out or not give out promotions or better jobs later. And second, for obscure reasons, participants often wish to become staff members in the future and to do this they must impress the present staff with their performance. To be sure it is hard to ferret out what kind of performance pleases the staff and leads to appointment in a staff role, the rewards for which are questionable; but people try, as they try for As in college.

As they struggle, one of the major difficulties in group life becomes apparent, namely the problem of knowing how *I* stand with the others. Am I pleasing my peers and the authorities or not? Of course, I will never know in detail for certain, but it is important to me to estimate and to be as accurate as possible in my estimate. The job of estimating and evaluating is much easier in a twosome since there is only one person besides myself to be concerned about, and since I started out in life developing expertise in knowing how I stand with one significant other, usually Mother. As Winnicott puts it,

Some babies . . . study the variable maternal visage in an attempt to predict the mother's mood, just exactly as we all study the weather. The baby quickly learns to make a forecast: 'Just now it is safe to forget the mother's mood and to be spontaneous, (i.e. to play) but any minute the mother's face will become fixed or her mood will dominate, and my own personal needs must then be withdrawn, otherwise my central self may suffer insult.'

In spite of or even because of this early training which we have all gone through, the forecasting of people in a group is not comfortable. Wilfred Bion's metaphor of the group as a sphinx, made up of disparate parts, some threatening, some more beneficent, expresses the frightening experiences which people live through in groups.

To judge from the lack of spontaneity in many groups, it could be assumed that the members have looked around and predicted that they had better be careful about expressing their personal needs in order not to suffer insult to their central selves. When they consider their fellow group members, instead of seeing something related to themselves and their needs, as they would in a good mother, they see their peers preoccupied with the same question with which they are preoccupied, namely trying to find out how they stand with each other. And there are so many of them! Even in a small group one has to deal with three or four potential friends, two or three potential enemies, and one or two impenetrable ones. As the group increases in size to 30 or 60 people, perhaps divided into subgroups, it becomes really impossible. One cannot even see everyone at once, so how can anyone predict from which quarter to expect an attack or friendly support or indifference? This holds true of self-study groups as well as of communities or boards or agency staffs or university departments which one has newly joined. It takes some time before one knows how the wind will blow in any of these situations; and even after years one may find oneself surprised by sudden shifts.

In a residential conference composed of members who do not know each other in advance and will probably never see each other afterwards, it is re-markable how quickly the evaluation of one's peers, to say nothing of that of the persons in authority, the consultants, comes to be of enormous importance. The statement that one is free to experiment or to play because one's behaviour will have no real consequences back home and in the world outside is both highly rational and reasonable, and also manifestly untrue. It matters that these people are judging each other right now. And behaviour, alas, becomes rigid and compliant, compliant with heaven knows what expectations, but certainly not free to play or to experiment. There are, fortunately, exceptions. People do loosen up, decide they are going to try out something new, take risks, etc. But one has only to observe a new group in the process of formation to be astounded over and over again at the fear which grips human beings in each other's presence. The preoccupation seems to be with the question: 'How am I impres-sing them? What will they think of me?' And above all: 'How will the people in authority respond to me?'

To be sure, the major task of the conference involves teaching the members, or rather giving them opportunities to learn, to work through their problems about authority. The staff teaches, or rather provides opportunities to learn, that the members are living under an illusion of powerlessness in the face of a staff which is usually highly articulate, but has actually no power to make members do or not do anything. The truth is that the members had the power from the very beginning. They could have done and can do what they like with it. The strict rules which they saw and imagined were for the staff, not for them. The discipline was the staff's discipline. No one was telling them, 'Do this, do that.' They had that coveted possession called freedom and had been complain-ing about it. They had been denying their own authority and wishing to put it on the staff, and, of course, denying their own responsibility in the process.

And this is perhaps the heart of the educational events which are called group relations conferences. There are wide applications to be made of this teaching, especially in universities. Students have to discover every year **for** themselves that when they fear to challenge authority, many professors would welcome their inquiries and their opposition, their playing with new ideas.

But the question arises: 'What is now the new anxiety, if we have worked through the one about the powerful father and the castrating mother who will not let us be potent and competent?' There is a new anxiety and a new illusion: namely that there is a right way if we can only find it, if we will only work hard enough and be clever enough to learn the right skills and techniques. But if we do not, we shall surely not survive. We shall be cast into outer darkness, not by a powerful father, but by our own doing or not-doing. This is more fearful, and the anxiety associated with this idea is more paralysing than that associated with authority. It leaves people less capable of performing the task of the conference, which is a game to be played with the best resources of heart and mind that are available. And the same is true of the larger task of living in the world.

Some other kinds of groups in the current group scene, with which the A. K. Rice Institute has little in common, actively encourage games and playfulness. In some encounter groups people leave their names and old professional identities behind them and choose new names and new identities quite playfully and sometimes quite imaginatively.

Group relations conferences have a spartan attitude in this respect. There is no *artificial* playing. It has to be real. In traditional conferences lists are printed of members with full names, addresses, titles, and professional or occupational identities. The game has to be played straight. It is like a drama without any stage set and without any costumes. But never fear; like the mime who gives the illusion of climbing the stairs, though no stairs are visible, roles will be taken and the drama will be played without help from any props. The lack of props, the stern refusal to use any gimmicks, and the deeply serious intent, have often led staff members to say severely, 'This is not a game; no one is acting; we are not wearing masks; we are simply doing our jobs.' Undeniably true, but the job is a rehearsal; a trying out of roles, playing hard, sometimes even with fire.

Staff members often talk about work and task in these conferences with a kind of religious fervour. Bion's technical term, 'work group', and A. K. Rice's term, 'primary task' suit the Protestant work ethic well. No time for fun and games here. The staff performs the same function that the skull performs in medieval paintings, which says, 'Look what is beneath the exterior. The surface may be pretty smiles and rosy cheeks, but they quickly fade; the death's head is what lasts; it is the enduring reality. *Memento mori.*'

Have we perhaps drawn the wrong conclusion from the death's head? Should we not, in view of our mortality, dance and sing, play our harps and flutes, as well as hammer our shields and plant our vegetables? It may be said that there is a place for dancing and singing; only the conferences are not it. But in a metaphorical sense, they are exactly the place, and so are our universities and our schools.

The leadership of the conferences, and perhaps of our educational institutions in general, is suffering from the illusion that what we do is not just serious, but deadly serious; that play has no part in it, but technique may save us from death. The anxiety associated with this illusion is so severe that it has to be pushed under the rug. One of the best ways to do this is the way a competent surgeon does it, namely to become such a proficient craftsman, skilled, so experienced in his technique that he can be confident about his performance. He also becomes absorbed in his performance so that during an operation he need not be bothered by anxiety about its success. One of the side effects of this is that he often becomes intolerant and impatient of incompetence in others, especially in those who assist him. He knows the right way and will brook no interference. It is quite possible for a surgeon to develop sufficient skill that he can feel and *be* competent in life and death situations. He can say with some confidence that if he did not succeed in the operation, success was very likely not possible.

The leaders of a conference, however, are not dealing with one organ of an anaesthetized body. With all due and great respect for the task of the surgeon, it can be argued that the responses of 50 unanaesthetized bodies are more complex than what goes on on the operating table. When conference leaders, therefore, feel that they are in a life and death situation, their task becomes well nigh unbearable. One of the ways to deal with the anxiety is the surgeon's way. Consultants become highly proficient technicians, skilful in their jobs, 'knowing' the right way, intolerant of interference and incompetence, arrogant in their attitudes.

Members often get the message from the staff: 'There is a correct technique. You can learn it from us, though we don't instruct you in words.' In universities and in the world outside there is also a tendency to look to technicians for leadership, for they are thought to have magic power over life and death.

Underlying all this is the assumption that there are knowable criteria for ultimate success and failure in the conferences and in life itself. Conference leaders shake their heads wisely and say: 'This last one was a good conference', or 'A lot of learning took place that time.' There is even evidence for such statements. Members in their application groups towards the end of the conferences indicate that they understand better how their organizations work and how they can be improved. Letters come in later saying that people have reorganized their programmes at home in the light of what they have learned. In fact, if none of these things happened, the conferences would probably soon cease to exist. They are part of the export system of the conferences and they constitute the products which make a new import possible. Similar things are said about all our ventures—about graduate schools, the national economy, in war, and in peace. A programme must have a measure of success from some partial point of view if it is to survive.

But must we survive? Is this perhaps the true question to be learned from looking at the death's head underneath the rosy cheeks? Must the conferences survive, and our universities, and our society itself? Might it not be better to play creatively and to risk being unsuccessful—to play without attachment to the consequences even if these should turn out to be the end of our institutions and our lives? This may be thought to be a counsel of old age when death is close in any case. But it is a lesson which youth knows better than old or middle age, for it is in youth that people are most careless of survival.

There is a way to live with the anxiety which remains when the fear of authority has been worked through and we are faced with the remaining uncertainty about the correctness of our performance and its consequences for us and our world. It is the way of nonattachment in play. But the consequences of this way are unknown.

Chapter 4

The Pseudomutual Small Group or Institution*

James P. Gustafson

There are many ways to preserve the *status quo* of a small group or institution. The traditional methods are the use of literal force and favour and the cultivation of irrational hopes and fears that will assure loyalty. Bion (1961) has argued that we are prone to three types of irrational group formation which may be used to prevent development: the basic assumption dependency group which acts as if it only need wait for the godlike leader to provide for all the group's needs; the basic assumption pairing group which acts as if it only need wait for a pair of people to produce a messiah or messianic idea; the basic assumption fight–flight group, which acts as if it only need flee from or attack the supposed danger. Bion suggests that the major conservative institutions are based on specialized use of one of the three basic assumptions: the church (also, the medical profession) uses basic assumption dependency, the aristocracy uses basic assumption pairing, and the army uses basic assumption fight–flight. While all of these modes may be very powerful, and crude, at least they are familiar. Since we may define these assumptions, we are less apt to lose ourselves in their spell.

We have less definition of, and thus less distance from, other common, more subtle modes in which the *status quo* is maintained. In my view, one major principle of these modes is to blur distinctions and boundaries. We seem to be increasingly aware of how language is muddled by public figures. My purpose in this paper is to show how a group or institution may, as well, obscure its external group boundaries, internal disagreement and opposition, the outline of the leader's role, and the distinctness of the individuals who are its members.

What I describe here in reference to public small groups and institutions has been described precisely and repeatedly in reference to family relations of schizophrenics. The clearest, brief account is that of Wynne *et al.* (1958): the 'pseudomutual family' is the result of systematic family effort to blur distinctions and boundaries, which is felt to be necessary because these allow clear disagreement and disagreement is felt to be catastrophic. The child who is to become schizophrenic is thought to be unable to define an identity in this blur. The adult who has already established an identity in other contexts may

*I am grateful to Dr. Nicholas Ward for his comments on earlier drafts of this essay.

better tolerate pseudomutuality in the family or in the public small groups or institutions that I will describe here.

In summary, this pseudomutual defence against differentiation and change relies less on a show of strength and more on camouflage. *A consultant's work, correspondingly, shifts from interpretation of irrational forces to insistence on clarity of definition. With explicit awareness of how a group may obscure itself (systematically), we know better how we will be confused by the group and what questions may not be evaded. I will first describe the extreme case; secondly, its relation to the previous literature; thirdly, the events of my consultation to a particular group of this sort; and, finally, summarize a strategy for the consultant in these situations.

The extreme case

One's first impression of such a group may well be a blurred collection of good-natured people. One is impressed by their goodwill. This impression is not dispelled as long as they are able to prevent any sharp focus, and this they do very well. Clear distinctions and boundaries make disagreement and even confrontation possible and could lead to individuation, change, and growth.

If one is able to focus on their blur, one may begin to hear what they do to language. For instance, one hears them use 'authority' (the right to do work on behalf of others) and 'power' interchangeably. 'Consultant' is the same as 'counsellor'. 'Contract' is the same as a sudden unanimity to do something with another group. 'Helping' means any activity initiated by the group. They are very fond of these vague words. Since language is the major internal tool for distinctions, the loss of clear language by itself may be enough to block anything from happening.

At the physical boundary of the group, they are equally ingenious. In no way can there be anything definite to come up against. The door is always open. Everyone is invited in, as members! No one may sit as a detached observer, without being invited into the circle. Few people come and few leave. Those who leave 'hurt' the group, but are always welcome back as members.

When pushed, they will admit that there are a few possible members with whom they would be 'uncomfortable'. These are people who are very 'selfish' and 'callous'. But should these people appear, they will be very 'concerned' and 'help' if they can.

Asked for a characterization of the 'we' that they are, they are extremely difficult to pin down. They agree they are a 'core group' or 'administrative group'.

The leader's role is often occupied by a virtuoso of charm. He graciously admits to the fault of 'taking too much responsibility' and that he always feels a need to be talking. Who would dare tell him to shut up? The group is senti-

---

*Rather than a biological metaphor, I could use a military or a political one: the change is from massive armament to mobility and deception, or from 'conservative' beliefs to 'liberal' evasion.

mental about him, the dear one. Anyone who makes a move must check with him first, at least waiting for his nod.

What about literal opposition? In the first place, this immediately evokes a mood of 'hurt', lifted eyebrows, and the sense that this is unnecessary 'nastiness'. The person with the objection is offered 'help'. If this is not enough, it is suggested, at first gently, then with greater 'concern', that the objector may have some personal 'problem' with the issue.

The outside world barely is represented in the group. One easily forgets about it. The members rarely make forays into it.

If disagreement finally breaks through all of this, and two or more individuals are pushing against one another, individuality now more evident than group membership, the group is in crisis. In Turquet's (1975) terms, they are, above all, 'membership individuals' and 'individual membership' is not possible for long. Individual members who cannot be browbeaten with 'help' have to be sent out as observers. When this fails to relieve tension, the last resort is rapid splintering.

In summary, the group colludes to blur the awareness of language, the boundaries with other groups, the boundaries of the self, the force of the leader's role, opposition or disagreement, and the fact of an outside, alternative world.

Previous formulations

What I have just described as an extreme case of blurring in a small group or institution is summarized by Wynne et al. (1958), in reference to families, by the term 'pseudomutuality'. Aspects of this total defensive solution have been described as well by many other writers.

In regard to language, Wynne et al. comment follows:

In some cases, the sweeping parental approval of any of the child's behavior is verbalized as respect for self-determination, 'freedom,' and family 'democracy,' and is typified by the oft-repeated response of one set of parents, 'we only want you to do what you want to do'. (p. 211)

Orwell (1946) emphasizes that the wish to hide leads to the use of this language, but that the habit of this language then makes the recovery of clarity impossible:

The great enemy of clear language is insincerity. When there is a gap between one's real and declared aims, one turns as it were instinctively to long words and exhausted idioms, like a cuttle fish squirting out ink. ... But if thought corrupts language, language corrupts thought. ... This invasion of one's mind by readymade phrases (*lay the foundations, achieve radical transformation*) can only be prevented if one is constantly on guard against them, and every such phrase anesthetizes a portion of one's brain. (pp. 167, 168).

In regard to external boundaries, Wynne et al. describe the following:

the family members try to act as if the family could be a truly self-sufficient social system with a completely encircling boundary. ... The unstable but continuous boundary, with no recognizable openings, surrounding the schizophrenic family system, stretches to include that which can be interpreted as complementary and contracts to exclude that which is interpreted as noncomplementary. This continuous but elastic boundary we have called the rubber fence. (p. 211)

Laing and Cooper (1964) emphasize the violence necessary to maintain this boundary, which the family is 'pledged' to defend: The

pledge ... can be seen as the resistance of the survival group against separationist action, whether of going away or differentiation; as guarantee of the future through a lack of change produced in the group by freedom. .... It is freedom wishing to become inert. ... (p. 135)

In the nexal family the unity of the group is achieved through the experience by each of the group ... [that the danger is] ... the dissolution or dispersion of 'the family' ... The 'protection' that such a family offers its members seems to be based on several preconditions: (i) a fantasy of the external world as extraordinarily dangerous; (ii) the generation of terror inside the nexus at this external danger. This work is *violence*. (Laing, 1967, pp. 58, 59)

Upon reading Laing and Cooper (1964), I was unable at first to recognize the violent 'pledge group' from my experience. What are more easily noticed are the ingratiating, 'unselfish' qualities of such a group, while the pledge is more covert and only crudely enforced under trying circumstances. I would stress that the presenting quality of such a group is often friendly and 'unselfish'. As will be apparent in my consultation report, prospective members of such a group are often drawn in, before they become aware of the price of oneness, of the 'pledge'.

In regard to internal boundaries and distinctions, Wynne *et al.* describe the following:

We have already mentioned that even minor divergence may be experienced as threatening to precipitate, for example, a heart attack. Family legends about fury and violence may be pervasive reminders of the supposed consequence of divergence. (p. 211)

However, the force of this leadership is obscured as much as possible:

Hence they asked the ward administrator to tell their son to shave. When intermediaries participate in this way, the direct expectations in the family can be more easily blurred and the possible noncomplementarity remain untested. (p. 214)

The blurring of the boundary of the self may be quite extreme:

In order to document for us that 'nothing had changed,' the parents showed us the correspondence from him during the four months prior to hospitalization. These letters actually portrayed extremely vividly the marked changes in the son, which the parents were unable to recognize even when the letters were discussed with them directly. (p. 212)

The ideal of 'unselfishness' may often be what defines a family member from one who is not a family member, as if to say that one cannot be both a family member and 'selfish', as captured in the famous song of the Beatles, 'Sergeant Pepper's Lonely Hearts Club Band':

She (we never thought of ourselves) is leaving (never thought of ourselves) home . . .
She's leaving home after living alone for so many years.

The boundary between outside the family and inside is between the selfish individual who 'is leaving' (outside parentheses), and we 'who never thought of ourselves' (inside parentheses).*

I would emphasize, in summary, that thorough pseudomutuality is the extreme case, in which all possible sources of divergence are blurred. A less thorough defence may obscure any one or more of the possible boundaries or tools of the group or institution: namely, language, external boundaries, internal boundaries and opposition, the force of leadership, and the boundaries of the 'self'. Families may do all of this, defensively, as illustrated in the work cited. I will now proceed to illustrate the parallel phenomena in a small group which I served as a consultant.

A consultation

The consultation took place in the context of an intergroup exercise of a group relations conference.† In this exercise, which involved more than 40 conference members, the members initially convened with the conference director who essentially told them that they could form whatever groups they pleased and study the relations between the groups formed. They would have seven periods of an hour and a quarter each to go about this, and could get consultation as they proceeded from consultants stationed in five rooms.

Seventeen members came to my room, clearly led by an influential doctor. Asked about their reasons for coming, they spoke of the coolness of the room— it did have air conditioners—and said that they all were heads of things, i.e. in power. After nearly an hour of such talk, I suggested they knew very little about the outside world, and wondered if they were interested in it. Three of the most active people (including the influential doctor) quickly volunteered as observers. However, when these three could get no sanction to go on behalf of the group, they impulsively left on their own! It was as if the struggle between individual needs and those of the group could not be tolerated. In Turquet's (1975) terms, one was either a 'membership-individual' or a 'singleton'. One could not be an individual and a member.

By the second session, the group had learned that one of the three had defected to another group. They were 'hurt'. Two striking features I commented on after a while: first, I said that the women had begun to lead the group (13 of

---

*In Turquet's (1975) terms, one must either be a 'singleton' (outside groups) or a 'membership-individual' (wholly a loyal member). One may not be an 'individual-member'.

† For a description of the rationale and technique of the intergroup, see Rice (1965).

16 were women), but had backed down in defence to the doctor; secondly, the doctor and a powerful older woman were stationed by the door so that anyone leaving would have to pass between them. I was angrily told to keep silent, and chairs were pushed closer together, leaving me out.

They then discussed their 'openness'. When I inquired if this were completely the case (my own exclusion being evident to me), they agreed that there was a certain bossy, intrusive individual in the membership they would not be comfortable with. Clearly, a certain individualism continued to be anathema— that of the defector, myself, and the bossy member just referred to.

In the third session, 'isolation' was the theme. Was the isolation of the bossy individual his problem? Probably so. When I suggested they might investigate this with observers externally, while continuing their internal discussion, three active women volunteered, again could get no sanction to go on behalf of the group, left impulsively on their own, never again to return as members! They settled then into a very dependent posture with the doctor, and began picking on a young woman who by her low power status and her questioning attitude was the clearest 'outsider'.

In the fourth session, they were in 'mourning' over the defections, now a total of four. I asked if it were a sin to put individual learning ahead of group membership. They allowed it might not be, but suggested that the defectors had worse motives. They made their doctor 'chairman', when I suggested a chairman might help them delegate responsibility for external tasks, but continually referred to him as 'leader' in a deferential manner.

In the fifth meeting, they became interested in 'honesty'. How could they honestly talk to the bossy person, who held some real power over many of them outside the conference. They sent two representatives to discuss this issue with the 'boss'. The questioning young girl told them they were making the 'boss' too accountable for their own failure to be direct. She was told she was naive. I suggested that their own dishonesty was to deny the possibility that the defectors went to the boss's group for advancement, that they were envious, and oppressed by their need to deny individual ambition in everyone but the 'boss'. This made the influential doctor very selfrighteous and angry about his devotion to the welfare of one and all, and effectively closed off individual selfishness as a viable possibility in this group. The representatives then returned and the group marched off to meet with the boss's group *en bloc*.

In the sixth session, after their fruitless meeting with the boss, they sat in gloomy comfort, in turn justifying themselves to me and the questioning young girl. Five members in turn claimed evidence for their openness to the members in the other groups, which they had demonstrated by conversations during dinner.

In the seventh and final session, they had no patience with their 'chairman— leader'. He resigned barely in time. Several said they were tired of him being 'responsible'. One lady surprised everyone by an impassioned statement: '*We* are those who want things to stay the way they are. *I* do. *You* all do.' The other doctor in the group volunteered to take over as chairman. He said that he had not wanted to come to the group last session, that he was very curious about what was happening in the other groups, and that he had a plan. They should break into three subgroups and try to merge with the other groups. The tension and energy were running very high. They marched off within minutes. Again the divergent wishes of individuals cannot be contained within the pseudomutual group. There is some gain in being able to delegate roles to individuals. Rather than leave as singletons, they are able to leave in small subgroups, but the group is fractured.

The strategy of the consultant

I have emphasized the blurring of language, external boundaries, opposition, the leader's role, and individuality (except as pathology). All of these aspects may be effectively countered. The plainer meaning behind 'being hurt', 'openness', 'honesty', and so forth, may be said. The covert external boundaries may be clarified, such as in pointing out the doctor and powerful older woman at the door. The leader's role in keeping the group undifferentiated may be challenged. In short, the consultant may counter the vague boundaries by sharply questioning or defining them. He thus shows the possibility of opposition that is devoted to the work task of the group. Two issues deserve further emphasis. In these groups, only deviant individuals are interested in the outside world. What builds up, however, is an enormous yearning to 'be oneself', to feel the clear outline of oneself in motion, rather than the blurring of member into member. This individuation is felt to be intolerable within the group. Hence, the consultant must continually bring in the outside world, and what they may be missing out there. The lost parts of the individuals seem to be cast 'out there', rather than buried inside. Hence, the contact with these lost parts may be made through going away.

However, the consultant is subject to these same powerful forces himself. He is apt to become either lost or outrageously individualistic—denouncing their stuffiness, and so forth.* The consultant thereby feels his own outline in the blur. The teenager with such a family does the same. This does not move them. It rather hardens their resistance; the consultant represents individuality and its isolation (the 'singleton' role), which they vicariously participate in, while snug in their nest. We thus act out the hatred between individuals (the 'singleton') and the loyal group (the 'membership-individual') but do not get any further towards a new solution (towards 'individual membership'). The skill, rather, is in posing the difficulty inherent in the situation: whether clear individual expression will be tolerated in the group, or whether it is necessary to leave for that to be experienced? Is it necessary to have pure loyalty at home and free expression sent abroad?

---

*Turquet (1975) describes the same polarization of the consultant in large group situations.

References

Bion, W. R. (1961) *Experiences in Groups and Other Papers*. New York: Basic Books.

Laing, R. D. (1967) *Politics of Experience*. New York: Pantheon Books.

Laing, R. D., and Cooper, D. G. (1964) *Reason and Violence: a Decade of Sartre's Philosophy: 1950–1960*. London: Tavistock Publications.

Orwell, G. (1946) 'Politics and the English language'. In *A Collection of Essays by George Orwell*, New York: Harcourt Brace Jovanovich.

Rice, A. K. (1965) *Learning for Leadership—Interpersonal and Inter-group Relations*. London: Tavistock Publications.

Turquet, P. M. (1975) 'Threats to identity in the large group'. In L. Kreeger (ed.) *The Large Group: Therapy and Dynamics*. London: Constable.

Wynne, L. C., Ryckoff, I. M., Day, J., and Hirsch, S. I. (1958) 'Pseudo-mutuality in the family relations of schizophrenics'. *Psychiatry*, **21**, 205–220.

Chapter 5

Another Source of Conservatism in Groups

Robert H. Gosling

The ways that groups resist change in the face of good reason have often been the subject of comment. What Lewin (1951) called 'quasi-stationary equilibrium' can be seen in the way groups from the very smallest, the pair, to the largest, a conglomerate of institutions such as a state, cling to the *status quo* despite a widely agreed need for change and considerable internal and external pressure to bring it about.

Psychodynamic studies have usually pointed to two sources of this conservatism: reluctance to give up established relationships, and fear of the unknown and the unfamiliar. A third source will be described in this paper suggested by Winnicott's work on transitional phenomena and their importance in creative and cultural activities.

Two familiar sources

1. *The reluctance to give up a relationship and the pain of loss*

In the animal kingdom attachment behaviour can be observed universally between the mother and her young. Depending on the biological maturity of the neonate the efforts made by the young to maintain proximity to the mother are variously intense (Bowlby, 1969). If separation exceeds a certain point, vigorous efforts are made to overcome it. In the case of human beings, because of the notable and prolonged immaturity of the baby, attachment behaviour is both intense and elaborate.

While it is true that with increasing maturity self-reliance comes to replace reliance on the attachment figure, and as a result of sufficient 'mothering experience' the individual can come to 'mother himself', he yet remains disposed to seek attachment to others. Depending on the emotional centrality of this other person, his or her sudden loss in later life can trigger off a marked loss in *self-confidence*, as if the loss of this external attachment figure took with it the internalized figure that formerly provided the self-mothering. Subjectively the loss of a significant figure in the individual's emotional life causes *pain*—the pain of grief, that can sometimes even be localized within the body,

*Based on the Chairman's Address to the Psychotherapy Section of the Royal College of Psychiatrists given on 18 November 1976.

e.g. heartache, or a painful void. This pain is the result of two injuries to the self; first, an amputation of the attachment figure which besides being an object of attachment in itself has also come to contain a number of projected parts of the self; and second, an abandonment by a reflected and corresponding archaic internal figure that has in the past provided a sense of confidence in the self.

2. *Fear of the unknown*

At the same time that this familiar and relied upon figure is lost both externally and in the private world of subjective experience, there is also an experience of *anxiety*. From an external point of view this anxiety may be described as a fear of the unknown; subjectively, however, it is a fear of all sorts of hobgoblins and foul fiends that may spring out of the unknown. Where once the individual felt optimistic about the world he was in, as if he contained within him a benign and reliable 'good mother' who would look after him, he now feels fearful of what the world may hold for him and very ill-prepared to deal with it. This change from a self-confident person to a pessimistic misery can be triggered off by the loss of a present-day attachment figure, as if the external loss caused not only an equivalent and additional internal loss of a 'good' figure but also her displacement by a host of 'bad' and threatening ones. No wonder, therefore, that groups try to preserve their membership and sanctify 'things as they are' for the sake of familiarity. Changes threaten to remove people or social structures and so to revive experiences of undermining grief; changes also threaten a degree of the unknown which at once becomes peopled with horrors. So much for the well-known causes for resistance to change.

A third source

In a series of papers between 1953 and 1971, Winnicott described and conceptualized the gradual development of a child's capacity to acknowledge the world about him as something in itself and beyond his private world of wishes and fantasies. In his efforts to comprehend the infant's transition from a supposed world of total subjectivity to a world in which objective events are acknowledged by the infant as having a life and significance of their own, he introduced the concept of 'transitional phenomena'. He supposed that when the infant is still in the uterus and for some (undefined) time thereafter there is no distinction the infant can make between what is himself and what is his environment; sensations and changing states of feeling, such as a momentary wish to move a limb that is relieved by a wriggle, or a growing sense of hunger that is removed by a feed, are all experienced exclusively as features of the infant's own world; that is to say, infantile omnipotence holds sway and the part that the mother is playing in it all is not acknowledged.

Ultimately, however, if all goes well in the infant's development, he comes to know that though all things remain possible in his dreams and imagination, in social reality what he experiences is very much a result of the actions of others who are to some degree independent of him, and that, though they may be influenced by his wishes, they are not identical with them. He thus comes to inhabit two worlds simultaneously, one a private one that is subjective and subjectively conceived, and the other a world shared with others that in this sense is objective, though it is still, of course, subjectively conceived.

Winnicott argued that there must be a process of transition by which omnipotence is partially given up in favour of acknowledging a shared world of objective reality, the kind of reality that engages mature common sense and the imagination of natural scientists, for example. This process, he said, can be discerned in the use the young child makes of so-called transitional objects, such as a soft toy, a favourite blanket, a bundle of wool plucked from a blanket, etc. These Winnicott described as the child's 'first non-me possessions'. They are not part of him, as the foot is that he can play with or the thumb is that he can suck, but they are much more his possessions than his mother's whereabouts or, one might say, her breast. The adult world intuitively acknowledges the special rights the infant has over his transitional objects and treats them accordingly; no one in the household for a moment supposes that *the* blanket is just an old blanket. Furthermore, there is among the adults an unwritten agreement never to confront the infant with the implied question: did you create that blanket or did you just find it lying about? There is a self-evident need for sufficient tact to allow this paradox to remain unresolved. In the state of omnipotence it is supposed that the infant dreams up an object that corresponds to its needs, one that would assuage its craving. The attentive mother provides what is needed to fit in with this craving and so gives substance to the infant's dream. In this state the infant may be said to create the breast within its own subjectivity while the attentive mother allows the infant to find her actual breast at just the right moment so that the experience is clinched; or as Bion (1963) puts it: the mating of pre-conception and realization brings into being the conception. If the mother's breast intrudes too soon, it preempts the child's creativity and states a hunger that has not yet had time to flourish in the imagination to the point of being recognizable and memorable; if it fails to appear in time, the hopeful dream collapses into a nightmare of disappointment.

From the observer's point of view, of course, the baby has in no way created the breast. It is characteristic of an attentive mother, however, that she is prepared and even enjoys playing this game that the baby has invented of letting it find in social reality what it has begun to create subjectively, particularly as the game carries with it a special sense of delight and accomplishment for both of them which is quite different from, for example, the pleasure of taking part in assuaging the child's lusty hunger. Winnicott asserted that it is out of playing that the infant (and maybe the mother, too) comes to trust his own capacity to be creative in the face of the unknown and that playing therefore constitutes one of the roots of later self-confidence. The belief that figments of the imagination can in fact bear fruit in the material world of shared experience thus seems to rest on the mother's capacity to indulge playfully her infant's omnipotent assertions. Her respect for his illusions provides him with a starting-point from which he can make of experience and its inevitable dis-illusionments that which is his own as opposed to his having to accept comp-liantly that which is handed down to him by others. Her preparedness to indulge his illusions therefore seems also to be one of the roots of what will later be known as his sense of his own identity.

The excitement of this game between mother and infant lies in that fact that it is conducted on a knife edge between two pitfalls: one, a suffocating need on the part of the mother to preserve at all costs her child's self-importance; and the other, her need to awaken him prematurely to the social realities that she has been forced to acknowledge herself, but at the expense of his capacity for even transient self-deception. To leave him lost in his own grandiosity will ill-prepare him for later life; to challenge his illusions prematurely will turn him into a competent and compliant dullard. An example may illuminate the point. A four-month-old boy was having his nappy changed and had recently begun to relish the occasion for the opportunity it gave him to stretch all his limbs to their utmost, to heave his body up and down, and to let out some loud sharp noises. His mother had begun to respond to this by calling him a lion and by showing how impressed she was with his strength; every time he exploded in vigour, she gasped and pretended, in a very unconvincing way, to be afraid. They both laughed uproariously. There was no reason to think that this compe-tent mother was under the misapprehension that her son was in fact a lion. But now we must be careful, because any description of the event that gives no weight at all to this crazy idea will rob the occasion of the dreams of future possibilities that both of them were being touched by; as an onlooker my dream was of a great and vigorous male who would send thrills of excitement and apprehension down the spine of some as yet unborn woman; what the dreams were of the baby and of the mother I have no means of knowing. If a baby's antics are not given an imaginative reception, then the antics are just antics. So a paradox has to be sustained in which the baby is a lion and, for heaven's sake, of course, is not a lion; in which his blanket is unique and irreplaceable, and is yet a common nursery commodity.

Just as infantile omnipotence is still present in an adult's life in his capacity for dreaming and for reverie, and his first acknowledgement as an infant of a 'non-me' world outside him is later practised by an adult in his appreciation of objectivity and social reality, so too this transitional zone is perpetuated in a great many playful and cultural activities of later life (Winnicott, 1967): schools of creative endeavour that allow images that start as private ventures to gain some social (objective) currency; religious sects that celebrate truths that are hidden from nonparticipants; scientific discovery that legitimates within a scientific orthodoxy a scientist's private intuition (Kuhn, 1962); 'psychotherapy is done in the overlap of the two play areas, that of the patient and that of the therapist' (Winnicott, 1971); and the most ubiquitous of all transitional phenomena: language itself. How ludicrous to require Shakespeare to say whether he invented English or just found the language lying around: it was all there for him to use, but has never been the same since.

Three realms of reality for a member of a group

Each member of a group inhabits three realms of reality. First, he inhabits his private world of thoughts and dreams, uncommunicated and largely incommunicable. Second, he inhabits a world that is shared by the others, conceived of in terms of time and space about which a good deal of agreement can be gained without much difficulty. This is the ordinary world of common sense that is objectively perceived. And third, he inhabits a world of shared creations of the mind, fantasies, attitudes, values, assumptions, and misgivings, that have little that is conclusive to show for themselves objectively, but by virtue of being 'held in common' have a great influence on the life of the group members and are in that sense extremely real.

Anyone who has taken part emotionally in the life of a group will be aware how quickly assumptions about the group tend to arise and, what is more, to be so widely shared and that no doubting or testing seems to be called for at all (the basic assumption groups of Bion, 1961). Members who have been absent from a meeting feel distinctly 'out of things' even though no one can say precisely what they have missed. Norms for behaviour spring up that are felt to carry weight by virtue of the fact that they appear to be widely held, even though no one seems inclined to test whether this is so or not. The events that a group have gone through together seems to add up to a 'matrix' (Foulkes, 1964) that goes beyond any one member of the group or all of them together individually. Groups with a long history, such as families, are embedded in myths about themselves that are so alive that anyone who challenges them is felt to be, at best, offensive and, at worst, a rank outsider. In some groups, therapy groups in particular, an individual is allowed to express diametrically opposed views within a matter of minutes without in any way stimulating concern in others or even mild interest. It is as if a group soon develops, along with its customary ability to recognize some hard facts for what they are, a similar capacity for indulging illusions and living along with inconsistencies and paradoxes, to say nothing of downright lies.

Although most groups, such as families, teams, working gangs, committee meetings, therapy groups, etc., create shared experiences of the imagination that reach no great heights of sophistication compared with such specialist cultural groups as schools of poets and artists or religious sects, it seems very likely that they are valued by their members for just this capacity. For many it is by virtue of feeling a secure member of a group that all shared experience does not have to depend on what is objectively defensible. In 'one's group' one is again allowed to be opinionated, inconsistent, inconsequential, and downright nonsensical. Here some indulgence of illusions is taken for granted and the place lies strewn with paradoxes. Whether or not the group is engaged in an explicitly avowed common task, such a group has high sentience for its members

(Miller and Rice, 1967). This being so, it would not be the least surprising if people clung on to groups that they know either as to membership or as to structure or as to both. For only in such a company where 'assumptions' are for the time being accepted as 'facts' will the individual feel he has some sanction for his 'omnipotence' and so be able to gain some faith in what he is dreaming about but has not yet been able to find in the shared world of objective experience. For this chance to be playful with fellow members of a group and for this reminder of how imagination was first led on by a playful mother, group membership may sometimes be stuck to through thick and thin, and all efforts to change its culture resisted to the death.

Change as inimicable to playing

For action to be initiated, however, some decisions have to be made, and in the realm of decision-making some alternatives have to be excluded: if a is chosen then b is rejected, or x has to be replaced by y. Dichotomous forms of thought of the either/or type must come into use. To the extent that the playful group rests on the paradoxical assumption that there is no such thing as 'either/or' and that contradictions are to be left *in situ* and not resolved, the forms of dichotomous thought found necessary for action are felt to threaten the very nidus of imaginative innovation that the group with all its paradoxes has come to value. Action is felt as 'once and for all' and as a death to the as yet unconceived alternative. At this threat conservatism rears its noble or ugly head!

As people who are often called upon to operate in groups, whether committee meetings, clinical teams, seminars, therapy groups, or what have you, I suggest it is of some importance for us to consider what opportunities for playfulness a group offers, what are the limits that are appropriate, and how are the opportunities for imaginative innovation set up. According to the task in hand the constraints on playfulness may be too great or not great enough, the former resulting in a stilted and sterile group that produces only what its leader already has in mind; and the latter, through its disregard of common reality, resulting in an omnipotence that expands beyond the boundary of the task and that provokes various kinds of artistic behaviour. Some illustrations may give body to these ideas.

1. *A highly constrained group*

A committee had come to be held so strictly to its agenda by its chairman that tangential issues were never given an opportunity to show whether they were predominantly diversions or were in fact indirect ways of casting new light on the item under consideration—whether they constituted a flight from the task or a flight of fancy that illuminated the task in the manner of a free association. In trying to find the best practical solution to the problems before it, the committee soon ceased to benefit from the fact that it contained quite a variety of viewpoints, and instead became a rubber stamp for well-formulated proposals put forward by its various subcommittees. There was no room for the members to contribute their diversity and playfulness. Almost invariably, however, before the meeting was over, there broke out a highly charged and opinionated wrangle over some trivial item low on the agenda. It was the first chance the members had had to get at a problem that had not already had its solution predetermined by some subcommittee. These outbursts were beyond the chairman's ability to harness to a deliberate process of decision making. In the end a guillotine had to be applied and often no one, not even the secretary, was quite sure just what decision had actually been reached.

2. *An underconstrained group*

A workshop consisting mostly of psychiatrists and psychologists had been working for some time on the problem of how to make available to general practitioners such psychodynamic understanding and skills as they themselves had and that might be valuable to a general practitioner in the course of his daily work. Refresher courses had become lifeless rituals, and under the leadership of Michael and Enid Balint a new and somewhat outrageous kind of mid-career development was being fashioned. In the staff workshop connected with this training scheme a good deal of excitement was generated. As the shibboleths of the doctor–patient relationship were progressively exposed in the GP seminars for the defensive hokum that they were, there was in the staff workshop a corresponding exposure by colleagues of the seminar leaders' group methods and leadership styles which were being used as vehicles for all kinds of secret agendas and the preservation of the leaders' blind spots. The workshop became as zealous in illuminating the relationship between the seminars and their leaders as the seminars were in illuminating the relationship between the doctors and their patients. In their discussions of verbatim transcripts the workshop teetered between reassuring collusion with the seminar leader whose work was in focus and a disruptive exposure of it; there was a constant danger of a destructive polarization in the workshop. One way or another, however, the requisite playfulness was maintained and kept within bounds.

An important part in maintaining these boundaries was played by the staff workshop which addressed the task of articulating some of the psychodynamic and group-dynamic features of this kind of learning; the discussions and skirmishes in it led ultimately to the writing of a paper entitled 'The use of small groups in training' (Gosling et al., 1967).

When, however, it came to juxtaposing the work of this workshop with similar efforts being carried out in other countries the story was quite different. Rivalry for leadership and superadded issues concerned with the succession of generations, though containable within the workshop itself, when transposed to the setting of an international colloquim, were acted out in a hideous way. In particular, the forthright mutual criticism that had been found through painful trial and error in the home group to be both constructive and enlivening was transported wholesale into an international group setting in total disregard of how strange we all were to each other, how rivalrous and how prone to massive idealization and corresponding contempt. What had been tolerable challenges in the home group became outrageous insults when conducted between strangers in the setting of an international conference. It was as if no one had noticed that the primary task had changed when an ongoing, home-grown, technical workshop undertook to interact with similar bodies from overseas. The playfulness of the workshop had proved so rewarding and enlivening in its own setting that there was now no holding it back, and members of it portrayed themselves as arrogant and omniscient and downright foolish when they moved into a wider context.

3. *A moderately constrained group*

At a meeting of a therapy group one day I noticed that on this occasion the men were sitting on one side of the circle and the women on the other. After listening to the discussion for a while I gave it as my opinion that the women were propounding a certain view about the importance of feelings and the unimportance of logic that the men were finding hard to bear, and that this argument was given added force by the way the men and women had arranged themselves in the room. One member, a Mr X, renowned for his faithful attendance, his resignation to the fact that nothing could change for anybody, and his propensity for getting the other members to listen to long tales of his innocence and of the way he was ill-used by the world, leaned forward and with a mixture of seriousness, anxiety, and disdain said, 'It looks to me, Doctor, as if you have got a real "thing" about men and women.'

At this point a number of relatively 'hard facts' might have been educed by me, such as that so far as could be ascertained I was one of only two people in the group who had been able to get married and also to stay married, while he, poor fellow, had told us of many painful sexual misadventures to say nothing of a broken marriage that was quite incomprehensible to him. Another 'hard fact' that could have been pointed to was that as the members had that night not distributed themselves round the room in a random fashion but had arranged themselves into two subgroups according to their apparent gender, there were others present in the room besides myself who seemed to be aware of sexual differences, and so forth. But the reader will be glad to learn I held back from saying any of these things.

My thoughts then turned in other directions: was it that this group had the misfortune to have a sex-maniac for a therapist? I did indeed believe that I had a 'thing' about men and women and had gained the impression that this 'thing' had enabled me to move about through social space without too many mishaps, not to speak of the intense enjoyment it had often given me. Was this man, Mr X, who was apparently worried about my condition, seeking a less problematic position for himself than the one he saw me occupying by showing everyone that he was not tainted with such troublesome propensities? And so on.

Luckily we were not alone in the room together and so were saved from getting locked into positions of irreconcilable differences of perception and belief. The other members of the group took up various features of the predicament we were in and made comments on it from their different points of view, such as that some of the women did in fact feel safer if they were sitting together, that it was a matter of pure chance where people were sitting, that one member at least sat where he did because he liked to be near the window, that the men did often appear to be oblivious of tender feelings in the group, that one woman, Mrs Y, didn't understand what anyone was saying anyway, that if we weren't allowed even to be logical we might as well all go home, that Dr Gosling was always criticizing the men and favouring the women, that Mr X never seemed to be able to get it right with Dr Gosling as some other lucky ones seemed to be able to, and so on. I thought I noticed a rising tide of irritation, rivalry, and jealousy in the comments and that to some extent, but by no means completely, the shots at my remarks seemed to be coming from the male side of the room.

My next contribution to the discussion, arising partly from the fact that I was feeling more at ease in my role in the group than I usually did, was along the lines that if we did allow ourselves to have sexual awareness and feelings about each other we might find ourselves in positions of rivalry with each other with consequent feelings of jealousy and fear, and that perhaps this particular man was offering us the possibility of avoiding such an unpleasant state of affairs by showing us how we are all really the same, provided, of course, we agreed to avoid all sexual feelings about each other.

This contribution by me was felt by the members to be more provocative than those made by the others, and for a time there was a movement to use this shared view about my remarks to indicate that I was hitting back at an assailant, was evidently sensitive on this score, and so must indeed be suffering from some sexual disorder. But for some reason that is hard to identify, except to recall that there was at the time a certain atmosphere of nerviness, excitement, seriousness, and readiness for the unexpected, the issue was not settled so simply, and we ended up with a number of accounts of our predicament that seemed to carry some conviction (as well as some that carried very little). The solution, if indeed there was one, was pluralistic, as perhaps befits a topic that can all too easily get prematurely closed by invoking the simple male/female duality.

In the session that followed this one, two very unusual things happened. The first was that a woman whose current life was full of the most dreadful experiences, but whose head became completely empty of all thoughts as soon as she entered the treatment room, said that she had begun to see what an effective defence 'not knowing' could be, and then began to share with other members of the group some of her more pressing concerns in a way that communicated some of her feelings most vividly. The other thing was that the man who was perplexed by my having a 'thing' about men and women began to reflect on his broken marriage and for the first time in our hearing to wonder whether he had not had a hand in its demise.

As I have indicated, in the session there had been moments of seriousness, wry humour, tediousness, and surprise. We seemed at various times to be caught up in contradictory but firmly held beliefs about each other: at one moment these beliefs seemed to be self-evident and at the next quite preposterous. At such a time neither of the alternatives could be confidently preferred over the other for long, and yet as time went on a certain confidence seemed to have grown out of the group's capacity to entertain and in that sense contain them both.

Conclusion

These three examples are of working groups under various conditions that permit playfulness among their members to a restricted, an abundant, and a moderate extent, three points on a continuum. It has been argued that it is in the realm of playfulness where transitional phenomena are rife that transformations can occur in the mental life of the group from the known into the new, where familiar things can come to be seen in a new light. Such a realm of group sentience, not unnaturally, is highly prized for its inventiveness and hopefulness. But, it is further argued, when a group is functioning in such a way as to tolerate paradoxes and to postpone for a time the reality-testing of its assumptions, the dichotomous forms of thought appropriate to decision-making and definitive action are experienced as a threat and are dispersed and discredited as much as possible. We are thus left with the picture that the nidus of invention and its promise of change must shun actual change and thus become the champion of the *status quo*.

References

Bion, W. R. (1961) *Experiences in Groups*. London: Tavistock Publications.

Bion, W. R. (1963) *Elements of Psychoanalysis*. London: Heinemann.

Bowlby, J. (1969) *Attachment and Loss, vol. I*. London: Tavistock Publications.

Foulkes, S. H. (1964) *Therapeutic Group Analysis*. London: Allen Unwin.

Gosling, R., Miller, D. M., Turquet, P. M., and Woodhouse, D. (1967) *The Use of Small Groups in Training*. Hitchin, Hirts: Codicote Press.

Kuhn, T. S. (1962) *The Structure of Scientific Revelations*. University of Chicago Press (Phoenix Books).

Lewin, K. (1951) *Field Theory in Social Science*. New York: Harper Row.

Miller, E. J., and Rice, A. K. (1967) *Systems of Organization*. London: Tavistock Publications.

Winnicott, D. W. (1967) 'The location of cultural experience'. *International Journal of Psychoanalysis*, **48**.

Winnicott, D. W. (1971) *Playing and Reality*. London: Tavistock Publications.

Chapter 6

Manifestations of Transference in Small Training Groups*

Edward B. Klein

This paper is a beginning effort to elucidate and demonstrate the meaning and utility of the concept of transference as it is applied to understanding some psychological issues in small training groups. It is a preliminary attempt to answer these questions: What are manifestations of transference in small groups? Is transference more apparent in some groups than in others? A theoretical analysis using personality and group systems will be employed in understanding transference in small training groups.

Most of our knowledge of transference comes from classical psychoanalysis. A recent definition from that context is given by Greenson (1965):

Transference is the experiencing of feelings, drives, attitudes, fantasies and defenses toward a person in the present which are inappropriate to that person and are a repetition, a displacement of reactions originating in regard to significant persons in early childhood. I emphasize that for a reaction to be considered transference, it must have two characteristics: it must be a repetition of the past and it must be inappropriate to the present. (p. 171)

Schafer (1968) provides a similar definition and adds the dimensions of object and self-representation: 'Whatever the composition of transference, it involves object representations preserved from the past (and preserved self-representations as well) and the unrealistic imposing of these on current objects (and subjective self)' (p. 132). It is implied that the occurrence of transference is not limited to the psychoanalytic situation but can occur in any relationship. Freud and others (i.e. Hoffer, 1956) are explicit in describing the ubiquity of transference. Freud wrote: 'Transference arises spontaneously in all human relationships just as it does between the patient and the physician' (1910). And: '[Transference] is a universal phenomenon of the human mind ... and in fact dominates the whole of each person's relations to his human environment' (1925).

To summarize then, the chief general characteristics of transference phenomena are the following: (1) They are inappropriate to the current situation. (2) They are repetitions of past experiences. (3) They are universal in inter-

*This work grew out of the Yale interdepartmental seminar on groups. The author wishes to thank Clayton Alderfer, Boris Astrachan, Elizabeth Bellis, Janet Braslin, Phyllis Kempner, Daniel Levinson, Maurice Marcus, Braxton McKee, Peter Newton, David Singer, and Jane Stitelman for their comments.

personal relationships. Thus, a person (subject) exhibiting transference in a relationship experiences the other (object) in a way that is not representative of the actual object and which cannot be accounted for on the basis of the current situation alone but is based on previous interpersonal experience.

From classical psychoanalysis we know that optimal conditions for promoting transferences occur when the subject is consistently confronted by an object in a constant and uniform environment, and the object gives minimal cues and responses, particularly regarding himself.* The subject does not have the opportunity of knowing or interacting with an ordinary, current 'real' object, and his perceptions are based on previous interpersonal experience (real and/or fantasied).

The central role of transference in group psychotherapy has been noted by many authors (Foulkes, 1948; Slavson, 1950; Rosenbaum and Berger, 1963; and Wolf, 1949), but with few exceptions (Ezriel, 1952) they stress the dyadic treatment situation and ignore the group dynamics aspect. Although there is some acknowledgement of its presence in nonclinical small groups (Gosling et al., 1967), there is no elucidation of the role of transference in such groups. Conditions approximating those that are optimal for promoting transference (similar to the analytic situation in most respects) do appear in certain nontherapy groups. Further, it seems likely that investigations of transference phenomena in such groups would contribute in a significant way to a better understanding of transference in extra-analytic settings.

Significant sources of data about transference in 'extra-clinical' settings are certain small groups: those that gather regularly to pursue a task other than treatment, are composed of individuals who are not patients, are led by a person not filling the role of psychotherapist, and meet under conditions similar to the analytic situation. The study of such groups, by extending our understanding of transference in nondyadic, nontreatment settings, would provide perspectives, data and formulations that contribute to a general psychology of transference.

Two group training orientations

Currently, there are two major training orientations, each marked by distinctive procedures and foci (Singer et al., 1975). One is a psychoanalytically oriented approach developed at the Centre for Applied Social Research of the Tavistock Institute, London, and is commonly known as the 'study group' (Bion, 1961). The other, the human relations orientation, is derived from the social psychological work of Kurt Lewin at the National Training Laboratories (NTL) and is popularly referred to as the 'T-group' (Argyris, 1967). In practice, there are a number of similarities between these two training approaches. First, they usually take place in a relatively isolated geographical setting ('cultural island') to eliminate normal daily distractions and to aid in looking at behaviour in new ways.

---

*Although the role and behaviour of the object (e.g. analyst) is in fact unambiguous (Newton, 1971), nevertheless the subject (e.g. patient) usually experiences him as ambiguous.

Secondly, both use unstructured or semi-structured exercises. They are designed to highlight certain aspects of group behaviour. Members learn by becoming actively involved in the exercises and by developing skills that allow them to further understand individual and group behaviour. An underlying assumption in both orientations is that individual learning is most effective when it is experiential, involving both feeling and thought.

Risking oversimplification we spell out some differences relating to task, structure, culture, and leadership. The primary task in a Tavistock conference is to provide members with opportunities to learn about the nature and difficulties of authority in group settings. The primary orientation in T-groups is more varied, but the task tends to be the development of interpersonal competence. The structure of the two training orientations reflects their different primary tasks. For example, Tavistock conferences have a clearly delineated authority structure with a director, administrator, and consultants. In addition, there is a division of labour between staff and members; and the boundaries around these different positions and roles are sharply spelled out and maintained. In the NTL tradition, trainers tend not to define a clear and distinct division of labour between themselves and group members. For instance, T-group trainers will join group members in relating personal experiences in order to establish greater 'mutuality'.

The Tavistock focus on authority relations emphasizes the learning task, leadership, power, and covert group dynamics. Consultants embody and personify these values. The consultants' approach is intellectual, objective, and nongratifying, yet it stimulates an atmosphere that most members find intense. The staff, nevertheless, emphasize *individual* authority, responsibility, and understanding. In contrast, NTL develops a culture that is peer oriented, stresses expression of feelings, involves trainers and members working together on group issues both in and out of the training events, and has a more optimistic flavour than the Tavistock psychoanalytically oriented approach (Klein and Astrachan, 1971).

One of the more dramatic differences is the behaviour of the small group leader (Harrow *et al.*, 1971). The term 'leader' is not used in a formal sense but rather a general term to describe both the T-group trainer and the study group consultant (Klein and Astrachan, 1971). In the study group, a specific task—the study of the group in the 'here and now'—is explicitly stated and pursued. Since all of the consultant's behaviour, so far as possible, is devoted to that task, he refrains from revealing his particular personality. His comments are predominantly about the group's behaviour rather than any single individual's, and he refers to himself only when it contributes to an understanding of the group process. The consultant focuses on group-level behaviour and therefore tends not to address members by name.

In direct contrast is the behaviour of the trainer of the T-group. He reveals as much as he can of his personality. The trainer presents himself as a warm, supportive, and accepting individual. He minimizes his authority and gives and requests support and 'nonevaluative' feedback. He directly engages individuals, refers to them by name and promotes a peer group situation.

The study group situation more closely approximates conditions conducive to maximal transference tractions to the consultant, while the T-group minimizes such responses to the trainer. In other words, the study group situation should elicit more 'pure' transference phenomena, while the T-group tends to be less conducive to transference relationships to the leader.

Setting and exploratory questions

The investigations were conducted in a course at the medical school in Study 1 and a group relations training weekend in Study 2. Both events were set up to provide opportunities for mental health and social science students to learn about group dynamics. A secondary task was research on student reactions to the group training exercises. The first study examined members' attitudes towards consultants and trainers.

After the first investigation, notable differences in members' ratings of leaders for the two groups were observed. Study group consultants received more diverse ratings than T-group trainers. These varying perceptions offered an empirical method for the measurement of transference.* In the second investigation, it was predicted that the variability of student ratings of consultants would be greater than the same ratings for trainers. The small Tavistock group approximates a psychoanalytic situation which would make transference maximal, while T-group trainers would be viewed more on the basis of their personality. There were a number of additional questions. Specifically, does transference vary in different stages of group life? Are some perceptions of the leader based more on transference than others?

Both investigations were part of a larger research project. The first study's findings were *post hoc*, and in the second, differential transference phenomena were predicted. All of the criteria for transference were not met by the data. Given the limitations of the investigations, only the 'inappropriateness of response in the present situation' was testable by the methods employed. In any case, the similarity of the findings across the two studies is marked.

Study 1

Research design

The overall research design involved two groups of students each attending five T-group and five study group sessions. The order of group exercises was reversed for each: one group had five T-group sessions followed by five study group sessions, the other set had five study group sessions followed by five

---

*That is, variability of ratings of the group leader is a statistical method of measuring differential perceptions of the same object. The greater the variability the more the group members differ in their perceptions of the leader. Since transference assumes unique reactions for each individual, group variability would appear to be one method for measuring the quantity of transference operating in a group at any particular time.

T-group sessions. Four experienced group leaders—two T-group trainers and two study group consultants*—each conducted one of the groups.

The participants were students from a course in group dynamics and psychotherapy at Yale University School of Medicine and knew each other. There were three medical students, five psychiatric nursing degree candidates, six graduate students in administrative science and sociology, and five students in other disciplines. The two resulting groups were relatively balanced by sex and academic discipline.

The students were told that they would participate in a small group experience but were not told about the change of the group leader or style. The switchover occurred at the beginning of the sixth session. The former group leader occupied the observer's chair and the former silent, nonparticipating observer became the study group consultant or T-group trainer.

The principal measure in this research was a modified form of the semantic differential (Osgood *et al.*, 1957). After each session, students were given pairs of bi-polar adjectives on a six-point scale. Students were asked to rate the group, the leader, other members, and self. The adjectives rated to what extent the leader, members, and self were trusting, rigid, authoritarian, knowledgeable, sensitive to deep group trends and undercurrents, strong or empathic, respected, close to other members, etc. For purposes of the current paper, only the variability of ratings for the concept 'group leader' will be reported. A list of 21 sets of bi-polar adjectives and the rationale for their inclusion are reported by Harrow *et al.* (1971).

Results

There were 420 comparisons: 21 adjectives × 4 meaningful group comparisons (each T-group compared to each study group) × 5 sessions. Study group consultants were viewed in a more variable manner than T-group trainers in 264 cases (61 per cent), 154 comparisons were the opposite, and there were two ties ($p < .05$). In terms of the mean of the standard deviations of all five meetings *combined* (84 in total), 59 comparisons (70 per cent) showed larger standard deviations for consultants, 24 for trainers, and two the same ($p < .01$). The data are highly correlated (each student made a large number of ratings); therefore, they were analyzed by the sign test (Senders, 1958), which, though not a powerful measure, is appropriate for this type of nonindependent data.

Members' ratings of consultants were more variable than ratings for trainers, particularly in the first meeting. This trend decreased until meeting 3; a reversal occurred during the fourth session and the trend reemerged in the final meeting.†The greater variability of members' ratings of consultants over trainers occurred in 77 per cent of comparisons in meeting 1 ($p < .01$); 76 per cent in the second session ($p < .01$); 52 per cent in the third session (NS); 44 per cent in the fourth

*Boris Astrachan and Portia Bowers were the T-group trainers while Martin Harrow and Edward Klein served as study group consultants.

†Due to the nature of the data, it was not possible to compute analysis of variance and trend analysis statistics, therefore conclusions about trends have to be tentative.

meeting (NS); and 64 per cent in the fifth and final session ($p < .05$).

Nine of the 21 adjectives show greater variability (mean standard deviations) for the study leader than the T-group leader in all comparisons. The nine are 'rigid', 'trusting', 'respected', 'sensitive to others' comments', 'pleasant', 'friendly', 'frank', 'inhibiting', and 'authoritarian'.

In sum, the first study, on a small number of students, suggests that there is more marked variability in ratings of the leader occurring in study groups than in T-groups. This differential variability effect was more manifest at the beginning and end than in the middle of the groups. In addition, the findings held for a particular subset of nine adjectives more than for the other twelve.

In order to further test attitudes towards consultants and trainers, similar data were collected at a four-day conference conducted at the Yale Interdepartmental Seminar on Groups* during the following autumn. To eliminate the effects of having seminar teachers as group leaders, the familiarity of course membership, the possible confounding effect of lack of knowledge of the switchover of group leaders, and any other effects, a different design was employed.

Study 2

Design and sample

Students were informed of the conference well in advance with a notice that included a statement of purpose, staff composition, notification that groups would switch leaders, an indication that the workshop should be regarded as an educational not a therapeutic endeavour, and a reminder that research was to be conducted as part of the normal procedure. The conference occurred over a four-day period. For the first two days only, the conference had three Tavistock study groups and three T-groups, which met for six sessions. Each of the three study groups had a Tavistock consultant and a nonparticipating observer. Similarly, each of the three T-groups had a trainer and a nonparticipating observer. A lecture was delivered by the conference director between sessions 5 and 6 for all members and staff. There were eleven members in each group, diversified as to age, sex, academic discipline; participants were selected on the basis of being strangers to each other. The total membership included 66 psychiatric residents, graduate nursing students, psychology trainees, and divinity school students.

Upon the completion of each study and T-group, members were requested to fill out a questionnaire composed of 25 adjectives using a nine-point scale and rating the three concepts of group leader, the group, and self. Adjectives were selected on the basis of theoretically derived expectations about differences

*Boris Astrachan was the conference director, Portia Bowers, Alvin Fitz and Herbert Shepard were the T-group trainers, while Edward Klein, Daniel Levinson, and Theodore Mills served as study group consultants. James Miller, John O'Connor, and Rachel Robinson functioned as observers. The conference was held in the autumn of 1968, approximately six months after the previous study.

and similarities between study and T-groups and in keeping with the findings from the Harrow *et al.* investigation (1971).

Results

Data representing the average variability of the three T-groups combined *v.* the average variability of the three study groups were analysed. This was a more robust test than Study 1 (more subjects). Also, one factor was working against the prediction: one of the T-group trainers was a woman, so there should have been more variability of ratings for T-group leaders since the woman was combined with two men trainers *v.* three men consultants. With 150 comparisons in all (25 adjectives × 6 sessions), 98 (66 per cent) of the standard deviations were in the predicted direction ($p < .05$); that is, consultants were viewed in a more variable manner than trainers.

The first and third meetings significantly (72 per cent, $p < .05$) differentiated the groups in the predicted direction. In general, the magnitude of differences decreased; the last three sessions (68 per cent, 60 per cent, and 54 per cent) led to nonstatistically significant results.*

Though the adjectives used in this second study were not the same as in the first investigation (in order to sample other dimensions, only 16 adjectives were repeated), there were overall similarities across the two studies. The adjectives that led to greater variability for study group than T-group leaders at least five out of six times, were: 'hopeful', 'expresses feelings', 'critical of members', 'unemotional', 'close to members', 'frank', 'inhibited', and 'authoritarian'. In both investigations there was greater variability on ratings for consultants than trainers on the adjectives 'frank', 'inhibited', and 'authoritarian'.

These findings are interpreted as manifestations of transference. But there could be another interpretation. Using the general paradigm that behaviour (including perception) is the interaction between an individual and his situation, one might argue that the results are due to real differences in the situation. For example, the leader might have treated some members differently, in which case members would show different ratings of the leader. As indicated above, however, an important aspect of the study group is that all members are confronted with the same situation, especially with regard to the behaviour of the consultant. His role dictates that he treat all members the same, and generally as a group. It is in T-groups that participants are in fact confronted by different situations, particularly with regard to the trainer. If situational factors provoke variability of ratings, then, if anything, there should be greater variability of T-group ratings.

*Transference manifestations in the last sessions were attenuated in the second study since all of the members were to continue in their same group though with a different leader on the third and fourth days, and they knew this. On the other hand, members in the first investigation experienced termination at the end of the second week since, indeed, the groups ended at that time. Therefore, the way the data was collected, the actual termination in Study 1 and the continuing nature of the group in Study 2, accentuated transference in Study 1 and attenuated it in the second investigation.

One of the main criteria of transference is that it is inappropriate to the present. In the study group, each member was confronted with the same, uniform, actual situation, especially in the form of the consultant's behaviour. Reactions that are 'appropriate' would reflect this actuality and be similar. The variability in these ratings indicates that members' reactions cannot be explained by the situation alone. This study provides no evidence to meet the other main criteria for transference: that the reactions are repetitions of past experiences. However, even granting this important limitation, no concept other than transference is as valid or applicable with respect to the results.*

Discussion

The research has attempted to ascertain whether transference manifestations are more likely to appear in psychoanalytically oriented (Tavistock) than in human relations (NTL) groups. The data suggests that transference reactions are indeed more apparent in the former; the discussion, therefore, will focus on study group phenomena from personality and group systems viewpoints and then in combination.

Interpretation of findings from a personality system viewpoint

Interpretation of the results of this study focuses on the individual personality system. First, there is the finding that transference phenomena in study groups as compared to T-groups are most manifest at the beginning, not so apparent during the middle, and show themselves again towards the end of the life of the group. It could be proposed that at the beginning, because the consultant and the situation are not familiar, the individual perceives the consultant in terms of his particular dominant transference reactions. As he becomes familiar with the consultant's style, he perceives the consultant as a unique individual and consequently transference elements diminish. As termination approaches, transference reactions associated with his particular early separation experiences are activated.

However, a more likely explanation is that transference elements are an important aspect of the individual's experience throughout the life of the group. They only *appear* to be less prominent in the mid-life of the group because of the nature of the measurements of the study, i.e. the measurements are of variability of ratings comparing T-group and study group leaders. There is one condition in which individual transference reactions could be prominent and yet there would be virtually no variability from member to member in ratings:

*Another way of viewing the obtained findings is that a social adaptation process occurred with mutuality as the explanatory concept. That is, since the consultant demonstrates lack of mutuality, many characteristics may be attributed to him leading to variability of perceptions. In T-groups, with mutuality between trainers and members, participants adapt to the situation and view each other and the leader with consensual validation (Sullivan, 1953). This position, though interesting, would not adequately explain greater manifestations of transference at the beginning, levelling out in the middle, and particularly the reemergence of greater variability of perceptions at the end.

when members of the group share the same transference perceptions of the consultant. That such a condition exists during the middle phase of small group life is a common, if not invariable, observation (Mills, 1964; Slater, 1966). It is manifested by the members of the group sharing the same fantasy about the consultant; and while each member may behaviourally contribute something unique to the fantasy, he does have perceptions of the leader similar to every other group member (Ezriel, 1950).

As Sutherland (1952) notes:

In the individual psychoanalytic situation, the often apparent disconnected thoughts of the patient, his so-called free associations, can become meaningful if we assume an underlying dynamic source—namely, a relationship with unconscious objects (object representations) which he is trying to enact with his analyst. In a group the various conscious themes of the discussion can be made meaningful in a similar way, if we assume as the dynamic source a relationship with unconscious fantasy objects (object representations) of the same kind in all members of that session. (p. 113)

As the individual is engaged in this process, his perceptions of himself (self representations) and other members (now, through projection, personifying some of the object representations) are influenced and modified. These changes are a reflection of several intrapsychic processes: the 'splitting off' of certain object and self representations and projecting them onto the consultant and other group members, and an exaggeration of other self representations—this by virtue of the internalization of other group members' projections. A concept introduced by Bion (1961) to describe this is valency, 'the capacity of the individual for instantaneous combination with other individuals in an established pattern of behaviour—the basic assumptions' (p. 175). Or, in Ezriel's (1950) words, 'every group member takes up a particular role characteristic for his personality structure because of the particular unconscious phantasy group relations which he entertains in his mind, and which he tries to solve through appropriate behavior in the group' (p. 63). In part, this occurs because the individual regresses in the group, and all members are in the same state of regression at any given time.

One consequence of the individual's membership in the group is that he acquires a particular 'personal role-definition' (Levinson, 1959), that is, an idea of who he is and how he should behave in the group. To be consistent in the utilization of an intrapsychic frame of reference, we should note that the inner experience of a personal role definition is a particular self representation, since self representation 'may be defined as an idea that the subject has about his own person' (Schafer, 1968, p. 25). Even more specifically relating the social psychological concept of role to the psychoanalytic concept of self representation, self representations 'serve as information, as guideposts to behavior' (Schafer, 1968, p. 27). As indicated above, the group member's most prominent self representation in the mid-life of the group has a number of determinants, most notably early life experiences of self and others (now manifest in transference reactions), externalizations and internalizations by him, and current influences (e.g. projections, expectations) by other group members. There are always interactions and relationships between self and object representations, which, to use Ezriel's (1950) term, could be described as 'fantasy group relations'. This implies some internal organization of these experiences and suggests somewhat well-defined boundaries for each set of representations and their relationships.

The member's experience of the group and of himself in the mid-phase of the group consists of such a bounded constellation (set of representations and their relationships). At any given time the individual member has, in addition to the constellation accurately reflecting the reality of the group and himself, others that consist more of nonrational, unrealistic self and object representations and relationships between them (i.e. transferences). The task for the individual in the study group is to understand these different constellations, their interpenetrations and their relationships.

At termination of the group, although there are shared fantasies about the consultant (and therefore shared transference perceptions), there is also an increase in individual, nonshared transference reactions. Termination stimulates memories of separations (involving early object and self representations) which are unique for each individual. Furthermore, as termination approaches, participants disengage from group membership, take back projected aspects of self and object representations, become more oriented to themselves (in contrast to viewing themselves as primarily group members), and thus are less prone to be involved in shared fantasies.

The finding that certain adjectives (as used in this investigation) are more susceptible to variability suggests that particular aspects of the individual personality system are more subject to transference effects than others. The terms showing most variability—'inhibiting', 'frank', 'authoritarian'—are characteristics of the super-ego as described from an experiential viewpoint. From a theoretical perspective, the super-ego is largely composed of early object representations of parents or parental figures. It is a common observation in the psychoanalytic situation that, particularly in early therapy, transference elements are predominantly projections of these early object representations. As Greenson (1967) notes, 'early in the analysis one can usually observe situations in which the analyst takes on the function of the super-ego, he is felt primarily as critical, hostile, rejecting and negative' (p. 241). This interpretation, that the consultant represents a super-ego figure, is also consistent with Freud's (1921) formulation that in a group the leader stands for the ego-ideal (i.e. super-ego).

Interpretation of findings from a group system viewpoint

The studies reported in this paper do not have direct data about the group, only the individual. Nevertheless, there are many concepts about the group as a social system which should aid in understanding individual reactions. Five major concepts will be discussed from both a structure and process perspective.

These are boundaries, role, splitting, basic assumption life, and developmental stages in small groups.

Boundaries define what is in and out of any system (whether person or group), and their crossing has major psychological significance for the individual and the collectivity. The total training conference has a boundary around it (the conference introduction delivered by the director has as its primary task distinguishing the training conference from the outside world or drawing a boundary; Astrachan, 1975). Similarly, the consultant defines the boundary of the study group. While the boundary around the small group exists from the first moment on, it takes time for members to consciously experience its existence. The first session of any group is felt as a highly anxiety-producing or threatening situation by most members. Part of the process members go through in the initial session involves the giving up of some of their individuality (and their traditional roles) and becoming a group participant. Members, particularly in the first session, begin to develop some identification with the group and experience the boundary which distinguishes this particular group from the rest of the environment. Crossing the boundary into the group takes at least a part of the first session and calls for a psychological adjustment on the part of the individual (i.e. a commitment to being a group member) and a collective response involving a beginning development of group identification, norms, sanctions, and culture (Klein and Astrachan, 1971).

The small group starts with two positions, those of consultant and member. The consultant's role is clear and spelled out in advance, whereas, initially, the member position is undifferentiated, although each member has the formal task of learner–participant; members often feel lost in a global sea. This occurs because members have individual, idiosyncratic expectations of the conference, and unique experiences of other group participants and the consultant. Over time, participants begin differentiating and a structure evolves within the membership. Members begin to play roles which are a combination of what the person brings and what the group does to, for, and with him. His role, therefore, is what he does in the position of being a member.

Individuals can be viewed as units of the group performing roles in terms of group functions. For instance, cultures need deviants to define norms. It is common for groups to have a deviant who defines the limits of acceptable behaviour. As an illustration, a number of members at various times may try to be in a 'mental patient' role, but groups often only allow one person to play that role. It is fairly clear that all applicants do not meet the group's need and usually a particular individual (with a unique personality, style of presentation, and potential for that role) is selected to be in this role at a given time in the group's history.

During the middle sessions of study groups, boundaries and differentiated member roles become explicit. At this time splitting begins: it is not unusual for subgroup formation to occur within the study group. Initially, such subgroups may involve obvious characteristics such as race (Klein et al., 1971), sex (Kohler et al., in preparation), and age. Each is seen as carrying something different (and often negative) from himself or his own subgroup. Splitting allows individuals and subgroups to feel virtuous and hard working while others are seen as resistant and destructive. As members begin to be more familiar with each other, conventional stereotypes may break down and divisions occur along more philosophical lines (Klein and Gould, 1973). Interpretation by the consultant and work by members may make splitting conscious and lead to a more integrated process, with an awareness of both positive and negative aspects in each subgroup and person, and a more collaborative atmosphere.

In middle sessions the group is psychologically formed: there is more of a shared sense of cohesion and an emerging, collective identity. As group process continues there is a pull towards work (i.e. understanding what is occurring in the 'here and now') and a simultaneous push towards the expression of other needs, involving feelings, ideas, and alternative ways of proceeding, which Bion (1961) conceptualizes as basic assumption life. During middle sessions it is not unusual for members to become invested with informal roles often symbolized as assistant consultant, clown, theoretician, disruptor, anti-leader, etc. These can be seen as one way for the group to attempt to meet other than work needs and develop a more comfortable posture to deal with a distant, rational voice of authority and work.

In middle phases, there are more shared fantasies about the leader (Slater, 1966) and individual transferences tend to be more integrated in the group culture, leading to basic assumption life. The initial basic assumption in the group is often dependency. Members act 'as if' the consultant is omnipotent and has all the answers. Flight/fight is noted by participants' fear of the consultant such that they wish to attack or flee from the all-powerful leader. Pairing is the fantasied expectation that two members or, more likely, a member and the consultant, can give birth to an ideology which will perpetuate the group. Turquet (1974) has added a fourth basic assumption, fusion. Here, members act as if they could all be one, both denying individuality and feeling deskilled, if not actually 'mindless'.

The basic assumptions noted in this paper all occur in the middle sessions when the group boundary is experienced as being real and impermeable (members tend not to miss sessions or come late) and when there is a sense of mutuality operating among participants. Although these are not linear, a speculative and preliminary formulation of a developmental sequence in groups suggests six stages. They would appear to occur in the following modal order: becoming a member of the group (leaving traditional roles); fusion; dependency; fight/flight; pairing; and divesting one's self of group membership (reclaiming individuality or more traditional roles).

We now turn towards a systems analysis of transference manifestations in study groups. In the first session (which is transitional in nature), the boundary of the group is experienced as highly permeable, the member position is ambiguous, splitting and basic assumptions are not yet operative, and individual responses to the clearly defined consultant, in his role, predominate. Middle sessions are more integrated: there is a structure within the membership (hierarchy), relatively clear role definition, splitting, and a beginning sense of cohesion. Members develop common group transference fantasies about the consultant. These are a direct expression of whatever basic assumption is predominant at the time. Common group transference fantasies occur at this stage because members are in the same state of regression; there is a loosening of traditional boundaries in individuals and new roles are called for in the novel environment of the study group. The basic assumptions can now be expressed since they seem containable (and safe) within the boundaries (time and space) of the room.

In the last session of the group, the boundary to the outside world is experienced as highly permeable. Member roles are fused; splitting, basic assumption life, and task performance decrease, and there is a lack of shared perceptions. Under these conditions individual responses are paramount and the group focuses on the clearly defined 'other', the consultant in his role. Since members are beginning to drop their group role in preparation for returning to the outside world, the very nature of this transitional stage heightens idiosyncratic responses, particularly towards the consultant who symbolizes the task of the 'dying' group.

A beginning integration of personality and group systems views of small group behaviour

The first section of the discussion involved the personality system, while the second was concerned with a group system viewpoint. Here we attempt to integrate the two perspectives. A number of phenomena such as boundary, role, and splitting have been shown to operate on a group as well as an individual level. Indeed, an intrapsychic viewpoint alone cannot adequately account for group behaviour. To understand an individual in a group, one needs concepts which bridge personality and social systems. One major concept is role. Unfortunately, as Levinson (1959) notes, role has been used in a number of ways which are primarily psychological (the individual's unique characteristics and interpretation of position) or sociological (the demands of the organization). A social psychological view of role, as a dynamic interaction between personality and social structure, would seem the most appropriate way to account for the behaviour of an individual in a group. This vantage-point is particularly useful in understanding transference in study groups. During the first session the individual experiences himself as being stripped of a conventionally defined role (professional, familiar, etc.). This type of role defusion, plus the experience of a permeable boundary around the group and a clearly defined other (the consultant as an authority figure pursuing his task), leads to members projecting various things (primarily from their distant pasts) onto the consultant. As the group continues, member positions become differentiated; individuals take on new, nontraditional roles that are a complex combination of their own personalities (most notably self and object representations), interpretations of the member position, group structure, and what others

expect of, and attribute (project) to, them; and they begin to experience themselves as being in bounded roles. As the group continues to develop a life of
its own, members experience the boundary around the group, splitting occurs,
and the consultant becomes somewhat less paramount. In the last session, as
time passes and the end is clearly in sight, members experience the group
boundary as dissolving, roles are fused, splitting decreases, and only the consultant is clearly in a bounded role pursuing the work task. The consultant
becomes prepotent and members fall back on formative life experiences and
death fantasies which lead to individualized, unique, early object representations
being projected onto the consultant. They enact earlier roles (son, daughter,
elementary school pupil) as the structure of the group (boundaries) is felt to be
weakened and group life draws to an end.

Another concept, operating at both an individual and a group level, is that
of boundary. In keeping with the work of Alderfer (1976) on the relationships
between individual and group, it would appear that there is a direct correspondence between the boundaries around each element. In this context, when the
group boundary is experienced as flexible, so too is the boundary of each
member, and this is a clear characteristic of the first session of study groups.
The beginning session involves searching for a common task and means of
expression. Since both the group and membership are poorly defined (members
only have positions, not roles, and the group boundary is not consciously
experienced), individual transference reactions to the clearly defined consultant,
in his role, are maximal. In middle sessions when the group boundary is clearly
defined and experienced (outsiders will be excluded), boundaries around
participants in their roles also tend to be better defined (each member plays
a role for the group). In these stages basic assumption life is operative, shared
perceptions and fantasies are maximal and individual, unique transferences
are minimized. In the last session of the group, members are preparing for the
outside world. Boundaries are experienced as dissolving and individual transference reactions to the consultant, in his clearly defined work role, are paramount.

The idea of a bounded role operating within a bounded group and the inter-
dependence between the two is a specific way of beginning to integrate
personality and social system analysis of small groups. This approach also
facilitates an understanding of the complex transference phenomena reported
in this paper.

There are many parallels between training groups, the dyadic psychoanalytic
treatment situation, and group psychotherapy. It is a common occurrence for
therapists in treatment groups and leaders in training groups to experience
their overt, all-powerful position at the beginning and end and their more
covert power in the middle of the life of the group. Groups often act as if the
leader-therapist is less than present in his full complexity, as opposed to a
simplified view consistent with basic assumption life in the middle stages of
groups. These attempts at simplification are manifestations of the regression
that occurs in small groups as a means of handling the anxieties experienced in

connection with complexities, ambivalence, and potentially overwhelming feelings encountered by participants. It is only interpretation by the leader and work on group process by the members that allows a focus on the complexities of his role.

Using a combination of individual psychoanalytic and group systems theories, certain characteristics of transference, as they occur in nontherapeutic groups, have been explicated. In subsequent articles we will attempt theoretically and empirically to link individual and group phenomena. Specifically, what are needed are investigations designed to directly test manifestations of transference taking into account the race (Klein *et al.*, 1971), sex, age, and other characteristics of group leaders which affect perceptions of members. In addition, participants' previous background, family constellation, and authority relationships with parents and other significant figures need to be investigated to more completely understand transference in groups.

References

Alderfer, C. (1976) 'Change processes in organizations'. In M. D. Dunnette (ed.) *Handbook of Industrial and Organizational Psychology*. Chicago: Rand.

Argyris, C. (1967) 'On the future of laboratory education'. *Journal of Applied Behavioral Science*, **3**, 153–183.

Astrachan, B. M. (1975) 'The Tavistock Model of laboratory training'. In K. D. Benne, L. P. Bradford, J. R. Gibb, and R. O. Lippitt (eds) *The Laboratory Method of Changing and Learning: Theory and Application*. Palo Atto, Calif.: Science and Behavior Books.

Bion, W. (1961) *Experiences in Groups*. London: Tavistock Publications.

Ezriel, H. (1950) 'A psychoanalytic approach to group treatment'. *British Journal of Medical Psychology*, **23**, 59–74.

Ezriel, H. (1952) 'Notes on psychoanalytic group therapy: II Interpretation and research'. *Psychiatry*, **15**, 119–126.

Foulkes, S. H. (1948) *Introduction to Group-Analytic Psychotherapy*. New York: Greene Stratton.

Freud, S. (1910) 'Five lectures on psychoanalysis'. Reprinted in James Strachey (ed.) *The Standard Edition of the Complete Psychological Works of Sigmund Freud*. London: Hogarth Press and the Institute of Psychoanalysis, 1953, vol. 2.

Freud, S. (1921) 'Group psychotherapy and the analysis of the ego'. Reprinted in James Strachey (ed.) *The Standard Edition of the Complete Psychological Works of Sigmund Freud*. London: Hogarth Press and the Institute of Psychoanalysis, 1953, vol. 18.

Freud S. (1925) 'An autobiographical study'. Reprinted in James Strachey (ed.) *The Standard Edition of the Complete Psychological Works of Sigmund Freud*. London: Hogarth Press and the Institute of Psychoanalysis, 1953, vol. 20.

Gosling, R., Miller, D. H., Turquet, P. M., and Woodhouse, D. (1967) *The Use of Small Groups in Training*, Hitchin, Hert: Codicote Press.

Greenson, R. (1965) 'The working alliance and the transference neurosis'. *Psychoanalytic Quarterly*, **34**, 155–181.

Greenson, R. (1967) *The Techniques and Practice of Psychoanalysis*. New York: International Universities Press.

Harrow, M., Astrachan, B. M., Tucker, G. J., Klein, E. B., and Miller, T. C. (1971) 'The T-group and study group laboratory experience'. *Journal of Social Psychology*, **85**, 225–237.

Hoffer, W. (1956) 'Transference and transference neurosis'. *International Journal of Psychoanalysis*, **37**, 377–379.

Klein, E. B., and Astrachan, B. M. (1971) 'Learning in groups: A comparison of study and T-groups'. *Journal of Applied Behavioral Science*, **7**, 659–683.

Klein, E. B., and Gould, L. J. (1973) 'Boundary issues and organizational dynamics: A case study.' *Social Psychiatry*, **8**, 204–211.

Klein, E. B., Thomas, C. S., and Bellis, E. C. (1971) 'When warring groups meet: The use of a group approach in police–black community relations.' *Social Psychiatry*, **6**, 93–99.

Kohler, T., Klein, E. B., and Miller, J. (in preparation) 'The relationship between sex of members and consultants in study groups'.

Levinson, D. (1959) 'Role, personality and social structure in the organizational setting'. *Journal of Abnormal and Social Psychology*, **58**, 170–180.

Mills, R. M. (1964) *Group Transformation: An Analysis of a Learning Group*. Englewood Cliffs, Prentice-Hall.

Newton, P. M. (1971) 'Abstinence as a role requirement in psychotherapy.' *Psychiatry*, **34**, 391–400.

Osgood, C. E., Tannenbaum, P. H., and Suci, G. J. (1957) *The Measurement of Meaning*. Urbana: University of Illinois Press.

Rosenbaum, M., and Berger, M. (eds) (1963) *Group Psychotherapy and Group Function*. New York: Basic Books.

Schafer, R. (1968) *Aspects of Internalization*. New York: Oxford University Press.

Senders, V. L. (1958) *Measurement and Statistics*. New York: Oxford University Press.

Singer, D. L., Astrachan, B. M., Gould, L. J., and Klein, E. B. (1975) 'Boundary management in psychological work with groups'. *Journal of Applied Behavioral Science*, **11**, 137–176.

Slater, P. F. (1966) *Microcosm*. New York: Wiley.

Slavson, S. R. (1950) *Analytic Group Psychotherapy*. New York: Columbia University Press.

Sullivan, H. S. (1953) *The Interpersonal Theory of Psychiatry*. New York: Norton.

Sutherland, J. D. (1952) 'Notes on psychoanalytic group therapy: I, Therapy and training'. *Psychiatry*, **15**, 111–117.

Turquet, P. M. (1974) 'Leadership—the individual and the group'. In G. S. Gibbard, J. J. Hartman, and R. D. Mann (eds) *Analysis of Groups*. San Francisco: Jossey-Bass, 349–371.

Wolf, A. (1949) 'The psychoanalysis of groups'. *American Journal of Psychotherapy*, **3**, 529–557.

Chapter 7

A Manager's View of the Institutional Event

Dennis Guereca

The 'institutional event' seeks to lead to an understanding of the internal life and behaviour of the conference. Members and staff have each joined from their own individual environments and have experienced the process of joining and creating a unique organization which, by the start of the institutional event, has written some of its own history, established its own myths and allocated its own stereotypes and roles for a variety of tasks. While conference life is internally generated, it is inevitably coloured by the importation by the members and staff of their own values and experiences gained from their normal operational environments. Conference experience may already have severely tested and challenged the attitudes and behaviour of conference members, which are matters of passionate importance to individuals. It is not surprising that members' resentment and anger is aroused and directed to the staff who have presumed to organize and participate in a conference where the primary task is to explore and understand human behaviour—not through a series of cosy theoretical lectures but simply by letting it happen with all its excitement and drama. The only constraints are those exercised by the members themselves and the only structure is the time boundary of conference events and the maintenance of professional roles and behaviour by the staff. Members are not bound as the staff are by this same minimal structure. They are free to pursue their learning experience in their own ways. Whether they choose to operate within or outside the framework of the design of the conference is in itself a piece of experience with which members and staff can work.

Critics of the design of conferences have sometimes expressed the view that timetables and events are too rigid and that by establishing them management style and behaviour is too authoritarian. The underlying rationale for arranging a number of different groupings with different tasks is to provide members with the experience of dealing with the boundaries between them. These boundaries and changing staff roles for different events do give members opportunities of testing and crossing them. If they did not exist, they could not be experienced or examined. Boundaries and roles are frequently issues around which staff and members exercise their individual authority, and learning about authority in institutional life is a principal conference task.

It is in the institutional event that the total conference, staff and members, can explore the relationship between these two principal groups. In institutional terms these represent the managers and the managed. Members can develop political machinery to enable them to carry out this exploration. The staff work on a completely open system in that any member or representative of groups of members can observe the staff group at work as a corporate body. Members of staff throughout the conference perform roles as consultants to small groups, large groups, review groups, etc., and as administrators. Prior to the conference each member of staff has agreed to accept the roles offered to him and the general disposition of roles of other staff colleagues. Within the conference all staff accept and work with the delegated authority they have been given and equally accept the corporate accountability that goes with that authority. In the institutional event, as in all other aspects of the conference, the staff as individuals represent the corporate body of staff in everything they do and in that respect are plenipotentiaries. To enable them to carry out their tasks effectively there is clearly a need for a corporate view or understanding to be formed, however limited and embryonic, of conference behaviour and issues so that staff have a general framework or brief within which to operate. The putting together of this general and constantly changing picture is a principal task for the staff. It is culled from the interpretations and reports from other conference events and from what can be perceived and interpreted from the overt behaviour of the membership in the groupings the members choose and the subconscious roles of the members' groups.

The staff attempt to formulate a view of the underlying processes in the institutional event, and at the same time within the framework of that view take managerial decisions on appropriate responses and initiatives to the membership. This management task provides plenty of scope for differing and opposing views to emerge within the staff group. To all intents and purposes the staff group is in a similar situation to the management committee or board of directors of any other institution. Conference memberships frequently wish to see a conference management as monolithic and undifferentiated which patently it is not. When observers who have seen the staff at work together report back to their membership groups on the differences which have been expressed, this is often seen as a split in the staff rather than a normal management process. The capacity to tolerate and manage differences constructively is a necessary attribute of politicians, trade unionists, and managers. In accepting an invitation to serve on conference staff each individual also accepts the corporate accountability or 'cabinet responsibility' that goes with the invitation.

The institutional event can illuminate many aspects of organizational life. Members are free to form themselves into any groupings they wish. The members' subgroups frequently reflect some aspect of the members' perception of the staff. This mirroring can simply be in the shape or form of a subgroup or in a more complex way represent in its make-up and behaviour some of the different facets of the make-up of the staff. Identifying mirroring or parallels in an organization can be very useful in quickly identifying aspects of its culture —important to any newcomer to the organization. A simple illustration of this was in one manufacturing company where there had developed a hierarchy of professional qualifications which matched the management organizational hierarchy in that the managing director held a second degree, the board members held first degrees, and the next level of management held technical qualifications at nondegree level. In parallel with this the 2000 manual workers so arranged their affairs that their six-man negotiating committee was led by a member of the highest skilled group. His deputy was a member of the next grade of skill. Three others were from the skilled grades and only one was drawn from the semi-skilled groups who accounted for some 80 per cent of the employees. This certainly indicated how skill, training, and qualifications were regarded in the company. In industrial relations terms this had considerable significance particularly when issues on differentials in terms and conditions of employment arose.

In the institutional event members explore in their subgroups various forms of internal organization which vary from the completely autocratic through various forms of so-called democracy to groups which are completely unstructured collections of individuals. This event highlights the relationship between the individual and the institution of which he is a member. For the staff there is a prior commitment to provide to the best of their ability opportunities for the membership to learn through experience. This primary task is the shared objective which gives the staff cohesion and enables it to make use of its individual differences by allocating tasks and roles on the basis of the appropriateness of the individuals concerned to undertake them. In the last resort this primary task of managing a learning institution overrides all other considerations and the director, the ultimate guardian of the primary task, may have to make decisions which are unpalatable to some of his colleagues. What is important is that these situations are part of the life of the institution and are therefore open to examination as part of the learning process. This may all sound rather like a prescription for perfection. It must be tempered with the reality that the staff undertaking is to do the best it can in the circumstances in which it finds itself.

Members' knowledge of each other generally stems solely from conference experience. The exercising of choice is often quite difficult. At the conscious level there are issues about identity—do members choose to identify with those with whom they have established a relationship in their small groups, or the large group, or socially outside the conference events? Do they offer themselves as potential leaders around whom some potential followers will collect? Or do they join a waifs and strays group? Choice, however, is often based on a less well-defined and more subconscious basis, and as the groups become established and start to function in the event the underlying basis of choice becomes clearer. Each conference is unique and generalizations about the covert reasons for the formation of members' subgroups are not really feasible as they are infinitely variable. As an illustration, however, each individual is ambivalent within himself towards the staff and towards the learning methods on which the conference is based. Members harbour both positive and negative feelings towards them. Subgroupings of members can serve to polarize these feelings so that within the institutional event subgroupings can be rather like refracted light, each representing different parts of the spectrum, some freeing themselves from ambivalence and uncertainty in order to pursue a role, while others contain the uncertainty, negativeness, and at times the chaos from the other subgroups and thereby perform a role on behalf of the whole system.

A further feature of the relationships between members' groups is their capacity to be self-cancelling or mutually self-regulating when one or more groups seek to take an initiative. On the surface this may seem to be rationalized on the basis of competition in a power situation or merely on the basis that another group is more interested in going in another direction to pursue its own objectives. It seems, though, that many institutions and organizations have this regulatory mechanism to preserve essentially a *status quo,* or at least if there is to be change then it has to be slow and controlled. This is why, perhaps, there are in the so-called free world so many minority governments, and why in the United Kingdom the electorate in recent years has given successive governments such limited mandates. People concerned with industrial relations and who deal with multi-union negotiating committees know this phenomenon only too well. There is so often one section of the organization unwilling to go along with the rest and posing a constant threat of withdrawing from the conference table and becoming a breakaway group. Such groups frequently frustrate or slow down proposed changes, and may well be expressing the subconscious uncertainties of the whole institution.

As the institutional event proceeds members' subgroups have to start to deal with their internal self-management. If they decide on a formalized structure this requires them to allocate tasks and roles and therefore to choose individuals from among their number to perform them. Groups rarely seem prepared to invest their authority fully and appoint a director. Quite frequently a group will appoint a chairman, sometimes on a rather tenuous, rotating basis.

As soon as structures start to take shape and roles are allocated to, or assumed by, individuals, members are creating for themselves a small institution with some political machinery within the framework of the event. In so doing, members are investing some of their own authority in other people. They have, on occasions, to subordinate themselves to others. Members cannot be involved in everything that is going on. When interactions take place with other groups only a few members can personally experience the interaction. Those who are directly involved act in a representative capacity while the others are observers or sit at home waiting for their representatives to return to relate, of necessity, an edited account of what has happened and so provide a secondhand experience for their colleagues. As the event proceeds and the political machinery and therefore the representative system develops, a majority of members find themselves inevitably more and more remote from what is happening in the total institutional event, while the minority who are acting as representatives can be having quite an exciting time interacting with representatives of other members' groups or with the management. Representatives need more and more authority to act on behalf of their group as the pace quickens. The generality of the membership correspondingly has less and less scope and opportunity to be involved. While the skill of a representative is in knowing the limits of his authority and the general wishes and objectives of his constituents, to be effective and for the institution to function he has to exercise more and more authority on behalf of others. The price of belonging to institutions which operate through representative systems is the loss for the majority of individual identity and individual freedom. Ultimately, the choice seems to be to stay or to leave—cabinet responsibility in the broadest sense.

Representation is essentially a delegating process, and delegation is a process of conducting affairs through representatives. In any organization representatives, whether they act on behalf of the management or the managed, need to understand the objectives and policy framework of those on whose behalf they are acting. The institutional event frequently illustrates the difficulties which groups have in agreeing objectives so as to provide an adequate brief for their representatives. Representatives without an understanding of the objectives which set the boundaries of their role and which provide the necessary support can soon become merely messengers and lose credibility as people with whom business can be done. In carrying out their role, managers (i.e. representatives) use judgement and need to have the authority to exercise discretion. Rarely do people see situations or exercise their judgement in precisely the same way. Just as the representative in the institutional event has to report to his group when he returns from an assignment, so the manager has to face his boss. The sort of reception he gets starts to condition his future performance. If the group (or boss) finds difficulty in tolerating the individuality which inevitably arises in the way in which the representative (subordinate) performs the role, and regularly adopts a critical stance, the representative's brief becomes narrower. The representative becomes less and less confident in exercising judgement and more and more dependent on those who are briefing him. Eventually he may be destroyed by being made ineffective so that he resigns, is dismissed, or is simply ignored.

The process of delegation and of briefing representatives can be fraught with anxiety both for the delegator and delegate. The delegator who can accept nothing less than a carbon copy of what he believes his own performance would have been, and who is unable to tolerate individual differences, will generate high anxiety in his delegates and a decreasing level of performance. The delegator who cannot cope with his own anxieties may well project these into his subordinate and so sow the seeds of failure. Many organizations no doubt have their quota of casualties whose only misfortune was to work for a boss who could not tolerate the uncertainties and anxieties that go with delegation.

The primary task of conferences is to provide opportunities for members to learn about authority and leadership and behaviour of and within institutions. Conference behaviour clearly reflects our notions about the society and institutions within which we live. The conference's primary tasks is not to strive to create new forms of organizational life, although there are no constraints on members attempting to do this. Members sometimes hanker after an alternative society and seek to experiment with various forms of 'democracy', but this has proved to be elusive. There is much talk in Europe of the 'democratic imperative' and 'industrial democracy'. Conference experience so far seems to suggest that the more 'democratic' institutions become, through the representative system, the more remote and less involved the generality of people become. Representative systems interpose a level of communication if not a level of management between managers and the managed. If management chooses or is only allowed to talk to and do business with a small number of representatives this is undoubtedly at the expense of the majority for whom the quality of life and sense of individual worth probably deteriorates in terms of their own identity in relation to the institution in which they work or live.

It is inconceivable these days that institutions of any appreciable size could operate without some sort of managerial hierarchy and some sort of representative system through which the generality of the institution's members can speak. The leaders of the ancient city state of Athens provided opportunities periodically for all the citizens to meet together to debate policy and to take decisions. Conference experience of the large group with all its hysteria and neurosis gives some insight into its unreliability as a decision-making body. Athenians lived to regret some of the corporate decisions taken at such meetings. There is no ready formula for arranging the affairs of institutions so that all can be equally involved in decision-making except in the negative sense that each decision is sanctioned by those affected by it. When decisions are taken authority is being exercised. The nature of the impact on individuals of the exercise of authority is the same irrespective of whether it is exercised by managers, trade union officials, or employee representatives. Unpopular decisions are not necessarily any more popular because one's representative has been party to them. Authority is a fact of institutional life and those who exercise it must judge the extent to which they will be permitted to do so by those who are subject to it. It is a myth which needs exploding that the nature of authority and the management process will change if institutions are jointly managed by management and representatives of the generality of members of the institution. Style may change and the primary task may be changed but the nature of authority will not. *Plus ça change plus c'est la même chose.*

Leicester conferences examine power and authority. They enable the underlying dynamics and processes of behaviour in an institution to be acted out and understood. The primary task of conference staff is to provide learning opportunities for the members. Adherence to this primary task is the unifying brief which enables the staff to accept corporate responsibility. Both the members and the staff generally have fantasies about each other and these can be checked with reality. Members frequently, however, see staff as a totally homogenized group and wish to deny that individual members of staff are in fact individuals. Presumably it is always easier in organizations to see managers as depersonalized roles held accountable for all the ills and shortcomings of the institution and at which can be directed whatever anger and hostility may derive from the disappointments and frustrations which are inevitably part of institutional life. Sometimes if management is seen as too powerful and unassailable the hostility can be turned inwards to another group or department resulting in a very nonproductive fratricide. Undoubtedly an important management function in institutions is therefore to be prepared to accept whatever hostility there may be in the system from whatever cause. It is a frequent experience in industrial relations that it is necessary to give time to working through the expression of negative feelings before constructive and positive work can be achieved.

Conferences raise many more questions that can readily be answered. How, for example, can individuals relate to institutions? Conference experience certainly demonstrates the shortcomings of representative systems, but at the same time experience shows that organizations cannot operate without them. Managements which rely entirely on the representative system to relate to employees will very probably not be satisfying individual needs for recognition and individual identity. They may well be subjecting employees to an alternative management system, namely the hierarchy of employee representatives which has its own inbuilt career pattern and of necessity its own authority base.

If involvement and participation are confined to a few managers and representatives the institution may well survive but we will only have succeeded in imperceptibly increasing the numbers involved in the management process. Perhaps we should be concentrating our attention on the tasks of increasing individual discretion within the jobs people do, and providing for the greater and not the diminishing exercise of individual authority within institutional life in order to refurbish the sense of individual worth and identity with the primary task of our institutions.

In the current debate on 'industrial democracy' there are those who envisage this being achieved by employee representatives on boards of companies but with their accountability to the sectional interests of those whom they represent. The ultimate primary task of institutions must surely be to survive through the successful provision of services or the creation of wealth. Acceptance of the primary task is a prerequisite of corporate accountability and the minimum requirement from those who seek to manage institutions.

Conferences do not seek to find a panacea but they do provide rich and rewarding experiences giving insights into organizational life which can be put to positive and fruitful use.

Chapter 8

Men and Women at Work: A Group Relations Conference on Person and Role*

Láurence J. Gould

Introduction

The exploration of issues related to gender, sexuality, and age seem particularly germane in our current work and personal situations. In recent years we have witnessed the dramatic upsurge of many sorts of incipient revolutions. Certainly one among these has been in the sexual realm—not only in the intimate and narrow sense of sexual, but in the broader areas concerning the nature of the family unit itself, and role shifts or changes in the world of work. However, there is much to suggest that the ability of men and women to work together effectively is still often seriously impaired by deeply held gender-linked attitudes, fantasies, and stereotypes that men and women have about themselves and each other. Adding to these dilemmas are the powerful ways in which age or stages of adult development interact with such gender-related issues. And finally, the loosening of sexual constraints, both internally and externally, confront us continually with the dilemmas of temptation, choice, and action which cross traditional boundaries. This constellation of gender, sexuality, and age may be viewed, therefore, as an increasingly salient aspect of group and organizational work settings as it influences or interacts with issues of authority and leadership.

The 'Men and Women at Work' group relations conferences to be discussed in this paper are specifically designed to provide opportunities to study the ways in which collaboration among and between men and women in group and organizational work settings is affected by attitudes and beliefs, both conscious and unconscious, related to gender, sexuality, and age. The aim is to

*Necessarily, my thanks go first to all of the people who attended the conferences described in this paper. Without their participation these conferences would not have continued evolving. Thanks also go to my many staff colleagues. The ideas in this paper are as much their collective contribution as they are mine. Finally, I would like to thank Dr Daniel Levinson, whose research in the area of adult development has made an important contribution to my thinking about these conferences.

Much of the material in those sections introducing and describing the group relations conferences come from a variety of conference brochures. Since many of my colleagues have produced copy, which we freely borrow and exchange, I can only gratefully acknowledge these, by now anonymous, contributions.

further the exploration and understanding of these attitudes and beliefs as they are manifested behaviourally in the various conference events and in the conference as a whole.

Conference origins

Initially, heightened awareness of the issues noted above were stimulated, of course, by the developing 'women's movement'—so towards the end of the 1960s a number of my colleagues and I began to think about new conference designs which would hopefully provide more sustained and direct opportunities for exploring various aspects of male/female interactions. While such study seemed to me timely, on a more personal level I was deeply influenced by a number of women who were involved in the 'movement' including some colleagues, women graduate students in my programme and, most directly, by the woman with whom I live. If anything was needed to convince me of the importance of these issues, it was the continual and often disturbing experience of living with a woman and working with women who had begun the painful and exhilarating struggle to redefine themselves, personally and professionally. For my part I had all of the awkward and self-conscious responses of a man with 'liberal' convictions—I assiduously practised saying Ms until it smoothly rolled off my tongue, tried to deny my anxiety, and attempted as best I could to support the efforts of the women that I knew wished to change, and I tried to change aspects of my own behaviour.

The confluence of these forces led eventually to my participating, in a bit of a role reversal charade, as administrator (I made the coffee, ran errands, etc.) at a conference, staffed entirely by women colleagues, called 'A Working Conference on Women in Authority'. This conference was designed to provide both men and women with opportunities to explore their attitudes towards women in authority roles. Our explicit rationale was as follows: a large gap existed for most men and women between their earliest experiences with women in authority—namely, mothers and elementary school teachers—and adult experiences with women in authority roles; we also felt that, increasingly, both men and women were going to be working with women in positions of authority and leadership; and finally, we believed that women needed opportunities to explore models offered by women taking authority and leadership roles as a means of facilitating their own development in such roles.

This conference, held in New York City, attracted 30 women and 20 men. I and the women who comprised the professional staff group had all worked in many conferences on authority and leadership, but none with an explicit focus on gender and a design which included a professional staff group composed entirely of women, single-gender events (the small group), and a professional man in the administrator's role. Today, we take such configurations for granted—especially work groups composed of women—but in early 1970, as I vividly recall, sitting in the staffroom on the first day of the conference, we were terribly anxious and excessively constrained.

In all, however, we were sufficiently excited by this conference to plan another. For the second such conference 75 women and only three men applied! While we considered an all-women's conference an interesting option (Taylor *et al.*, 1978), we felt that it would not be a substitute for men and women working together around these issues. Therefore, a conference with 75 women and three men was clearly not the ideal learning environment. As a result, I had the rather awkward tasks of trying to entice some of my male graduate students to participate. I finally did manage to cajole about seven or eight of them into the conference, and as of this writing most, I believe, have forgiven me. I think that the very small number of male applicants, and the experience of the men who did attend, say a great deal about the fantasies and feelings that men have about women in authority. The anticipation of being 'surrounded by women' in an organizational environment where the authority structure is composed entirely of women apparently was just too disturbing, and as such, it was an experience to be avoided. I might also add that for the men who did participate, injury was added to insult, since the only man with whom they could identify, namely myself, was 'wearing an apron' and making coffee. If these men, therefore, experienced the conference as a symbolic harbinger of the future (as I believe they did), their distress was indeed understandable.

The paucity of male applicants and the experience of the men who did attend led us to modify almost entirely the structure of these conferences. Their successor had a different design, a staff group composed of both men and women, and was called 'Male—Female Work Relations in Group and Organizational Settings'. These conferences, of which there were about ten during the next five years, did attract a sufficient number of men, although with few exceptions, and until recently, they attracted considerably more women. Almost all of these conferences, which were in weekend formats, went through a series of successive changes and modifications as our experience in them accumulated, and our thinking developed. In 1976 we felt ready to hold a full-scale residential conference (Gould, 1976), and during this past year (Gould, 1977) we held the second such conference, described in detail below.

Conference organization

Introduction and aims

When authority is vested in a person, he or she thereby assumes a work role which in a formal sense is the same regardless of sex, age, race, or personal characteristics. However, the way in which he or she performs in role, the difficulties encountered in filling the role, and the way he or she is perceived by others, are all influenced by such personal and demographic factors. In the 'men and women at work' conference the focus is on an exploration of how attitudes and fantasies about sexuality and gender in relation to age (more specifically, in relation to particular stages of adult development) influence the ways in which men and women exercise authority and leadership in their roles, and how their roles are perceived and influenced by others. It is in this context that conference participants have opportunities to study their own and others' behaviour in situations in which the characteristics of the person or persons in authority, as well as the other members of the group, vary. A major aim is the heightened awareness of issues related to sexuality, gender, and age which may have a significant influence in work situations, often unnoticed or not consciously experienced by the persons involved.

While the behavioural sciences are extending our understanding of gender, sexuality, adult development (e.g. Levinson *et al.*, 1974), and of group and organizational processes, a gap exists between such understanding and the day-to-day problems encountered by those who must exercise authority and leadership. Often intellectual formulations are too generalized to be applicable to a particular set of relationships. In addition, the pressures and involvements of the immediate work situation often make it difficult to stand back and attempt a dispassionate analysis. It is the further aim of this conference, therefore, to bridge this gap by providing a means through which experience can be studied, and at least partially understood, as it occurs.

Although the aims noted above are in general the same as those underlying other group relations conferences (e.g. O'Connor, 1971; Rice, 1965; Rioch, 1970), the special emphasis of this conference entails some change in design and in the definition of the primary task.

The primary task

The primary task of the 'Men and women at work' group relations conference is to explore the exercise of authority and leadership as it is influenced by gender, sexuality, and stages of adult development.

Conference design

The conference is designed to provide opportunities for participants to study relations among and between men and women in group settings which vary in task, size, composition, and staff presence, as well as in the conference as a whole.

The various group events, described below, are viewed as an integrated system of activities, which together with the staff and participants who engage in them, comprise the formal work organization of the conference institution. The conference, therefore, can be viewed as a temporary educational organization designed specifically for the performance of the primary task.

The conference begins with an *opening plenary* session in which the conference and staff are introduced to the participants, and proceeds through the following events (See Figure 1 for the schedule of events):

Small groups consist of from ten to 14 participants of the same gender. The tasks of the small group is to study its own behaviour. Each group has the services of a consultant of the same gender as the members to help it in its task.

Figure 1. Schedule of events for the 'Men and women at work' group relations conference (Gould, 1977)

Time	DAY 1	DAY 2	DAY 3	DAY 4	DAY 5	DAY 6
8 : 00 Breakfast						
9 : 00–10 : 30		SG	SG	SG	SG	RRCG
10 : 30 Coffee						
11 : 00–12 : 30		LG	LG	LG	RRCG	TCP
12 : 30 Lunch	2 : 00 p.m. PCO					2: 00–3 : 30
2 : 30–4 : 00	SG	——	IE	IE	——	RRCG
4 : 00 Coffee						
4 : 30–6 : 00	LG	IE	IE	IE	GCP	
6 : 30 Dinner						
8 : 00–9 : 30	SG	IE	GCP	——	RRCG	

PCO—Plenary conference opening   IE—Institutional event
SG—Small group   RRCG—Role relations consultation group
LG—Large group   GCP—Gender conference plenary
—— —Break   TCP—Total conference plenary

In the *large group* all of the men and women in the membership meet together. The task of the large group is to study male/female dynamics in a group consisting of more people than can comfortably meet face to face. In the large group, participants have the opportunity to experience the ways in which the constellation of gender, sexuality, and age influences a situation in which sides appear to be taken spontaneously, subgroups form and dissolve, and myths emerge. Consequences for the individual with regard to gender, sexuality, and age as these influence the nature of roles taken, and of group support or its absence, are experienced and seen. The large group has the services of a male and a female consultant to help it examine its own behaviour.

The *institutional event* has the task of studying relationships among and between men and women in the conference membership, and between the participants as a total group, and the staff group within the context of the conference institution. The membership has the services of the entire staff to help in this task.

Three *conference plenaries* provide participants with opportunities for reflecting upon the experiences of the conference. In the first two *gender conference plenaries*, men and women meet separately with all staff members of the same gender. Their respective tasks are to review the role of the men and the role of the women—both members and staff—in the conference up till that point in time. In the third and final *total conference plenary* the entire membership and staff meet together to review the experience of the conference as a whole and in its various parts.

Role-relations consultation groups have three related tasks:

(1) To provide opportunities for each conference participant to examine his

or her personal and social relatedness to the conference institution, and the varying experiences—both gratifying and frustrating—the institution has offered.

(2) To consider the relevance of the conference experiences to participants' own work settings, and their roles in them.

(3) To provide a forum in which to explore the dilemmas of leaving the conference and returning home.

The membership of these groups is mixed, and each group has a staff consultant to assist in its task.

The staff role

The task of the staff members acting as consultants in the various events is to help the groups with which they are working to carry out the task of the event. They seek to behave in such a way as will, in their view, provide the best opportunities for participants to learn about the nature of authority and leadership in relation to sexuality, gender, and stages of adult development, as well as how participants' experience relates to the conference institution as a whole. Staff consultants intervene only when they believe that their interventions will facilitate the work of the group.

Since the focus of the conference is on the nature of authority and leadership, the behaviour of the men and women on the staff, who represent the management of the conference, is explicitly available for study in relation to gender, sexuality, and age.

Membership

There is no special prerequisite for participation except serious interest. The intention, so far as possible, is to draw together an equal number of men and women of all ages and form a variety of backgrounds and work settings.

A major value of the residential conference is the challenge provided by an unfamiliar situation. In order to obtain maximum benefit, we suggest that not more than one member of an immediate family apply. However, in the interests of applying conference learning to one's work setting, there is some advantage if participants attend with colleagues from the same institution, and preferably with colleagues of the other gender.

Technical issues in design and interpretation

The basic conference method (e.g. Rice, 1965; Rioch, 1970) is to construct situations in which conventional defences, both personal and institutional, against recognizing or acting upon attitudes, beliefs, and fantasies are reduced. This facilitates an examination of the covert forces which continually influence interactions at all levels, from the interpersonal to the organizational. In this conference, these interactions focused on age and gender, as they relate to authority and leadership, occur within the context of the various events which are group situations that differ on a variety of dimensions (see 'Conference design' section above).

Further, there are two particular aspects of the design of this conference which should be highlighted. First, the conference is not designed to address itself to questions about the origins of attitudes, beliefs, and fantasies in the realm of gender, sexuality, and age—whether, or the extent to which, for example, gender differences do, or do not have, biological bases. Rather, the conference is designed to illuminate experience and behaviour in the 'here and now', and it does make the assumption that attitudinal and behavioural differences (as well as similarities) do exist between men and women whatever their original source. Why else have a 'Men and Women at Work' conference? This relates to the second point that I would like to make about the conference design. In a number of the conference events, men and women, both participants and staff, are in separate groupings (e.g. the small group and the gender conference plenaries). It may be argued that such groupings create dilemmas, stimulate feelings, and exacerbate a divisiveness that would not exist if the groups were structured otherwise. Within the confines of this paper, I can only suggest, on the basis of experience in these conferences, that I do not believe this to be the case. Rather, I view this feature of the conference design as a structural vehicle for highlighting various dimensions of male/female interaction. By creating these group boundaries (e.g. Miller and Rice, 1967) rich material is elicited for study and examination. For example, participants have opportunities to experience the sorts of gratifications, anxieties, and defences that are stimulated by the different settings. That is, this design feature allows participants to experience differences and similarities in behaviour, affect and process in single-gender settings as contrasted to mixed-gender settings. It is useful, therefore, to have these settings juxtaposed. The partial structural separation of men and women has the further advantage of making more manifest gender-linked aspects of sentient bonds—that is, the nonrational aspects of affiliation or loyalty, as distinct from rational or task groupings (Miller and Rice, 1967). What, for example, is the quality and emotional strength of 'sisterhood' as compared to 'brotherhood'? What is the fate of these ties in mixed-gender situations? How do such ties either facilitate or hinder the development of appropriate task groupings or forms of task organization? Or yet, how do these ties influence the assessment and attribution of competence? If the conference design, in fact, raises these questions for the participants, as I believe it does, it is serving the aims of the conference.

A parallel issue to the above concerns the nature of interpretation. This conference specifically focuses on how a person's characteristics, namely, his or her gender, sexuality, and age, interact with his or her work roles as a member of a group and an organization. If interpretations are focused on these aspects of the person/role boundary and group processes, it may be argued that issues relating to gender, sexuality, and age are exaggerated or are spuriously created.

Again, I can only say that I do not believe this to be the case. Rather, I would suggest that this situation is more adequately conceptualized as a 'figure/ ground' phenomenon. In other group relations conferences, person characteristics tend to be 'ground', while role, group, intergroup, and organizational processes are 'figure'. By contrast, the emphasis in the 'Men and Women at Work' conference is on how various dimensions of these unfolding processes are accounted for by the gender, sexuality, and age of the participants. In practice this means that certain other aspects of these processes are either neglected or simply noted in passing. Put another way, the staff are continually faced with choices in providing interpretations. If the primary task is adhered to, some learning opportunities will be forsaken or minimized. However, it should be noted that the pursuit of any task necessarily constrains the pursuit of others—no less so in this than in any other enterprise.

Conference processes and culture

It is beyond the purpose and scope of this paper to provide an analysis of the specific processes and dynamics which develop in relation to the exercise of authority and leadership as it is influenced by gender, sexuality, and stages of adult development. Rather, I will attempt to provide an overview of the 'Men and Women at Work' conference from the perspective of the general processes it sets in motion, and aspects of the culture which develop during the life of the conference.

The appropriate starting-point is, I believe, the particular person/role focus of this conference. That is, this conference, more than others, directly touches very intimate and personal concerns and anxieties in ways which compared to other group relations conferences, are more difficult for the individual to defend against. While we do, in fact, believe that issues of authority, leadership, and work are quite personal, in other conferences there are somewhat greater possibilities for splitting off concerns about work relationships from what we ordinarily think of as personal relationships (with loved ones, family, friends, etc.). In this conference, however, the participant can be viewed, and may experience himself or herself, for example, as being as much an implicit representative of the family as he or she is explicitly a representative of a work organization. Therefore, the issues and anxieties around gender, sexuality, and age that are mobilized in this conference can be as intimate and personal, in the ordinary sense, as they are work-related. Hence, the boundary between the personal sphere and the realm of work, in whatever manner it may be conceptualized, is at best extremely tenuous. By implication, this aspect of the 'Men and Women at Work' conference raises anew the issue of training *v.* therapy (see Rice, 1965, Chapter 12, for a complete discussion), and the appropriate boundaries between these activities. While I do not believe that the 'Men and Women at Work' conference is in fact a therapeutic enterprise, the 'pull' in this direction is none the less generally somewhat stronger than in other group relations conferences. In practice, therefore, the staff must remain alert if the appropriate tasks boundaries are to be maintained, lest they inadvertently go into collusion with the participants to subtly shift these boundaries towards a therapeutic, as distinct from an educational, stance.

One other aspect of the conference culture requires elaboration, and that is the immediate emergence of quite powerful nonsexist and nonageist norms. This is not surprising given the ideology and conscious convictions of the majority of both participants and staff. That is, while participants attempt to collaborate in an exploration of nonrational and nonconscious aspects of attitudes and beliefs about gender, sexuality, and age, there is, at the same time, often massive denial, since everyone also tends to be quite selfconsciously on 'good behaviour'. The resulting culture of nonsexism and nonageism and the suppression of sexist or ageist attitudes and behaviours make new learning, of course, quite difficult. The staff for their part struggle with the same dilemmas. They also attempt to be nonsexist and nonageist, and as a result they may initially engage in a collusive avoidance with the membership, or project their own unconscious attitudes and beliefs onto the membership, making them the repository of all gender-linked and age-linked 'badness'. The participants may in turn engage in similar sorts of projections in an attempt to avoid their own dilemmas. It is often remarkable what details are used as a basis for these projections. The fact, for example, that the conference brochure was blue became, in the view of one participant, *de facto* evidence of staff sexism. In addition to a collusive avoidance, and the fight stance (Bion, 1961) and defensiveness that may ensue when powerful mutual projections dominate the group process, a third type of collusion may develop and alternate with the above to provide a social defence system (Menzies, 1967). This process is characterized by subtly shifting the appropriate 'figure/ground' emphasis of this conference, noted in the preceding section, to the more familiar emphases of other group relations conferences. This process tends to develop when, as is often the case, a substantial number of participants have attended other group relations conferences, and are, therefore, able to use such familiarity defensively. Further, since most of the staff have also had considerably more experience in other conferences as well, the likelihood that they will collude in this process is exacerbated for similar reasons. As a result, the 'Men and Women at Work' conference may, at times, have its particular focus in name only. Therefore, as with the boundary between the training enterprise and the therapeutic enterprise, noted previously, the staff must struggle against these collusive internal and external pulls if the requisite task boundaries of a 'Men and Women at Work' conference are to be maintained.

Summary and conclusions

By way of a summary, I would like to enumerate several aspects of the 'Men and Women at Work' conferences that are implicit in the foregoing discussion.

First, the emphasis on work-related processes in these conferences continues to provide unique learning opportunities compared to other types of groups such as encounter and sensitivity training. For the most part, these tend to focus almost exclusively on the more narrowly intimate, personal, explicitly sexual and/or interpersonal aspects of male/female relationships.

Second, the focus on group and organizational aspects of male/female relationships in these conferences provides a perspective which is markedly different from the large body of research on the male/female dyad. That is, this perspective may help us to understand aspects of dyadic relationships in a new light (whatever the personal and demographic characteristics of the pair). What, for example, are the forces which influence the nature of the boundary that defines a dyad, and hence the quality of the relationship, whether these originate in the larger family, the social network, or the organizational environment? After all, the problem for Romeo and Juliet was that they were members of groups!

Third, these conferences can be conceived as a laboratory in which the emergent behaviours provide an enormous amount of data and stimulate almost endless hypotheses about gender-related and age-related aspects of authority and leadership, group functioning, and organizational behaviour. Many of these can then be more carefully investigated under controlled conditions. Numerous instances are available in which the conference experience led, directly or indirectly, to a variety of systematic formulations and empirical investigations (e.g. Bayes *et al.*, 1977; Bayes and Newton, 1976; Beauvais, 1976; Chandler, 1975; Gould, 1975; Wright, 1976; Wright and Gould, 1977). These in turn have enriched our ability to conceptualize aspects of the conference, as well as provided an opportunity for retesting the validity of these formulations and research findings in subsequent conferences.

Finally, while the above are important, these conferences have the primary task of helping men and women in their struggle to collaborate more effectively and with greater satisfaction. The hope is, therefore, that the conference setting will provide opportunities for an authentic and passionate engagement of issues related to gender, sexuality, and age in mode which will facilitate continued learning and change for the individual's personal, social, and institutional roles in the 'back-home' environment.

References

Bayes, M., and Newton, P. (1976) 'Women in authority: A sociopsychological analysis'. Presented at the Scientific Meetings of the A. K. Rice Institute.

Bayes, M., Wisnent, L., and Wilk, L. A. (1977) 'The Mental Health Center and the Women's Liberation Group: An intergroup encounter'. *Psychiatry*, **40**, 66–78.

Beauvais, C. (1976) 'The family and the work group: dilemmas for women in authority'. Unpublished doctoral dissertation, City University of New York.

Bion, W. (1961) *Experiences in Groups*. London: Tavistock Publications.

Chandler, E. (1975) 'Choosing to work in groups: A naturalistic study of four women'. Unpublished doctoral dissertation. City University of New York.

Gould, L. J. (1975) 'Attitudes toward women in authority'. In E. Zuckerman (ed.) *Women and Men—Roles, Attitudes and Power Relationships*. Radcliffe Club of New York, 150–156.

Gould, L. J. (1976) 'Male–female work relations in group and organizational settings'. Conference brochure, Washington-Baltimore Center of the A. K. Rice Institute.

Gould, L. J. (1977) 'Men and women at work'. Conference brochure, Washington-Baltimore Center of the A. K. Rice Institute.

Levinson, D. J., Darrow, C. M., Klein, E. B., Levinson, M. H., and McKee, B. (1974) 'The psychosocial development of men in early adulthood and the mid-life transition'. In D. Ricks (ed.) *Life History Research in Psychopathology*, vol. III.

Menzies, Isabel E. P. (1967) *The Functioning of Social Systems as a Defense Against Anxiety. A Report on the Study of Nursing Service of a General Hospital.* Tavistock Pamphlet No. 3.

Miller, E. J., and Rice, A. K. (1967) *Systems of Organization.* London: Tavistock Publications.

O'Connor, G. (1971) 'The Tavistock method of group study'. *Science and Psychoanalysis*, **XVIII**, 100–115.

Rice, A. K. (1965) *Learning for Leadership: Interpersonal and Intergroup Relations.* London: Tavistock Publications.

Rioch, Margaret J. (1970) 'Group relations: Rationale and techniques'. *International Journal of Group Psychotherapy*, **XX**, 340–355.

Singer, D. L., Astrachan, B. M., Gould, L. J., and Klein, E. B. (1975) 'Boundary management in psychological work with groups'. *Journal of Applied Behavioral Science*, **11**, 2, 137–176.

Taylor, S., Bogdanoff, M., Brown, D., Hillman, L., Kurash, C., Spain, J., Thatcher, B., and Weinstein, L. (1978) 'By women, for women: A group relations conference'. This volume.

Wright, F. (1976) 'The effects of style and sex of consultants and sex of members in self-study groups'. *Small Group Behaviour*, **7**.

Wright, F., and Gould, L. J. (1977) 'Recent research on sex-linked aspects of group behavior: Implications for group psychotherapy'. In *Group Therapy 1977: An Overview*. New York: Stratton Intercontinental Medical Book Corporation.

Chapter **9**

By Women, for Women: A Group Relations Conference*

*Susan Taylor, Marcia Bogdanoff, Danielle Brown, Linda Hillman,
Cheryl Kurash, Julie Spain, Barbara Thacher, and Lissa Weinstein*

In psychodynamic studies of group process, the behaviour of women in groups, and women's relations to those in authority and leadership roles, have usually been studied in mixed-sex settings (e.g. Freud, 1950; Gibbard and Hartmann, 1973; Slater, 1966). Yet women find themselves with increasing frequency in task groups of their own sex: in a work context (even in occupations which are not traditionally female-dominated), in civic, religious, and voluntary organizations, or in groups gathered for 'consciousness-raising'. Do such groups manifest concerns that are gender-specific? Do women encounter particular difficulties around leadership, authority, and participation in same-sex groups?

In order to pursue these questions, the authors planned and staffed a three-day, nonresidential group relations conference which focused on issues of authority and leadership among women. This article will describe the conference and the dominant psychodynamic themes which emerged when women came together to study the functioning of all-women's groups.

Origin and design of the conference

This conference evolved as a training opportunity for a group of advanced doctoral students pursuing degrees at the institution sponsoring the conference (the Clinical Psychology Doctoral Program of the City College of New York), who were to serve as the conference staff. It began as a project of a nucleus of students interested in group relations work, conducted in the tradition of the Centre for Applied Social Research of the Tavistock Institute and the A. K. Rice Institute (see Rice, 1965; Rioch, 1971), under the auspices of a faculty member who had taught and supervised such work. Each of the prospective staff members had already been consultants to several self-study groups, and many had worked on the staff of a student-run group relations conference held at the sponsoring institution the previous spring.

*This paper is the product of a work group consisting of the authors, who delegated to the first author the task of synthesizing and codifying their ideas. The authors would like to thank Dr Laurence J. Gould for providing the opportunity to hold the conference, for his help as a consultant to the staff group, and for his critical reading of the manuscript. The authors would also like to thank Dr Zeborah Schachtel and Dr Carol Beauvais for consulting with the staff during the preconference phase.

The six women and three men of this original staff group shared complex, long-term sentient ties as classmates, collaborators in a number of settings (including co-consultantship in undergraduate self-study groups), friends, and—with two exceptions—former members of a semester-long self-study group which had existed two years earlier. Three of the women were planning to spend a year's clinical internship together at another facility, beginning three months after the conference, and two other women would be remaining in the programme for an additional year. Thus, the sentient life of this group (Miller and Rice, 1967) extended beyond the work of staffing the conference, both forwards and backwards in time.

It was due in part to sentient processes that the original staff group contained more women than men, and that within the first few weeks of preliminary meetings, the men withdrew from the staff group, one by one. This loss of male staff stimulated two fantasies which dominated the subsequent work of the six remaining women, as well as infusing the conference itself. First, there was a belief that women who were allowed to compete, exercise competence, or seek leadership would be capable of great damage and destruction: they could 'kill off' men, and each other. The second fantasy theme was based on the group's perception of the departed men as having been relatively less powerful, more ambivalent about assuming leadership, and more needy and vulnerable than the women. Their absence came to signify the women's wish to export such qualities as weakness and neediness from their group, and to maintain an image of themselves as unambivalently task-oriented, without the distraction of 'softer' feelings.

Early in the work group's history, then, powerful norms began to develop against the fantasied dangers of female leadership and competition, and feelings of neediness and vulnerability. It is striking that the 'weaker' attributes were located in the men, in a dramatic reversal of sex-linked stereotypes. But the life of this conference contained a number of such paradoxes, and a blurring of the attributes projected onto women and men. If it appeared that the men had 'become' women for the staff group, it was equally necessary, as we will see later, that some women in the conference must 'become' men.

Because the staff planned to meet weekly during the two months prior to the conference, they would clearly have available a great deal of data regarding issues of authority and leadership among women, drawn from the staff's own processes. In fact, the staff's examination of their own preconference behaviour (at one point with the services of a consultant) pointed to certain core conflicts which were mirrored in the conference weekend.

One example of the mirroring process was the ongoing difficulty experienced by the staff in fully authorizing one member to act as director. (The sponsoring institution had authorized the group as a whole to conduct the conference, rather than authorizing a director who would then choose her staff.) The confirmation of one woman's authority to direct had become bound up with all the dilemmas of peer leadership, envy, and rivalry. Similar difficulties occurred for the conference members in their attempts to evolve work leadership, and it was largely through recalling their own preconference struggles that the staff could effectively interpret these conflicts.

The group which ultimately staffed the conference consisted of the six consultants, and two administrators recruited later: one a clinical psychology doctoral student, and one a practising dance therapist who had returned to the college and studied group process with one of the consultants. A small group–large group design was adopted, with four consultants in the small group team, and a team of two (including the director) consulting with the large group.

The membership of 32 women, ranging in age from 19 to 53, contained roughly equal numbers of women working in educational or mental health settings, and preprofessional graduate students and undergraduates. Only three women were from minority groups (Hispanic and Asian-American). And while only a few members had outside ties with the consulting staff, fully one-third were dance therapists who had been recruited, from overlapping work settings, by one of the administrators.

Before discussion of the dynamic themes evident in the conference, a brief description of the experiential texture of this institution is in order. To begin with, the overall conference experience seemed to be an unusually frightening one for members, paralleling some of the fears which arose in the staff when they first began preconference work. The women seemed reluctant to engage in any form of self-disclosure within the conference boundaries. For instance, emotional expressiveness, whether in the service of work or of basic assumption activities (Bion, 1961), was absent for a significant part of the weekend; it seemed difficult for members to tolerate both experiencing feelings, and working to understand them in the context of group process. Throughout the early part of the conference, members generally clung to a sophisticated, pseudowork structure, with occasional outbursts of basic assumption activity which were later disowned. Often they expressed their dynamic concerns concretely— especially in spatial terms—rather than verbally.

Finally, it was strikingly difficult for members to join with the staff, either around work or around basic assumption themes. The work which did take place towards the end of the conference seems to have been possible both because of interpretive work by the staff, and because members succeeded in finding a means of relating to the staff on a symbolic level. Based on this symbolic resolution of underlying dynamic concerns, a working alliance was established within which individuation around work could occur.

Conference themes: leadership, envy, and aggression

The membership of this conference, like the staff, were a relatively 'liberated' sample from the female population. Most had chosen professional careers and were either in positions of authority in their outside work settings, or were working towards assuming authority roles. Judging from their career achievements, there was no demonstrable lack of leadership ability, ambition, or competence among them. It was, then, quite striking how *little* striving for leadership these women manifested within the boundaries of the conference institution.

For one thing, the groups would not allow any exercise of peer leadership, ignoring or criticizing individuals who attempted to structure the work. Even members who sought basic assumption leadership were given only temporary support. For instance, one member, a forceful older woman with significant outside authority over several conference members (and, formerly, over one administrator), managed to evoke intense feelings of dependency in her fellow small group members, who tried as best they could to please and placate her. But when she attempted to gain followers for a fight–flight movement in the large group, she was silenced by the utter unresponsiveness of other members.

Colluding with this passive–aggressive refusal to allow another woman to differentiate as any kind of leader, individuals were noticeably reluctant to seek out or assume leadership positions. Women in the staff group tended to experience conflicts about taking strong leadership actions, and members also appeared reluctant to compete openly for leadership. The director's inner experience of terror at the prospect of managing the staff's work, early in the preconference phase, probably reflects some of the feelings which kept the women from trying to differentiate themselves in their groups.

In fact, it was around the director, in the first large group session, that the membership played out its most powerful 'morality tale' regarding the consequences of differentiation and a woman's assumption of authority over other women. Seated in the innermost of three concentric circles, the director was clearly experienced as director, not as one of a pair of large group consultants. The membership entered the large group with a great deal of resentment at her for having delivered a formal address in the opening plenary, and having described at length the conference's structure of authorization. One member grumbled, to the approval of others, that the director apparently believed she had been 'authorized by God'.

When the director made her first interpretation, members briefly remarked on her 'critical', 'punitive' tone, and there then ensued a dramatic physical shift in the room, as all the members moved their chairs away to form a single, large circle. The director was then alone in the centre, and her co-consultant was left outside the perimeter. As she continued to speak, two members rushed into the centre and dragged her chair out into the large circle, where she was left for the rest of the session.

This series of responses embodied two of the attempts made by the women to deal with another woman's differentiation into a position of authority. They first tried to pull away, just as the staff had initially tried to 'neutralize' the director by emotionally distancing themselves from her in the preconference phase. Similarly, in one small group the consultant was physically extruded, while in another the consultant was always left with an empty chair on either side. When one member of that group ventured to occupy a chair next to the consultant, she soon changed seats, saying she felt the consultant's 'power' too strongly and was afraid of being overwhelmed. There was evidently a quality in the power attributed to a woman, by virtue of her authority alone, that made it necessary for other women to save themselves, and her, by separation; the price for demonstrating competence and assuming a position of authority was, in these instances, to be excluded from the group and to suffer isolation and emptiness.

But the sight of a woman so obviously differentiated (even spatially) from other women was intolerable too; she must be returned to the undifferentiated circle. So the group turned to a second means of defending against the fears and fantasies evoked by a woman in authority: they attempted to fuse her back into the homogeneous mass. This process was also in operation in several small groups in which the consultants reported that they were being treated as 'idiosyncratic members'.

The staff's preconference experience, as well as further data from the large group, indicates the nature of some of the fears and fantasies which were in operation in this area. A woman who differentiated herself on the basis of attributes valued in the prevalent group culture—in this case, through work competence, leadership abilities, and the power which was assumed to go with an authority role—became the object of other women's envy. She would then be, in fantasy, subject to their murderous attacks; in the female analogue of castration, she would be ripped apart, internally damaged, and depleted. Great terror accompanied this fantasy of the violence one woman might do to another. Paradoxically, the object of envy and aggression was seen as both fragile and omnipotently vengeful. If one attacked another woman, she might be equally likely to succumb at once, or to respond with a devastating fury of her own.

A member of the large group alluded to this set of fantasies (among others) when she expressed her unwillingness to attend the large group because of 'the emptiness in the centre'. This phrase names the terror of having succeeded in destroying another woman's 'centre', aggressively depleting her of envied internal riches. Such success is fearsome because of the talion threat implied in her emptiness, a 'black hole', a vortex which could engulf and destroy everything.

The psychotic nature of this anxiety (Klein, 1952), which was elaborated elsewhere in the conference as well, seems particularly noticeable when it is a woman who envies and a woman who is envied. One defence against the anxiety was to act as if the envied figure were a man, so that the fantasies of reciprocal female violence would not be evoked. Members in the large group made use of this process in an attempt to defend against the fantasied consequences of their 'attack' on the director. Ultimately, they came to see her as a man, 'more like a stern father than a mother', and on that basis could respect her authority and recognize her competence. She was endowed in fantasy with a penis to replace the threatening female part-object; members spoke of 'castrating' her, and commented that 'if we looked between her legs, I'm not sure what we'd find'. No longer a woman with the vulnerable and terrifying 'centre', she was kept in the inner circle after the first session, and listened to with polite interest.

The other consultant, however, was spatially excluded from each large group session by members in the outer ring who moved their chairs to close her out. For she had become the female member of the pair, and to her were attributed all of a woman's vulnerability and destructive power. She was not even given a name during the first half of the large group's life, so seemingly unspeakable were the attributes which were located in her. At one point a member responded to her interpretation by covering her ears and saying desperately, 'She's driving me crazy!' Only by shutting out such a woman did members feel they could preserve their own ego boundaries, which this female figure was seen as capable of disintegrating.

In sum, the women's difficulty in assuming or granting peer leadership, and in dealing with the authority structure present in the staff, was closely linked to fears of experiencing envy, and of becoming oneself the object of envy. In the group's fantasy, one woman's envy of another would lead to unmanageable aggression in which both individuals would be consumed. The specific threat of a woman's aggression was that she would vengefully engulf another woman, destroying individuality in the whirling chaos of her 'empty centre'.

Conference themes: neediness and contempt

If women could not accept competitive, envious, or angry feelings in themselves or others, we might at least expect them to accept 'softer' feelings such as the wish for warmth and closeness. It has traditionally been women's task to provide nurture for others; at the same time, women sterotypically need emotional supplies (love, acceptance, approval, caring) and are viewed as finding affiliation more rewarding than achievement. Moreover, if women in this conference had difficulty in attaining and exercising competence in work leadership, we might expect them to be content with forming emotional bonds as a way of deriving something positive from the weekend.

As it happened, however, for most of the conference it was difficult for women to express or even experience their wishes either to give or to receive emotional support. The few small group members who voiced neediness were treated with contempt or clinical interest, and were soon silenced. In the large group, only the excluded, denigrated consultant dared to speak of the feelings of alienation and loneliness, and the wishes to be accepted and recognized, which were apparent in the group. These comments were experienced as incoherent and chaotic; the consultant was ridiculed and considered too full of feelings to be competent. A similar process occurred often in the staff group; the few members who voiced such feelings had to struggle to overcome the group's tendency to treat them as incapable of competent work.

Sanctions against signs of vulnerability and neediness resulted in a noticeable decrease in the expression of such feelings. Members and staff alike came to believe that emotional needs were shameful, and must be fended off so that one could appear self-sufficient and invulnerable, and hence avoid the group's contempt. A woman could be soft and needy outside the conference boundaries, often with 'the man back home'; for the staff, experiences of dependency and vulnerability were often 'postponed' until after the day's work was over, or even after the weekend itself had ended. Or a woman could explode in a 'crazy', hysterical outburst which rendered her a casualty, to be cared for with solicitude that was tinged with contempt. But the possibility of using feelings in the service of work was effectively closed for the members, and at times for the staff, for much of the weekend.

Along with the rejection of neediness, there was a rejection and devaluation of those who actually offered nurture. Early in the conference, one small group member, an older woman who had been a nurse, attempted to comfort another member who voiced distress. The 'mothering' member was isolated and criticized for being insincere and condescending. Eventually her position in the group became so untenable that she left the conference early, in evident pain, communicating her decision to the only other recognizable 'mothers' in the conference institution—the administrators.

It was towards the two administrators that both members and staff expressed the greatest devaluation of the mothering role which recognized and responded to neediness. One member referred to the administrators as 'babysitters'; they were often ignored during coffee breaks, and never seen by members as 'real' staff. Interestingly, the only woman on the staff who had actually borne children was one of the administrators, and she experienced a continual struggle to be heard as a contributor to the staff's conceptual work.

During the closing plenary, when an administrator made some interpretive comments, there was a sense of universal astonishment, shared even by the administrator herself. This reflected the strength of the group myth that no woman who recognized or ministered to neediness could also do conceptual work. It appears that once a woman became locked into the devalued nurture-giving role (just as with the devalued nurture-seeking role), she could exercise other kinds of competency only after an internal and external struggle to break out of that shared fantasy.

In an important sequence of actions beginning in the third large group session, a member group violated the norms against expressing neediness or nurture, and provided members with an opportunity to confront the under-lying fantasies more directly. The process began when six members of a small group attended the large group as an avowed unit. They declared that they had found 'the answer' to all the dilemmas of the conference, by sharing feelings with each other, accepting each other, and becoming close and loving. They did not explicitly tell the large group that this closeness had developed after two of their members had admitted having sexual relationships with other women; but their tones of mysterious fulfilment conveyed the sexual impli-cations quite clearly. The large group reacted with curiosity, some envy, and a hesitant acceptance of 'the answer'.

This incident, whose further ramifications will be discussed later, points to homosexual anxiety as one of the threats preventing expressions of neediness and nurture between women. The group which embodied homosexuality in the conference defied a pervasive taboo which had prevented other members from seeking out closeness and warmth in a same-sex setting. But once homosexuality was accepted as 'the answer', an even deeper fantasy threat surfaced—that of fusion. Members of the 'loving' small group discovered that they had gained closeness at the expense of individuality, and that fusion was a particularly powerful threat when gender-related differences were not present to promote individuation.

From this perspective, much of the women's resistance to sharing feelings appears as a defence against their anxiety that such sharing would dissolve their self–other boundaries irrevocably. Further evidence regarding the power of this threat was present in the large group, where members had difficulty acknowledging that their individual feelings and fantasies might be the outcome of a group process—as though an individual could remain intact only by unwaveringly defending her separateness from others. It is hardly surprising that the women preferred to endure silent, lonely anonymity, rather than risk engaging with the ultimate engulfing mother: a group of other women.

Thus women, in entering close relationships with other women, were confronted by fears and fantasies of a symbiosis as destructive as the aggression thought to arise out of anger. The threat of merger made it difficult for the women to use positive feelings to temper whatever aggressive impulses they felt towards each other, in the way that the possibility of sexual closeness can modulate aggression in mixed-sex groups. The result was that women felt it necessary to maintain a wary distance from each other for the first two days of the conference, since feelings of either love or anger were thought to imply the individual's disintegration.

Towards individuation

It was fortunate that in this conference members had an opportunity to work explicitly with a number of the themes described above, following the appearance of homosexuality as 'the answer'. What occurred in the third large group session, sparsely attended due to absences after a meal break, was a symbolic separation of the issues of love and anger as embodied in the presence of the 'loving' women, and the absence of another subgroup who were, by consensus, the contemptuous, 'angry' women. These two subgroups represented the 'good' and 'bad' consultants, respectively. The 'good' group had six members, mirroring the six consultants, and even displayed its own 'director', a member who was described as enfolded in the centre of her group 'like a queen bee'. The other women, in effect, incorporated this 'good member of staff' into the large group, and were able to enter a new phase in their relationship with the actual consulting staff as a result of this symbolic rapprochement.

Members began by naming and examining fears about joining in any way with other women, expressed in their fantasies about the 'loving' group.

Enough resolution took place so that they felt for the first time able to join collaboratively with the consultants. This working alliance helped them in dealing with their fantasies about the 'angry' women who returned the next day. Simultaneously, a small but stable work group developed, with several members seeking and defending leadership roles. In this context, the remaining work of the conference—re-owning the wishes and attributes which had been projected into individuals, subgroups, and the conference institution as a whole—could be undertaken.

An important development in this work was the women's recognition of how they had separated power and authority from femaleness throughout the conference. In the large group, one consultant was made powerful but male, and the other was experienced as female but powerless. The administrators, who by their role were recognizably female, were relegated to near-invisibility. Small group consultants reported that when they were recognized as being in positions of authority, they were treated as male or neuter figures. The image of a powerful woman seemingly evoked too much envy, and too much terror, to be tolerated. By stripping an individual either of power or of femaleness, members protected both themselves and her.

In this and other areas, members developed enough emotional distance from their defences to begin work, and by the closing plenary they had articulated and collaboratively examined many of the key processes contained in the conference. Productive competition was allowed to surface, even in the large group where fears of aggression had been most intense. One member allowed herself to be recognized both as demonstrably competent and as obviously full of feeling, insisting on her right to contain both parts. In short, many of the defensive polarizations could be overcome, freeing members to confront their experiences and work with them.

The consulting staff were uniquely able to interpret processes such as these because of their history of preconference self-examination. Having painfully and with great difficulty voiced and examined some of their own fears and fantasies surrounding intrastaff process, the staff could use to some advantage their sense of the commonality of psychodynamic issues in women's groups.

Concluding remarks

The themes represented in this conference were partly derived from its same-sex composition, and partly reflect issues particular to women in groups. A complex integration of historical, socio-cultural, and intrapsychic perspectives is necessary if we are to understand these themes.

For instance, women's ambivalence about assuming work leadership in this setting certainly reflects the historical fact that intellectual work has usually been reserved for men, and the cultural consequence that women have not usually been socialized to compete overtly for leadership roles. On the other hand, the fact that a conference like this could be given at all reflects the broader social movement through which women have become more aware of their historical roles, and have begun explicitly to recognize various options for change. The conference staff and membership—professionals and pre-professionals—were probably a fairly typical sample of educated women struggling to come to terms with these societal changes.

But the next step in our analysis must take into account prevalent group fantasies and the imagery regarding a woman's power to destroy other women. The women perceived themselves and each other alternately as fragile little girls, and as superhuman 'giantesses of the nursery'. It was the uncanny power of these archaic images which seemed, fundamentally, to account for the women's terrified ambivalence about allowing any leadership differential to exist among themselves. A powerful female figure seems to call up primary pre-oedipal fantasies regarding the symbiotic mother whose ability to give and sustain life is matched by her power utterly to annihilate life.

This level of essentially psychotic concern for one's very existence as a separate individual, was also manifested in the women's inability to tolerate closeness with each other. We might point to the societal tendency, internalized by women as well as men, to locate neediness and nurture in woman and then experience contempt at her 'weakness'. Or we might observe that any woman who tries to make her way in the male-dominated work world will experience pressures to seem 'as competent as a man', even if that 'competence' requires that she deny an important aspect of her experience: the wish to give and to receive emotional support.

Yet these processes themselves may be seen as collective defences against the terrifying possibility that closeness between women might actually occur, bringing with it the threat of engulfment, fusion, and loss of ego integrity. This terror is overdetermined: in the first place, the other woman bears an uncomfortable resemblance to the symbiotic mother, and evokes archetypes of that earliest female–female relationship. At the same time, she bears a striking resemblance to oneself, in the absence of visible, gender-related differences. So it is not difficult to see why fusion operates as a continual threat in the fantasies of women in same-sex groups.

Finally, the absence of men in this conference allows us to speculate a bit about the customary nature of male–female interactions in mixed groups. Given the host of conflicting wishes and feelings which each individual contains, it is indeed convenient that the other sex is usually available as a repository for one's disowned parts. A clear theme in this conference was that conflicting wishes and attributes are bound to be split apart, either to remain defensively separated or to be worked through one at a time, whether or not the attributions are congruent with patterns established by society.

We might say that even where no men existed, women had to 'create' men out of their own number, both to promote differentiation, and to temper anger with love. Only then did an adult, sexually female identity, composed of both manlike and womanlike attributes, become conceivable.

References

Bion, W. (1961) *Experiences in Groups*. London: Tavistock Publications.

Freud, S. (1950) 'Group psychology and the analysis of the ego'. In *Complete Works of Sigmund Freud*, vol. 18. London: Hogarth Press.

Gibbard, G., and Hartmann, J. (1973) 'The oedipal paradigm in group development: A clinical and empirical study'. *Small Group Behavior*, **4**, 305–354.

Klein, M. (1952) 'Notes on some schizoid mechanisms'. In Klein, M., Heimann, P., Isaacs, S., and Riviere, J., *Developments in Psycho-Analysis*. London: Hogarth Press.

Miller, E. J., and Rice, A. K. (1967) *Systems of Organization: the Control of Task and Sentient Boundaries*. London: Tavistock Publications.

Rice, A. K. (1965) *Learning for Leadership: Interpersonal and Intergroup Relations*. London: Tavistock Publications.

Rioch, M. J. (1971) ' "All we like sheep . . . " (Isaiah 53 : 6); followers and Leaders'. *Psychiatry*, **34**, 258–273.

Slater, P. (1966) *Microcosm*. New York: Wiley.

Chapter **10**

A Model for Distinguishing Supportive from Insight-oriented Psychotherapy Groups

Robert H. Klein

Frequent discussions of the features characterizing group therapy appear in the literature. Some descriptions focus upon structural aspects of groups, e.g. size (Castore, 1962; Wolf and Schwartz, 1962), duration (Mintz, 1971; Stoller, 1968), setting (Jacobs and Spradlin, 1974), specific techniques and format utilized (Kaplan and Sadock, 1972; Sager and Kaplan, 1972), etc. In other instances, the leadership (Lieberman *et al.*, 1973; Turquet, 1974), the population served (Friedman, 1976; Neighbor *et al.*, 1958; Reddy and Lansky, 1974), the curative factors (Corsini and Rosenberg, 1955; Lieberman, 1976), and the theoretical persuasion of the therapist(s) (Cohn, 1970; Durkin, 1964; Whitaker and Lieberman, 1969; Yalom, 1971) have received considerable attention. At a somewhat broader level, psychotherapy groups are often differentiated in terms of whether they are 'supportive' or 'insight-oriented'. 'Supportive' generally refers to groups composed of more severely disturbed patients in which limited goals of symptomatic relief are pursued, while 'insight-oriented' is usually applied to groups for neurotic outpatients which aim at uncovering and working through unconscious determinants of patients' behaviour. Experience suggests, however, that such descriptions usually confuse rather than clarify matters by their lack of precision. These terms frequently are used as if they are mutually exclusive, and as if they identify a dichotomous classification, whereas, in our opinion, these labels refer more accurately to a continuum along which a given group may be characterized as more or less supportive or insight-oriented.

The present paper is designed to provide a model/schemata for making meaningful distinctions between groups along this continuum from supportive to insight-oriented treatment. Specifically, ten dimensions will be employed to characterize psychotherapy groups: (1) group goals; (2) participant roles; (3) level of anxiety; (4) cognitive/emotional balance; (5) locus of reinforcement; (6) content areas; (7) topographic level; (8) structural components; (9) domains of data; (10) process levels. These variables can be used to both describe the operations of the group as a whole, and to conceptualize therapist behaviour in relation to that of group members.

135

Group goals

Singer *et al.* (1975) suggest that psychotherapy groups can be thought of as temporary institutions whose manifest goal or task is to provide some psychological benefit to the group members. Ideally, the structure of the group, which concerns the utilization of time, space, and material and human resources, is designed to facilitate task accomplishment. In order to plan effectively and compose the group, establish screening procedures for applicants, articulate the participant roles, etc., the therapist needs to be aware of the task and the benefits offered prospective members, i.e. the goals of the group. These goals should serve as the primary criterion in relation to which such decisions are made.

The goals for psychotherapy groups vary widely, and unfortunately many group therapists fail to respect the importance of treatment goals. In the course of conducting supervision, one often discovers that trainees are unable to verbalize their actions, desired outcomes, and the relationship between these two variables. Furthermore, trainees who are able to identify a set of treatment goals frequently are reflecting their exclusive view; the notion that goals are to be specific, conscious, explicit, and agreed upon by both the therapist and the participating patients seems to go unheeded.

Whatever goals are established and agreed upon must be related in a meaningful way by the therapist to the size of the group, the number, duration, and frequency of meetings, the length of time available for conducting therapy, the financial costs required, and the level of therapist training, sophistication, and capacity for working towards these goals. Perhaps the single most important factor in these considerations, however, is the importance of achieving some congruence between the identified tasks and goals, and the level of ego functioning and motivation patients have available for working towards the attainment of such goals. As Ferber and Ranz (1972) suggest in their discussion of family therapy: set reachable goals and give workable tasks. For a successful outcome in a psychotherapy group, it is necessary that the group's tasks and goals fit the members' needs and resources. To the extent that the tasks and goals of the group remain ambiguous, implicit, not consciously agreed upon by the participants, not related to realistic constraints, and beyond the work capacities of group members and/or therapist(s), it is likely that the participants are colluding to avoid doing meaningful work and are instead engaged in the establishment and maintenance of basic assumption operations (Bion, 1961; Rioch, 1970, 1971).

Most psychotherapy groups espouse tasks and goals involving psychological change, e.g. altering coping capacity or response repertoire, as compared with learning tasks which more typically involve cognitive/perceptual changes. Examination of a group's goal permits classification in terms of more supportive or insight-oriented change goals. Specifically, to the extent that psychotherapy groups espouse change tasks which are broadly defined and aim towards promoting greater self-awareness coupled with extensive working through leading to structural changes in personality, they are more insight-oriented. Piloting members towards the most adaptive solution of unconscious pathogenic conflicts, removing distortions with which members came into psychotherapy, developing more satisfactory and flexible modes of defence and coping, and promoting personality reintegration and maturation, typically require significant effort and emotional investment to be successful, and frequently represent a long-term, expensive venture for both the patient and the therapist.

In contrast, those psychotherapy groups which pursue more limited, practical, symptom-oriented, circumscribed, and/or shorter-term goals operate in a fashion consistent with a more supportive approach. For example, some psychotherapy groups may be designed specifically to change or eliminate a single self-destructive or undesirable target behaviour shared by the members, e.g. alcoholism or drug abuse. Though such groups may make use of confrontational and encountering styles, the circumscribed nature of their goals plus the fact that they are oriented towards relief of symptoms, places them more towards the supportive end of the continuum. A group established for chronic psychotically disturbed persons in which the goals involve curtailment of disruptive psychotic behaviour and reduction of immobilizing levels of anxiety, plus the development of more adequate patterns of interpersonal socialization, also constitutes a more supportively oriented psychotherapy group.

Thus, insight-oriented therapy is directed towards resolution of unconscious conflicts and towards promoting more effective personality organization development, and maturity. Immediate symptom relief is secondary; the hope is that, following the resolution of unconscious conflicts, patients will be able to give up symptom formations as they are no longer necessary. In contrast, supportively oriented psychotherapy typically involves limited goals and direct relief of symptoms. The focus is maintained on alleviating current conscious conflicts, and on supporting and strengthening defensive and adaptive ego functions in order to reestablish a dynamic steady state. Little effort is devoted to altering unconscious conflicts and personality distortions.

Participant roles

Role definitions are critical aspects of any group's structure and provide an effective means for describing the nature of a given psychotherapy group. The roles of participants in a group should be derived from a mutually agreed upon contract, and should be consistent with the therapeutic goals of the group. More specifically, the question needs to be raised as to what role prescriptions will best enable the group to move effectively towards attainment of its goals. In addition, the establishment of an overt contract concerning participant behaviour is essential for assessment of the extent to which a participant is fulfilling his/her role.

Therapist role

Let us begin with an examination of the role of the therapist. Yalom (1971) notes that the basic tasks of the therapist are group maintenance and culture-building. Certain features of the maintenance task are performed by the therapist prior to the first meeting of the group. Specifically, he selects and composes the group, formulates a contract, establishes the time and place for meetings, etc. Once the group has begun, the therapist attempts to create an atmosphere in which patients can speak freely, and to recognize and resolve any factors which threaten to disrupt the integrity of the group, e.g. absences, subgroupings, scapegoating, etc. He also attempts to shape a set of norms in the group which are consistent with the therapeutic goals. His basic roles in the group, according to Yalom, are that of 'technical expert' and 'model-setting participant'. The therapist functions as a social engineer when he uses his expertise to select and compose the group, prepare the patients for treatment, establish the norms and ground rules of therapy, and define roles for the participants. As a model-setting participant, the therapist attempts to demonstrate various behaviours which will promote the development of desired group norms, encourage patients to experiment with new kinds of behaviour, promote nonjudgemental acceptance and appreciation of others, reinforce interpersonal honesty, etc.

Another way of conceptualizing the role of the leader is offered by Rice (1969) and elaborated by Singer *et al.* (1975). They maintain that the major function of leadership in a small group event is the management of its boundaries—both internal and external. Management of the external boundaries involves relating the psychotherapy group to the outside world (deciding what population will be recruited, who will be permitted entry into the group, and what tasks will be worked on for what purposes). These authors suggest that the management of the internal boundaries involves 'monitoring the relationship between the task of the group and its structures . . . to insure that form is appropriate to function, monitoring the relationship between the task of the enterprise and the personal and emotional needs of the individuals and subgroups within it' (Singer *et al.*, 1975, p. 13).

Since the role of the therapist in the group is to mediate between the group on the one hand and the consciously agreed upon task and goals on the other, he must be alert to the nature of the therapeutic tasks and goals. Indeed, he must be instrumental in defining and continuously redefining the tasks and goals of the group (Turquet, 1974).

As a technical expert who mediates between the group and the primary task, the therapist can utilize a variety of behaviours and techniques. The therapist's interventions may be in the form of reflective and empathic statements, clarifications, support, suggestions, questions, interpretations, etc. Similarly, he may establish a variety of formats for the group, some of which involve the use of special techniques such as role playing, psychodrama, marathons, etc. Whatever the therapist's role, the specific techniques and/or formats he selects for use in the group, and the type of interventions he employs, it is essential that these features remain consistent with the primary task of the group.

In insight-oriented psychotherapy groups, the therapist tries to maintain a relatively consistent, neutral, participant-observer role. DeWald (1964) notes that the therapist role, which primarily involves listening in a therapeutic sense, is implemented by an active process which occurs silently within him. Thus, he tries to become aware of the full range of patients' behaviours, and of his own associations and emotional responses to the material presented. By permitting himself to regress in the service of the ego, he is able to search for connections, associations, and meanings, and to establish empathic understanding through a partial and reversible identification with patients. Following this process he returns to the objective position and secondary process thought of a therapist interacting with a patient in which capacity he evaluates and organizes the understanding so achieved in the light of his own theoretical and clinical knowledge (Greenson, 1967).

In supportively oriented groups, the therapist is likely to use himself as an instrument for introducing active interventions aimed at promoting the specific supportive goals of treatment. The therapist usually surveys the various defences available to the patients and determines which of these can be most effectively introduced or strengthened, while encouraging the maintenance of those defences already in use unless they are resulting in symptoms or excessive anxiety. Through model-setting, a supportive group leader attempts to promote and encourage identification with him as therapist by establishing rapport and maintaining a positive relationship and active participation in patients' efforts to deal with their concerns. By suggesting new mechanisms for patients to use, exploring different ways of looking at or resolving problems, and revealing some healthier aspects of his own personality to patients, the therapist encourages patients to accept him as a model and to internalize his ways of working with psychological issues. The hope is that patients' ego and super-ego functioning will be modified and strengthened as a result of this identification process.

Patient role

In a more insight-oriented group, patients are encouraged to engage in spontaneous interactive communication, to share candid thoughts, feelings, and associations, to bring into the group their fantasies and dreams, to aim towards self-disclosure, and to pursue the discovery of latent meaning in their presenting symptoms and modes of relating to one another and to the therapist. Another feature of the patient role in an insight-oriented approach has to do with self-observation. Specifically, the therapist encourages patients to develop a capacity for self-observation which involves fostering a split in ego functioning between emotional reaction and intellectual reflection. That is, in addition to experiencing, patients are encouraged to stand off, examine, and reflect upon what they have just felt.

The patient role in a more supportively oriented group, by contrast, is defined to assist patients in maintaining a more narrowly focused, goal-directed posture intended to reinforce and encourage the development of adaptive, socially acceptable modes of coping and defence. Such a role definition, in general, aims at promoting greater awareness of reality factors rather than of internal emotional factors. Therefore, patients are encouraged to focus upon observable, concrete, pragmatic, practical aspects of their lives, to diminish concern and preoccupation with wishes, fantasies, dreams, fears, and transference distortions, and to try to understand the realistic consequences of what they say and do in relation to others. Secondary process, i.e. rational thinking, is emphasized, and patients are urged to remain logical and to edit their remarks.

Level of anxiety

An important dimension of any group has to do with the level of anxiety that typically characterizes the group's operations. The level of anxiety is closely linked with the nature of the population being served, the goals of the group, and the quality of the interaction. The therapist's behaviour, however, is particularly crucial in this connection and therefore is the element upon which I wish to focus in order to sharpen the discriminations along the continuum between supportive and insight-oriented psychotherapy groups.

In every psychotherapy group the therapist must monitor the level of anxiety to ensure that it does not interfere with effective work. By maintaining a silent, enigmatic, depriving posture and limiting his interventions to interpretative comments, the therapist tends to increase the level of anxiety within the group; conversely, to the extent that the therapist adopts an empathic, accepting, nurturant posture he reduces the level of anxiety within the group. Therefore, the therapist will ideally shape his behaviour and techniques in accord with an estimate of the level of anxiety that will be most beneficial in propelling the group towards the accomplishment of the agreed-upon task. Too high a level of anxiety will serve to incapacitate patients and to inhibit and disrupt task accomplishment, while too low a level of anxiety may result in patients losing interest in the task, feeling the group is moving too slowly, experiencing a sense of boredom and complacency, and perhaps terminating their group membership.

Groups which operate more towards the supportive end of the continuum are those in which the therapist's efforts appear to be directed towards allaying anxiety and maintaining it at a low level. This usually reflects an assessment on the part of the therapist, that the patients cannot effectively cope with the task in the presence of heightened anxiety. Such groups are often composed of patients who, in the face of mounting anxiety, resort to more genetically primitive, less adaptive means of defence and coping. Temporary and, in some instances, sustained episodes of psychotic functioning are likely to result in groups with more severely disturbed patients when their levels of anxiety are not adequately controlled. Unfortunately, the patients themselves often are unable to maintain such controls on their own behalf, and therefore tend to rely upon the therapist's available ego functioning to provide the needed assistance. When the therapist fails to recognize the presence of mounting incapacitating anxiety and consequently does not attempt to reduce the tension and stabilize patient functioning at a more adaptive level, patients often feel abandoned and panicky. Their increasingly extreme and/or bizarre and regressive behaviour seems, at some level, designed to gain the therapist's attention and to solicit the use of his ego control mechanisms.

In a more insight-oriented group, composed of healthier patients, the therapist's efforts are more likely to be directed towards permitting the group to maintain a higher level of anxiety without his feeling the need to relieve this increased pressure on the participants and/or himself. Indeed, the therapist may reason that in order to accomplish major structural changes in personality it is necessary that patients undergo some form of therapeutic regression to permit a lengthy and detailed working through process for healthier reintegration of previously warded off aspects of the self. The patients in such a group must have sufficient difficulties to warrant exposure to such a process, but yet have sufficient ego resources to recover from such a therapeutically encouraged regression.

Cognitive/emotional balance

Closely related to the level of anxiety is the cognitive/emotional balance maintained within the group. A group in which the therapist endeavours to 'keep the lid on' emotional expressions is likely to be functioning towards the supportive end of the continuum. Such groups often appear as if they are seeking to suppress or avoid more intense emotional expression. The therapist frequently provides detailed cognitive structure for the group in order to assist members to adaptively integrate their experiences. Basic to the therapist's behaviour is an assumption that, if he does not assist patients in controlling their feelings and impulses by monitoring the level of effective expression and by actively introducing cognitive synthesizing operations into the group, the members will derive limited benefit from the process. Therapists working with such groups often reason that group members need a 'tightening up' of controls, potentials for regression, and integrative capacities as opposed to the 'loosening up' of repressive and constricting postures more typically prescribed for neurotically disturbed persons.

Patients in more insight-oriented groups are perceived as able to tolerate, and to be in need of, more impassioned emotional expression. They engender in the therapist less pull to provide a cognitive framework for the members since depth and intensity of affective expression is encouraged without extensive modulation and control by the therapist. In most instances, the membership of such groups is better able to engage in such expression, examine its effects, and integrate this learning independently.

Locus of reinforcement

Various forms of reinforcement, e.g. praise, encouragement, support, 'strokes', etc., exist within a group. On an interpersonal level, a patient can obtain reinforcement from another patient, the therapist, the entire group, or any combination of these. In addition, reinforcement may be self-initiated and achieved on an intrapersonal level as a result of a patient's own sense of growth and accomplishment. To the extent that reinforcement is largely provided from external sources, and in particular from the therapist, the group is more likely to be operating on the supportive end of the continuum. Conversely, those groups in which patients are expected to provide their own reinforcement are more likely to be operating on a more insight-oriented level. Reinforcement provided by the therapist in supportively oriented groups is designed to encourage patients to attempt new methods of adaptation. The gratifications achieved via these new modes of coping will themselves hopefully provide further reinforcement for patients to continue to use and develop them. Thus, in a supportively oriented approach, there is reliance upon external authority for motivation, control, and judgement (DeWald, 1964). In contrast, in an insight-oriented approach the therapist does not provide reinforcement or reward specific types of behaviour or change. Rather, patients are encouraged to make their own way.

Content areas

The content areas explored within psychotherapy groups obviously vary widely; hopefully, however, there is some meaningful relationship between the goals of the psychotherapy and the content discussed within the group. Indeed, careful articulation of the goals for psychotherapy may well provide a means for determining what content is relevant and within the purview of the agreed-upon tasks of the group, and what content is irrelevant and outside the task boundaries. (In this regard we are referring primarily to manifest as opposed to latent content.)

Though it is difficult to examine the dimension of content areas without simultaneously considering the depth and intensity with which these areas are experienced and processed, some meaningful distinctions can be drawn between those groups which are more supportively oriented as compared with those which are more insight-oriented. In the former, content areas tend to be circumscribed, practical, concrete, and closely related to current life problems. In insight-oriented groups, the content discussed usually varies over a wider range consistent with the broader goals of such groups. Apart from the level at which content is examined, the specific areas which arise for consideration are more likely to be linked with neurotic distortions and transference preoccupations, e.g. issues which exist beyond their immediate representation in a specific discrete event.

Topographic level

All groups operate on a variety of topographic levels. A group may be simultaneously dealing with and processing conscious, preconscious, and unconscious levels of functioning. Any event which occurs within the life of the group can be examined from each of these perspectives, none of which is mutually exclusive. Though the precise level of psychological functioning with which the group is concerned may vary from moment to moment, it is possible to identify the level of psychological functioning with which the group is primarily concerned when one examines broader segments of the group's life, e.g. several group sessions.

Of course within any group, countless events and transactions occur within and between members and leader. It is unusual for a group to have the luxury and ability to examine thoroughly the meaning of their experiences at each of these topographic levels of functioning. Therefore, most groups implicitly select one or more of these levels as a primary focus of attention. Ideally, one can meaningfully relate the goals of the group, the task and role specifications, and the desired level of anxiety to the topographic level selected for examination. Thus, in a group which has as one of its goals the working through of unresolved transference distortions, and where the therapist role is defined as primarily involving interpretation around such issues with the patient's task centring around exploration of his inner experience, then such groups should be dealing with preconscious and unconscious levels of functioning in addition to more immediately accessible conscious phenomena. Conversely, in a group which has as its goals symptomatic relief and/or the modification of disruptive socially undesirable behaviour, and where the therapist role emphasizes his model-setting behaviour, then one would expect such a group to be much less concerned with examination of unconscious levels of psychological functioning in relation to which the therapist seeks to promote group concern.

In general, the more concerned the group is with conscious phenomena in an exclusive fashion, the more likely it is to be functioning towards the supportive end of the continuum. Rather than attempting to elicit unconscious material, the therapist discourages relaxation of defences and primary process explorations in favour of maintaining a closer allegiance to conscious and preconscious issues. More typically, the therapist seeks to support and maintain repression, not to mobilize unconscious conflict or to promote further regression. To bring into consciousness, through the process of regression, unconscious material that more severely disturbed patients are unable to deal with effectively, is to subject them to unnecessarily unpleasant and up-setting experiences. Similarly, as the patients' capacities to recover from regression are limited and ineffective, then to encourage them to regress is to severely tax already burdened egos.

To the extent that the group is willing and able to explore meaningfully preconscious and unconscious levels of functioning in addition to conscious material, it is operating more towards the insight-oriented end of the continuum. Efforts are made to promote therapeutic regression so as to recover, reintegrate, and work through previously repressed, dissociated unconscious material.

Structural components

Consideration of which structural components of personality receive the most attention in a given group yields additional important, though often complex, information about the group's behaviour.

Any interaction between members in a group can be examined in terms of drive, defence, and concordance with conscience and ego ideal. However, as a general strategy, more supportively oriented groups devote most of their efforts to developing and strengthening adaptive ego functioning. Those strategies of coping and defence which are more genetically primitive in nature and which involve more severe distortion of reality are not supported but are identified, discouraged, and, if possible, replaced. Logical reasoning, realistic perceptions, less primitive and socially disruptive modes of defence tend to be reinforced. Other supportive groups emphasize the building of delay capacity and inhibitory controls, establishing more socially acceptable modes of drive expression, and developing more adequate social judgement so as to enable participants to understand better the consequences of their behaviour. Thus, more supportively oriented groups tend to focus attention upon ego and super-ego functioning. Relatively less attention is devoted to uncovering and exploring libidinal or aggressive wishes and fears, though some gratification may be provided for derivatives of unconscious drives.

In contrast, insight-oriented groups devote more attention to drive-dominated aspects of functioning in relation to which emphasis is placed on exploration and integration rather than inhibition and control. Insight-oriented groups composed of individuals with unresolved neurotic problems typically tend to adopt more 'restrictive' rather than 'enabling' solutions (Whitaker and Lieberman, 1969). That is, they are more concerned with protecting their reactive fears than they are in satisfying underlying disturbing motives. Therapists, therefore, tend to become involved in working with such groups in an examination of the nature, origin, and intensity of the defended against drive-dominated component of the conflict. Ideally, of course, the membership of a more insight-oriented group is sufficiently equipped in terms of ego functioning to tolerate and benefit from such efforts which are conducted in a state of relative deprivation of gratification of drive derivatives.

Domains of data

Data from several different domains can be examined within a group. These domains of data include: (1) the 'here and now', (2) the current life situation, (3) the 'there and then', and (4) the transference.

1. The 'here and now'

A strong case has been made by various writers (e.g. Berne, 1966; Bion, 1961; Yalom, 1971) that the therapist ought to focus his attention upon the here and now, i.e. what is happening at the moment in the group. Yalom (1971) maintains that focusing attention on this domain of data enables the therapist to promote interaction and a sense of cohesiveness which derives from the group's engaging in a common, lively task, open to all for examination. When members, in addition, turn their attention upon themselves they create further opportunities for interpersonal learning, a critical curative factor in group psychotherapy. Exclusive examination of here and now data, however, may result in a lack of integration between these and other important experiences in patients' lives.

2. The current life

Patients nearly always bring data into the group from their current life situations, often related to unsatisfying experiences in dealing with people or events. They experience the derivatives of unconscious underlying conflicts in immediate, concrete, but disguised ways in their daily lives and these manifestations of difficulty bring them into psychotherapy. Most patients, particularly in the beginning of treatment, are quite eager to talk about their current life problems, often from a practical, concrete point of view. However, when such matters are discussed, the group must rely upon data furnished by the patient in his or her account of some outside event, i.e. one which is not directly observable by the other members. Selective reporting renders such data especially prone to individual filtering and distortion. These features are not as readily detected as when examining the shared experiences and observations of other group members which are available when processing here and now data.

3. The 'there and then'

The there and then domain of data refers to past events, relationships, and experiences which are often reviewed by group members. Careful examination of relevant past life experiences is, of course, a crucial element in the exploration of unconscious determinants of behaviour. Mutual exploration of historical data may also serve to disclose similarities in life experiences between patients and consequently may result in an increased sense of cohesion from a shared task. However, such historical reviews may constitute a form of resistance when the data remain disconnected from their representation in patients' current life situations and their interactions within the group.

4. The transference

Closely intertwined with the other three domains of data are those data which stem from transference distortions and preoccupations. These are realistically inappropriate, unconsciously determined modes of perceiving and relating to the therapist and other group members (parataxic distortions) which derive from significant past relationships. Some psychotherapy approaches, principally psychoanalysis, place primary emphasis upon the analysis of resistance and transference (e.g. Wolf and Schwartz, 1962) while other approaches regard this as a less important aspect of treatment (e.g. Berne, 1966).

In general, more supportively oriented groups tend to focus on the problems patients experience in their current lives outside of the group and with the representations of these difficulties as they are manifest in the here and now process of the group. Relatively less emphasis is placed on exploration of past significant events and relationships, and even less attention is devoted to eliciting, exploring, and interpreting unresolved transference phenomena.

In contrast, more insight-oriented groups deal with data derived from each of these domains, and are likely to pursue efforts to integrate such data. Particular attention may be paid to transference material in that the development of the transference provides a vehicle through which previously unconscious conflict is mobilized and brought into a patient's consciousness. Once there, it can be examined, interpreted, and worked through with the aid of other patients and the therapist.

Process levels

The processes occurring within a group can be examined in terms of (1) intrapersonal processes, (2) interpersonal processes, and (3) group processes. Each process level is a system different from but related to the others. Singer *et al.* (1975) point out that since behaviour is multidetermined, any event that occurs within a group can be understood as the product of processes occurring concomitantly on all of these levels.

Three models of psychotherapy groups can be considered which are based upon the manner in which these individual and group processes are integrated (Astrachan, 1970). These models are (1) member to therapist, (2) member to member, and (3) group to therapist. In the context of a psychotherapy group engaged in the task of changing behaviour, this notion of levels refers to the processes utilized as the vehicle for intervention to produce change.

The *member to therapist* model stresses the central role of the leader as a transference figure and appears primarily to represent the application of a classical psychoanalytical approach to the group situation. This model proceeds with the analysis of the individual within the context of the group. The analysis occurs primarily through examination of an individual patient's transference reactions to the therapist. To a lesser extent, other group members serve as multiple transference figures. Individual members strive to relate separately to the therapist, while the therapist endeavours to establish a climate within which individual members can learn about their responses to authority figures.

In contrast, the *member to member* model appears to derive from social psychological research and intervention strategies (Argyris, 1964, 1967, 1968; Bennis and Schein, 1964; Lewin and Lippit, 1938). This model stresses the importance of examining ongoing interactions between members of the group. The group leader assumes a position which, over time, approaches that of group member. The leader uses his authority to establish group norms of trust, openness, and risk-taking, rather than the encouragement of fantasy, regression, identification with, and working through of feelings about persons in authority. The establishment of a suitable climate and the reliance upon intermember feedback permits members to lower defences, build trust, provide nonjudgemental feedback on another's behaviour, and try out new behaviours as they acquire information from others regarding their manner of functioning within the group.

In the *group to therapist* model, the relationship of the total group to the therapist in the here and now is subject to examination (Bion, 1961; Foulkes and Anthony, 1964; Ezriel, 1952; Sutherland, 1952). Bion described the group setting as one which was conducive to the development of certain underlying unconscious group themes which he labelled the basic assumptions. These 'as if' states focus upon the manner in which the group is relating to the leader, specifically in terms of what they are seeking to elicit from him. Thus, the collective wishes and fears in the form of expectations of the leadership are examined.

Whitaker and Lieberman (1969) have also proposed a group to therapist model in which they postulate the notion of a 'group focal conflict'. Such a conflict, which involves the total group, is marked by efforts to resolve the tension engendered by an underlying disturbing motive (wish) and the reactive fears it arouses. The role of the leader involves the identification of such group focal conflicts, and members responses and contributions to them, as well as assisting the group to develop enabling as opposed to restrictive solutions.

The different levels of processes occurring within a group serve as the vehicle by which change is accomplished, and can themselves be the object of examination. Thus, the therapist can encourage group members to focus upon the process at an intrapersonal, interpersonal, or group level. Examination of the group process is typically initiated by the therapist early in the life of a group, though patients also often adopt this mode of working as the group progresses. When the group does examine the process, its attention is turned upon itself, which often leads to heightened awareness of the here and now, and a deepened appreciation of the diversity and complexity of members' experiences.

Furthermore, some predictable consequences tend to occur as the result of which particular level of the process the therapist encourages the group to examine. For example, to promote identification of unresolved transference issues, a therapist might choose to intervene in the ongoing process of the group on an intrapersonal level and to encourage group members to examine what happens when he addresses his remarks to a particular member. The examination of the process on an interpersonal level tends to reduce preoccupation with the leader, to diminish regressive transference reactions, and to encourage more interdependent behaviour among group members. On the other hand, inviting the group to examine group level processes frequently results in intense preoccupation with the leader, heightened levels of anxiety, feelings of deprivation among individual members, and potentially increased awareness of the roles members play in the group.

Regardless of the nature of the particular psychotherapy group, the therapist should encourage examination of the process of the group only when such examination is relevant to the agreed-upon task and goals of the group, and when it seems timely to do so. Strachey's (1934) concept of the mutative interpretation and the notion of the corrective emotional experience (Alexander and French, 1946) are critical in this regard. Specifically, the examination of the process within the group should be undertaken at a time when the data derived from such an examination can be effectively integrated with and promote a clearer understanding of an important emotionally engaging event in the life of the group. It is also important to note that as a therapist one can remain aware of the processes occurring within the group but choose not to examine them.

In general, more insight-oriented groups tend to make use of the process for purposes of examination; exploration of ongoing processes in the group often seem relevant and timely. In order to promote a deepened understanding among members of the determinants of their behaviour within the group, many insight-oriented groups aim towards integrating data derived from intrapersonal, interpersonal, and group levels. More supportively oriented groups are, of course, also marked by processes occurring at each of these levels. As is the case with insight-oriented groups, they too seek to make sophisticated use of these levels of the process in order, for example, to develop a more accepting, safer, more cohesive group atmosphere. However, owing to the nature of the limited and specific goals in a more supportively oriented group, and the limited capacities of patients for working towards increased awareness and appreciation of the complexity of their experiences, relatively less energy is devoted to examining the process. Such examination in many supportively oriented groups would remain inconsistent with the agreed-upon tasks and goals and hence would be less relevant.

Summary

In summary, then, a useful description of a supportively oriented group implies conformation to a majority of the following criteria: (1) therapeutic goals are circumscribed in scope, largely focused upon symptomatic relief, and do not involve working through neurotic difficulties in the hope of achieving structural changes in personality; (2) the therapist adopts an accepting, supportive, noninterpretative posture in which advice may be offered along with the identification of behavioural alternatives, which encourage focused, realistic, goal-directed patient posture designed to foster more adaptive, socially acceptable strategies of coping and defence; (3) the therapist carefully monitors the level of anxiety among group members and attempts to prevent it from going beyond a minimal level; (4) he simultaneously ensures that emotional and impulse expression are accomplished in a controlled fashion, and that cognitive/emotional balance is maintained with appropriate synthesis and integration of experience; (5) reinforcement, praise, encouragement, and support are provided largely from external sources, particularly the therapist; (6) relevant content areas tend to more narrowly focused around symptomatic manifestations and specific, concrete, practical current life problems; (7) the therapist discourages relaxation of defences and primary process explorations in favour of maintaining a closer allegiance to conscious and preconscious phenomena; virtually no effort is devoted to eliciting and examining unconscious material; (8) the group's work is largely confined to examination of ego and super-ego structural personality components; drive-dominated determinants of behaviour receive relatively little attention; (9) the group is primarily concerned with examining the immediate here-and-now aspects of experience and patients' current life situations, with little effort devoted by the therapist to promoting regression for the purpose of eliciting and interpreting unresolved transference issues; similarly, there and then, that is, the relevant significant past relationships and events, does not gain extensive and/or intensive examination; (10) relatively little attention is focused upon examining the group process as an object of study, though sophisticated use is made of various levels of process through which social influence is exerted.

In contrast, a group can be described as more insight-oriented when: (1) the mutual consciously agreed-upon goals of the therapy are broadly based in scope and primarily involve the working through of neurotic difficulties with the hope of achieving structural changes in personality; (2) the role of the therapist is implemented primarily by his observing, clarifying, and interpreting resistance and transference; patients are encouraged to adopt an explorative, introspective posture in which they engage in free interactive communication, attempt to be spontaneous and candid in their thoughts, feelings and associations, bring into the group their fantasies and dreams, and pursue the discovery of latent meaning not only in their symptoms but also in their modes of relating to one another and to the therapist; (3) to the extent that the therapy is designed to achieve a corrective emotional experience, the level of anxiety among patients is permitted to go beyond a minimal level to encourage the development of a therapeutic regression in the service of the ego; (4) group norms permit intensive and extensive emotional and impulse expression; synthesis and integration of experience is achieved largely through patients' own efforts rather than as a result of the therapist's initiative; (5) similarly, reinforcement is self-generated for patients as a result of their own sense of growth and accomplishment; (6) relevant content areas are broadly defined and likely to be linked with explorations of neurotic distortions and transference preoccupations; (7) the therapist attempts to promote a therapeutically induced regression to enable the uncovering, exploring, and working through of repressed unconscious phenomena as well as conscious and preconscious material; (8) the group's work includes examination of ego and super-ego structural personality components plus the drive-dominated (id) aspects of behaviour; (9) the group is concerned with examination, processing, and integration of data from all four domains: the current life situation, the here and now, the significant past genetic material and the transference; it differs from a supportively oriented group in that considerable attention is devoted to the recovery and reintegration of unresolved transference issues and relevant genetic history; (10) the group process is not only regarded as a means through which social influence can be exerted, but also is itself an object of study in that the therapist encourages the group to turn its attention upon itself in order to achieve heightened awareness of the here-and-how experiences and deepened appreciation of the diversity and complexity of members' experiences.

References

Alexander, F., and French, T. (1946) *Psychoanalytic Therapy: Principles and Applications.* New York: Ronald Press.

Argyris, C. (1964) *Integrating the Individual and the Organization.* New York: Wiley.

Argyris, C. (1967) 'On the future of laboratory education'. *Journal of Applied Behavioral Science*, **3**, 153–183.

Argyris, C. (1968) 'Conditions for competence acquisition and therapy'. *Journal of Applied Behavioral Science*, **4**, 147–177.

Astrachan, B. M. (1970) 'Towards a social systems model of therapeutic groups'. *Social Psychiatry*, **5**, 110–119.

Bennis, W. G., and Schein, E. H. (1964) *Interpersonal Dynamics.* Homewood, Ill.: Richard B. Erwin.

Berne, E. (1966) *Principles of Group Treatment.* New York: Oxford University Press.

Bion, W. R. (1961) *Experiences in Groups.* London: Tavistock Publications.

Castore, G. F. (1962) 'Number of verbal interrelationships as a determinant of group size'. *Journal of Abnormal and Social Psychology*, **64**, 456–457.

Cohn, R. C. (1970) 'Therapy in groups: psychoanalytic, experiential, and gestalt'. In J. Fagen, and I. L. Shepherd (eds) *Gestalt Therapy Now.* Palo Alto, Calif.: Science and Behavior Books.

Corsini, R., and Rosenberg, B. (1955) 'Mechanisms of group psychotherapy: processes and dynamics'. *Journal of Abnormal and Social Psychology*, **51**, 406–411.

DeWald, P. A. (1964) *Psychotherapy: A Dynamic Approach.* New York: Basic Books.

Durkin, H. E. (1964) *The Group in Depth.* New York: International Universities Press.

Ezriel, H. (1952) 'Notes on psychoanalytic group therapy: II. Interpretation and research'. *Psychiatry*, **15**, 119–126.

Ferber, A., and Ranz, J. (1972) 'How to succeed in family therapy: Set reachable goals—give workable tasks'. In A. Ferber (ed.) *The Book of Family Therapy*, New York: Science House.

Foulkes, S. H., and Anthony, E. J. (1964) *Group Psychotherapy.* New York: Penguin Books.

Friedman, W. H. (1976) 'Referring patients for group psychotherapy: Some guidelines'. *Hospital and Community Psychiatry*, **27**, 121–123.

Geller, J. J. (1951) 'Concerning the size of therapy groups'. *International Journal of Group Psychotherapy*, **1**, 1–2.

Greenson, R. R. (1967) *The Technique and Practice of Psychoanalysis.* New York: International Universities Press.

Jacobs, A., and Spradlin, W. (eds) (1974) *The Group as Agent of Change*. New York: Behavioral Publications.

Kaplan, H. I., and Sadock, B. J. (eds) (1972) *New Models for Group Therapy*. New York: Jason Aaronson, Inc.

Lewin, D., and Lippit, R. (1938) 'An experimental approach to the study of autocracy and democracy: A preliminary note'. *Sociometry*, **1**, 292–300.

Lieberman, M. A. (1976) 'Change induction in small groups'. In M. R. Rosenzweig and L. W. Porter (eds) *Annual Review of Psychology*. Palo Alto, California: Annual Reviews.

Lieberman, M. A., Yalom, I. D., and Miles, M. B. (1973) *Encounter Groups: First Facts*. New York: Basic Books.

Mintz, E. (1971) *Marathon Groups: Reality and Symbol*. New York: Appelton-Century-Crofts.

Neighbor, J. E., Beach, M., Brown, D. T., Kevin, D., and Visher, J. S. (1958) 'An approach to the selection of patients for group psychotherapy'. *Mental Hygiene*, **42**, 243–254.

Reddy, W. B., and Lansky, L. M. (1974) 'The group psychotherapy literature'. *International Journal of Group Psychotherapy*, **24**, 477–517.

Rice, A. K. (1969) 'Individual, group, and intergroup processes'. *Human Relations*, **22**, 565–584.

Rioch, M. J. (1970) 'The work of Wilfred Bion on groups'. *Psychiatry*, **33**, 56–66.

Rioch, M. J. (1971) ' "All we like sheep ..." (Isaiah 53 : 6); followers and leaders'. *Psychiatry*, **34**, 258–273.

Sager, C. J., and Kaplan, H. S. (1972) *Progress in Group and Family Therapy*. New York: Brunner Mazel.

Singer, D. L., Astrachan, B. M., Gould, L. J., and Klein, E. B. (1975) 'Boundary management in psychological work with groups'. *Journal of Applied Behavioral Science*, **11**, 137–176.

Stoller, F. (1968) 'Accelerated interaction: A time-limited approach based on the brief intensive group'. *International Journal of Group Psychotherapy*, **18**, 220–235.

Strachey, J. (1934) 'The nature of the therapeutic action of psychoanalysis'. *International Journal of Psychoanalysis*, **15**, 127–159.

Sutherland, J. D. (1952) 'Notes on psychoanalytic group psychotherapy: I. Therapy and training'. *Psychiatry*, **15**, 111–117.

Turquet, P. M. (1974) 'Leadership, the individual and the group'. In C. S. Gibbard, J. J. Hartman, and R. D. Mann (eds) *Analysis of Groups*. San Francisco: Jossey-Bass, 337–371.

Whitaker, D. S., and Lieberman, M. A. (1969) *Psychotherapy Through the Group Process*. New York: Atherton Press.

Wolf, A., and Schwartz, E. K. (1962) *Psychoanalysis in Groups*. New York: Grune & Stratton.

Wolfe, M., and Projansky, H. M. (1974) 'The physical setting as a factor in group function and process'. In A. Jacobs, and W. Spradlin (eds), *The Group as Agent in Change*. New York: Behavioral Publications.

Yalom, I. D. (1971) *The Theory and Practice of Group Psychotherapy*. New York: Basic Books.

Chapter 11

The Adolescent, the Family, and the Group: Boundary Considerations

Roger L. Shapiro and John Zinner

I

In this paper we want to discuss the boundary concepts which have given orientation to our work in a research treatment programme for disturbed adolescents and their families. Boundaries are demarcations which are crucial to the definition of any system, in that they separate it from its environment and from other systems in its environment (Miller and Rice, 1963; Rice, 1965, 1969). As such, boundary concepts are central in explicating a psychology of the individual personality system, of the family system, or of the group. Boundaries are also constructs which speak of the relationships between parts of a system and thus provide an essential framework for conceptualization of differential aspects of psychological processes within the individual or family or group (Landis, 1970).

We assume that there is an important correspondence in the structure of the personality system and its subsystems, and the structure of external reality—especially the social system and its subsystems—which impinges on that personality (Edelson, 1970). The same concept, then, would be expected to have an important homology in each system. The correspondence between the boundary concepts of individual psychology and the nature of boundaries in the family system and the group is the focus of our study. The aim of this study is to define the relation of boundary characteristics of the family system, in particular, characteristics of the boundary between the family and the individual adolescent, to the nature of self boundaries which have developed within the adolescent himself (Shapiro and Zinner, 1976). In addition, we consider how characteristics of self boundaries in the adolescent relate to the role boundaries he establishes in new interpersonal and group situations. Where there is pathology in the adolescent and in the family, we design treatment situations so that the manifestations of pathology in boundary problems, or the origins of pathology in boundary problems, may be explored (Shapiro, 1966, 1967, 1968, 1969).

The major boundary concept in psychoanalytic psychology is the ego. Freud defined it as the coherent organization of mental processes which relate the individual to his drives and to the external world (Freud, 1923). Certain boundary characteristics of ego functions are conceptualized as self boundaries, a structural concept which refers to boundary properties of the self representation, which differentiate the phenomenal self from other aspects of the personality and from the world of reality external to the person as subjectively experienced (Hartmann, 1950; Jacobson, 1964; Landis, 1970). Throughout development, biological maturation and experience bring changes in the functioning of the ego and its discriminations of internal and external reality; and related changes in the boundaries which differentiate the self. Our research concerns aspects of experience which effect these differentiations of self and determine characteristics of self boundaries in adolescence.

During adolescence there is important change in the individual's relationship to his family, to his peer group, and to other groups in society (Shapiro, 1963). This change follows maturation in the ego and the id during puberty which results in new cognitive and affective capacities (Freud 1936, 1958; Inhelder and Piaget, 1958). These capacities may or may not be free to develop, depending in part upon the nature of internalizations of family experience which have occurred through infancy and childhood (Schafer, 1968). Adolescent development brings about a reorganization of childhood internalizations in relation to ego-id maturation and new experience.

New capacities for abstract thought in the adolescent are clearly demonstrated in the work of Inhelder and Piaget, who describe a consistent change in the individual's ability to conceptualize and to generalize between ages 11 to 15 (Inhelder and Piaget, 1958). There is progression from concrete operations in the thinking of the child to a new capacity for abstract thought in the adolescent. The capacity for hypothesis formation develops with the utilization of hypotheticodeductive reasoning and experimental proof. We consider this cognitive growth in early adolescence to be evidence of autonomous ego development (Shapiro, 1963). It is the cognitive basis of the abstract differentiation of the self which occurs in the adolescent, resulting in a new definition of boundaries of the self.

Jacobson has conceptualized adolescent development in terms of remodelling of psychic structure and increase in the secondary autonomy of the ego (Jacobson, 1964). This implies increased strength and definition of the boundary between conflict-free ego functioning and ego functioning which continues to be determined by the internalizations of experiences of anxiety and conflict in childhood. Increased autonomy of the ego is also evidenced in increased strength and definition of the boundary between the individual adolescent and his external objects. Reorganization of roles and modifications of libidinal investment within the family are seen. The adolescent is also redefining himself in his peer relations and in the group life of social institutions outside of the family. His increasing freedom to act in new roles in society is a further aspect of the increased strength and definition of his self boundaries.

Erikson has conceptualized alteration in the self and new definition of its boundaries during adolescence as the establishment of ego identity (Erikson, 1956, 1958, 1962). In Erikson's formulations, change in the ego of the adolescent and in the definition and resilience of self boundaries is a precondition for extensive change in the adolescent's experience with his family, with his peers, and with other groups in society. Familial and societal response to adolescent muturation facilitates or interferes with the development of ego identity with stabilization of new self boundaries. Where either the internalizations of childhood experience or lack of nutriment in current adolescent experience interfere with ego reorganization and increasing autonomy in the adolescent, there is a failure in the coherent differentiation of the self, with chaotic boundaries and a clinical picture of identity confusion. Disturbances of adolescence are thus a consequence both of the continuing power of internalizations of disturbed family relationships of childhood causing ego impairment in the adolescent, and of failure of the current family and group relations of the adolescent to facilitate progressive differentiation and integration of the self.

II

These considerations regarding disturbance in the individual adolescent determined the design of our research and residential treatment programme at the National Institute of Mental Health from 1960 to 1974. This programme for adolescents aged 14–21 included both individual psychotherapy for the adolescent, conjoint family therapy, and study of the hospital group in which the adolescent lived and worked. It combined three hours per week of individual psychotherapy for the adolescent with a weekly one-hour conjoint family therapy session; one hour per week of marital therapy for the parents; and four patient–staff meetings per week, including a study group examining peer relations and authority relations on the psychiatric unit. In designing the programme we attempted to articulate the psychological maturation of the individual adolescent with his experience within his family, within his peer group, and within the social institution of which he was a part. The task of our programme was to design and manage the conduct of situations for study and treatment which promote relative ego autonomy in the adolescent, leading to his individuation and psychological separation from his parents.

In this discussion and review of boundary concepts we have utilized in our work, we want to define the following subtasks within the overall task of the programme. First, to explore and modify the internalizations of childhood experience which are manifested in disturbance in the development of relative autonomy in the adolescent's ego with impairment in his individuation. This is the task of individual psychotherapy.

Second, to explicate and modify the actuality of current family dynamics which are interfering with adolescent individuation and separation. This includes clarification of the nature of the boundary between the parents as a marital pair and the adolescent. This is the task of conjoint family therapy and marital therapy.

Third, to study and modify the adolescent's functioning in a new social organization away from the family in which he has the opportunity to develop a more mature and responsible relationship to peers and to authority figures than was present in his family relations. This is the task of the unit study group.

What boundary considerations are involved in the implementation of these tasks? We investigate how chaotic self boundaries in the individual adolescent are related to the nature of his internalized objects and their boundary characteristics; how they are related to the current dynamics at the boundary between the adolescent and his family; and how they are related to the boundaries of the roles he seeks to assume or is put into in new interpersonal or group relationships. Individual psychotherapy, family and marital therapy, and the unit study group are situations in which we explore these questions. In these therapy situations we investigate characteristics at the boundary between two interacting psychological systems. This study is facilitated by recognizing that these may be considered intergroup situations. Each of them involves two systems in a situation of mutual exchange. We observe and define characteristics of boundary regulations between them and infer the relation of these regulations to the inner coherence of each system.

The group therapy of A. K. Rice has helped us to recognize and articulate this situation (Miller and Rice, 1963; Rice, 1965, 1969). Rice's basic propositions in applying to individual and group behaviour a system theory of organization are, first, that every relationship—between individuals, within small groups, and within large groups as well as between groups—has the characteristics of an intergroup relationship; and, second, that the effectiveness of every intergroup relationship is determined, so far as its overt purposes are concerned, by the extent to which the groups involved have to defend themselves against uncertainty about the integrity of their boundaries. A corollary of this is that the making of any intergroup relationship carries with it the possibility of a breakdown in authority, the threat of chaos, and the fear of disaster.

Rice's formulations about the intergroup situation thus specify an interrelationship between the integrity of the boundary, that is, the adequacy of boundary regulations between two systems, and the state of internal coherence within each system. Integrity of the intergroup boundary implies that each system has a clear inner sense of differentiation from the other. This depends upon the presence and effectiveness within the system of sufficient internal authority for integrated functioning. Here, authority is defined as the capacity within each system to be able, to some degree, to determine task definition, to be self-regulating, and to control task implementation including intergroup transactions.

Conditions at the boundary between the two systems are determined by covert definitions within each system of the intergroup task. If each system has a different definition of the intergroup task, or if change in one of the systems requires a change in definition of the intergroup task, authority in each system is strained, with anxiety arising over the possibility of breakdown in authority in each system. The integrity of the intergroup boundary is threatened if there is insufficient differentiation between the two systems to promote clear intergroup transactions, or if authority is too fragile within either system to maintain integrated functioning, or if authority is too inflexible within either system to find a framework for intergroup transactions within a changing situation.

Under these circumstances abrupt separation from the intergroup situation occurs or there is breakdown of boundaries between the two systems with accompanying chaos.

Conceptualized as intergroup situations, individual psychotherapy, conjoint family therapy, and the unit study group highlight different determinants of the self boundary problems of the developing adolescent. We have defined three tasks which these intergroup situations are designed to accomplish. We will next discuss our efforts to implement these tasks through study and modification of the characteristics of the crucial intergroup boundary in each situation. This involves a focus upon the interrelationship between the nature and extent of boundary integrity, and the state of internal coherence within each system in these intergroup situations during a period of rapid change, the period of adolescence.

III

We return to the first task we have defined for our research and treatment programme: to explore and modify the internalizations from childhood which have rendered the adolescent's ego vulnerable and unable to achieve relative autonomy and individuation. We utilize the individual psychotherapy situation to implement this task. In Rice's terms, this is an intergroup situation between two individual personality systems where the task of therapy and the patient and therapist roles are clearly defined. Here psychoanalytic theory provides conceptual means in the structural, dynamic, and economic theories for articulating phenomena within each individual personality system; and the theories of transference and countertransference explicate the phenomena of the intergroup boundary between the individual personality systems.

In the individual psychotherapy situation the internalizations of the adolescent are studied through their projections in the transference. These internalizations may interfere with capacities maturing in the adolescent which alter his potentiality for individuation and for the finding of new libidinal objects outside of the family. If characteristics of the adolescent's internal objects militate against this development through engendering anxieties over separation, sexual anxieties, or anxieties deriving from deficient models for adult roles and relationships, these characteristics of internal objects will have manifestations in the transference relationship. The phenomena of the transference/countertransference boundary elucidate these internalizations and related anxieties which have determined weakness and confusion in the adolescent self boundary. The experience of psychotherapy involves the interpretation and working through of transference distortions in the context of a new relationship. As a more realistic perception of the relationship to the therapist occurs, the intensity of anxieties determined by old internalizations is diminished with consequent alteration and consolidation of self-boundary definition. The present is less pervaded by the past, chaos within the adolescent is reduced and the adolescent develops sufficient inner authority for integrated functioning. This allows progression in development of relative ego autonomy and individuation with increasing coherence and integrity of self boundaries.

IV

We utilize the conjoint family therapy situation to implement the second task defined above, that of explicating and modifying the actuality of current family dynamics which are interfering with adolescent individuation and separation. Study of the conjoint family therapy situation poses new conceptual difficulties. It is a more complex intergroup situation than is the individual therapy situation. The intergroup boundary between the individual adolescent and his family as a group is the major boundary to be examined in relation to the task. We conceptualize transactions across this boundary through use of the concept of delineation and through a related concept, that of unconscious assumptions in the family as a group. We observe interaction in family therapy with these concepts in mind to clarify the phenomena at the boundary between the adolescent and his family. We will discuss these concepts briefly in this paper. They have been discussed at length and with detailed clinical examples in previous publications (Shapiro, 1966, 1967, 1968, 1969; Shapiro and Zinner, 1976; Zinner and Shapiro, 1972).

Delineation is a concept closely linked to observable behaviour. We define as delineations, behaviours through which one family member communicates explicitly or implicitly his perceptions and attitudes—in fact, his mental representation of another family member—to that other person. Through use of the concept of delineation we make formulations involving three levels of inference from observations of family interaction. A first level of inference is that specified behaviours in one person imply a particular delineation of the other person.

A second level of inference is about the determinants of delineation. Delineations may communicate a view of the other person which appears to be predominantly determined by his reality characteristics. Or delineations may communicate a view of the other person which appears to be predominantly determined by the mobilization of dynamic conflict and defence in the delineator. We call the latter category defensive delineations. We pay particular attention to parental defensive delineations of the adolescent. When parental delineations are observed to be distorted, stereotyped and overspecific, contradictory, or otherwise incongruent with the range of behaviours manifested by the adolescent, we make the inference that these delineations serve defensive aspects of parental personality functioning. That is, they are not simply realistic responses to the current characteristics of the adolescent. And we further hypothesize that the parents, through their defensive delineations, seek to hold the child and adolescent in relatively fixed roles throughout development.

In addition, we make a third level of inference, that of characteristics of the family group as a whole. From excerpts of family interaction containing defensive delineations, we accrue evidence of shared or complementary characteristics of the family as a group and of the unconscious determinants of these characteristics. We conclude that this evidence of coordinated, shared, complementary behaviour in the family relates to a level of unconscious fantasy and defence in the family group analogous to Wilfred Bion's concept of small group behaviour organized around particular unconscious assumptions (Bion, 1961). The group theory of Bion derives from psychoanalysis and is a way of conceptualizing conscious and unconscious systems of motivation and defence in the group as a whole. Bion's small group theory characterizes the basic assumption group as one in which for defensive reasons the group appears to be dominated and often united by covert assumptions based on unconscious fantasies. The work of the group, its functioning and task performance, is impaired with deterioration of the ego functioning of the members. The realities of the situation and the task are lost sight of, reality testing is poor, secondary process thinking deteriorates, and more primitive forms of thinking emerge. There is new organization of behaviour which seems to be determined by fantasies and assumptions which are unrealistic and represent a failed struggle to cope with current reality. Thereby the group survives as such, though its essential functioning and primary task is now altered in the service of a different task (Turquet, 1974).

When the family is in a situation of anxiety leading to predominance of defensive delineations, there are interesting analogies to small group basic assumption behaviour. When defensive delineations predominate in family interaction, conflicting motivations, anxiety, and defences are seen with accompanying ego regression and behaviour determined more by fantasy than by reality. Work failure is evident in the family situation, similar to basic assumption functioning: there is emergence of confused, distorted thinking; failure of understanding and adequate communication; breakdown in the ability of the family to work cooperatively or creatively on a task, to maintain a progressive discussion in which family members understand each other, or to deal realistically with the problems under discussion. In short, the family is in a situation in which unconscious assumptions are mobilized with associated anxiety, a variety of defensive behaviours are seen, and there is disturbance in the family's reality functioning.

The work conjoint family therapy is an articulation of the ways in which family members delineate each other. In particular, we attempt to elucidate the dynamics of parental delineations of the adolescent and the relation of these to a dynamic of shared unconscious assumptions of the family as a group. The maturation of the adolescent has altered the intergroup situation between the individual adolescent and his parents, in that adolescent individuation involves the finding of new libidinal objects and gradual separation from his parents. However, the families we work with resist the changes required by the maturation of the adolescent. The dynamics of this resistance are conceptualized in terms of the unconscious assumptions of the family as a group. These assumptions determine delineations observed at the boundary between the adolescent and his family. Disturbance in the adolescent and in the family are manifestations of the breakdown in authority and the threat of chaos described by Rice in an intergroup situation in which unconscious assumptions militate against necessary change and determine uncertainty about the integrity of boundaries within a changing situation.

In addition to conjoint family therapy, we utilize marital therapy to implement the second task of explicating and modifying the actuality of current family dynamics which are interfering with adolescent individuation and separation. In marital therapy we want to clarify the nature of the boundary between the parents as a marital pair and the adolescent. Problems in the marriage are explored which have resulted in pressures against change and characteristic efforts to hold the adolescent in particular roles related to the parents' difficulties and dissatisfactions with each other. The boundary between the generations is often uncertain and unstable and this adds to the anxiety within the family as adolescent maturation occurs. The generational boundary is made explicit in the design of our programme by having a separate session each week of marital therapy for the parents. This in turn helps us to clarify in the conjoint family therapy the problems and uncertainties at the boundary between the parents and the adolescent and the contribution of this to the problems of the adolescent. Weakness and specific failures in the generational boundary are problems at an intergroup boundary within the family group which generate specific pressures against adolescent individuation and separation.

Another intergroup boundary in the conjoint family therapy is that between the therapists and the family. The individual therapist of the adolescent and the marital therapist of the parents shift roles to become co-therapists of the family as a group in the conjoint family sessions. The study as a part of this shift in role the ways in which parents and adolescent relate to the role shift. For example, there may be denial in the family sessions of the psychological presence and availability of the experience of marital therapy or individual therapy even when it is clearly relevant to what is happening in family therapy. Or there may be a perception of one of the therapists in family therapy which is dominated by his role as an individual or couple therapist and relates to attitudes towards the individual or couple therapy which are not being made explicit. Issues such as these become evident and interpretable through focusing on the intergroup boundary between therapists and family and between the therapy subgroups in the family session. The transference issues in this situation are complex and must be approached with the recognition that family therapy is an intergroup meeting with a number of subgroups present. The family's techniques for dealing with boundary problems in the meeting are studied to elucidate the unconscious assumptions which govern its management of boundaries within the family and of boundaries between the family and the world of relationships outside.

V

The third task defined above is that of study and modification of the adolescent's functioning in a new social organization away from the family in which he has the opportunity to develop new roles and a new relationship to peers and to authority figures. The situation we developed in our programme for implementation of this task is the 'unit study group' (Shapiro *et al.*, 1975). In this situation we study transactions at the boundary between the individual adolescent and the group which are expressions of the role the adolescent takes or is put into in a new group situation.

There were several one-hour administrative meetings each week in our psychiatric unit in which the unit administrative psychiatrist and the nursing staff met with all the patients to discuss the problems of living and working together in the hospital. In these meetings the rules which regulated life on the unit were evolved, issues concerning implementation of the school and work programme were discussed, activities away from the Clinical Center were decided upon, and community passes and privileges requested and discussed by the group. Efforts were made to examine the responsibility each patient was taking for therapy, school, work, and behaviour in the hospital and outside community.

Separate from the administrative meetings, the unit study group is an inter-group meeting consisting of all of the patients, the chief psychiatric nurse representing the nursing staff, the unit administrator representing the individual and family therapists, and the clinical director representing the research project chiefs and senior psychiatric staff. The tasks of this meeting is the study of authority relations and peer relations in the group life of the psychiatric unit. It is explicit that this is not a decision-making meeting but one in which the dynamics of roles and role relationships are studied, including the nature of attitudes towards those in authority roles. The work of the meeting is the examination of roles individuals take or are put into by the group in the hospital with whom they live and work. Patients are able to reflect upon the roles they take in relation to people in authority and to examine the dynamics of their relationships to peers and to authority figures. Staff members in authority roles are able to articulate role differences between themselves, experience differences in roles they take with the patient group and the ways they are related to by the patient group; and, despite definitions of difference, see and work with projections through which they are experienced as monolithic in the group. A whole range of issues of group life in the hospital are discussed in the meetings. In particular, phenomena defining the boundaries of the self are attended to in the group, the roles taken by the patients, and new roles which evolve in their relations with each other and with authority. Transactions at the boundary between the individual adolescents and figures in authority are studied with attention to real and fantasied characteristics of this boundary and the consequences of this for group behaviour. The adolescents define themselves in a variety of ways and as their experience in the group evolves, shifts occur in their transactions with peers and authority figures. Interpretations focus upon the dynamics of new roles patients take and the nature of transactions which eventuate in definition of new behaviours and role boundaries.

The following excerpt from a unit study group meeting contains transactions from which we infer different definitions of patient role. The excerpt exemplifies the kinds of themes which emerge in the group and the kinds of transactions which occur across the boundary between the individual adolescent, the authority figures he relates to in his group life, and his peers.

Unit study group meeting

Excerpt

DR S: One consequence I was thinking of is that if less talk has to do with having less authority, then the patients feel low man on the totem pole.

BRUCE: Yeah, but you know, the way I see it is that you cats can tell us things for ever, you know, but it wouldn't do any good, you know ... like 'cause each person is an individual and you can't, like if you're going to help somebody with their problems or something you're going to have to know that individual pretty well, and like you can't just come and tell people what's happening, they have to tell *you*, you know; if they don't tell you then you really can't do a very effective job. So you can sit and talk for ever and it's not gonna do any good. And you can tell 'em where it's at. It might even *be* that way ... but you really don't *know* where they're at 'cause they won't talk to you.

DR S: I couldn't agree more!

BRUCE: Well ... that's where it's at, I think ... .

DR R: It's not clear why you want to, for instance, leave me as unit administrator uh—not knowing where you're at so that it makes the administration not accurate, sort of imposed.

BRUCE: Well, I don't *know*, I just think, you know, *you* might feel it starts off like I'm leaving you there, but *I* feel like it starts off like you're imposing on *me*. You know what I mean?

DR R: So it's a debatable question as to who started imposing on whom, and there's a battle going on ... ?

BRUCE: [Interrupting] It really doesn't matter. I don't see any battle, really ... you know ... .

DR R: Sounds like it.

BRUCE: [Snickers.]

DR S: I think it's clarifying. Because you're speaking *for* the group at the moment. I have a lot of feeling of people feeling imposed on. Even Dr R, as the administrator of the unit, has felt imposed on in here. But you're also saying something about your knowing best of all where it's at for you.

BRUCE: That's right.

DR S: And that's true for everyone in this room.

BRUCE: [Low voice] That's right.

DR S:	And ... [pauses, does not continue].
DR R:	You know, it's interesting. I think that Fred was empathic with the position he felt me to be in, at least he could see that I was sitting alone.
Dr S:	His empathy's put him to sleep, apparently ....
DR R:	[Interrupting] Yeah, that's what I was going to say, it's almost as if pointing that out uh and making an effort seems to have worn him out. Takes a lot of work. Ann points out everybody's alone to some degree. Sounds like she felt very alone. Yet to work on what that's about ... maybe it's about being with ... people who tend to talk too much so you feel like they're imposing. It takes more effort than it seems to be worth.

[Pause]

ANN:	Well, I think each person in here was ... attempting to ... bound their own territory; you know ... create ... their own world, their own boundaries.
DR R:	I think that reflects the feeling I've had. Certainly I've felt that in a way Dr S has come onto the unit. Then I've been having to say, 'Hey, wait a minute, let's get clear at least if you're gonna come on the unit, in what way, and what our relationship is. I am here daily. You're my boss.' I run the unit directly in terms of being administrator—but it's not a usual experience until this kind of group for me to work this way and as closely with you—so I've had to do a lot of thinking about that, sort out my feelings about it. [Pause] How do you go about doing that, Ann?
ANN:	What?
DR R:	Sorting out—your place.
ANN:	I haven't been involved in that here ....
DR R:	You haven't at all? ... sounds like you've been thinking about it.
ANN:	About my—place?

[Long pause]

DR S:	I have the impression, Ann, you felt undercut by Dr R because you were trying to define your thinking here, your boundaries, your territory. I thought what you said implied you have been thinking about it. And he took your lead maybe to try to define his place and his task.
ANN:	Well, that's—that's cool.
DR S:	[Interrupts] I thought it was. But I thought you felt undercut by it in some way. I think that may be one of the problems in a group. Did you experience it that way?
ANN:	[Slight pause] No, not ... not really. No ....
Dr S:	Because then when he asked you, it was brought back to you,

and you said, well, you really hadn't been thinking about it, but you just had ... *told* us you had been thinking about it.

ANN: Well, I was ... thinking more in terms of my own place, not ... with other people, but with myself. Your way ... of forming boundaries is talking and ... getting everything in form, all your actions and interactions, so ... [pause].

DR S: Are you saying that's not your way?

ANN: I'm just saying that it's one way.

DR S: It is one way.

ANN: Yes.

DR S: I wonder what the problem is around defining one's self with words. Does it feel that it's just my way or Dr R's way. Bruce said he forgot what the meeting was for. Ann said it's one way and I don't think it is the only way, but I wonder what's wrong with the one way. There's something about it that seems to make for reticence so that Rennie, you, for instance, you listen and take it in but you don't find a way to work actively for quite a long time in this group. Sometimes it's interesting to listen and take in, but why does that role seem the only one for you? ... it's better than sleeping but there might be something better yet. Bruce has become the group artist; he draws people, doesn't talk about *them* but he talks about me and you today. Doesn't ... really say much about the other patients he lives with. You're all very careful with each other.

ARNOLD: [Pauses] Uhhhh ... I'm becoming an observer again.

DR S: You are, Arnold. You came in feeling released, but what happened?

ARNOLD: Lots—I couldn't ... maintain concentration. One thing I have noticed about this meeting is that it seems to be a rather odd relationship here between staff and patients in that they do interact but they never seem to work quite properly. It never seems to get anywhere, and I was wondering why. I just was reading the autobiography of Malcolm X; you know, the more you read the more you get turned on to the fact that the audience in certain parts of the countries that Malcolm X was visiting were actually putting on little vignettes; they were acting, so Malcolm X would be struck by this, just as Nixon was struck by that girl who was holding up the sign some place in Ohio. There is a definite inter-relationship between the actor or the audience, and uh ... the leader. Like they are two parts of the whole. And I was wondering why it seems that there's never that type of dialogue between staff and patients here. I think it's because ... all we talk about is why we don't talk about anything.

And we never seem to ... introduce anything from the outside that might be useful, to start up, you know, to get a little bit of conversation going into something that wouldn't be directly personal or wouldn't antagonize anybody. Then you'd, you'd also have the personal relationships the way people are interreacting as well. I don't know. You can't just talk about a vacuum for too long.

[Pause]

DR S: One could say that your model of Malcolm X and the countries he visited, or even President Nixon for that matter and the girl he saw saying 'Bring us together'—that there is something going on in this room similar to that.

ARNOLD: Similar, yeah, but it seems to be descending, spiralling downwards as opposed to the opposite, spiralling upwards.

DR S: I think it's felt so much as a slap in the face, for instance, I called Bruce the group artist and ... he ... winced as if I'd struck him and insulted him. I myself don't know what's wrong with being the group artist.

BRUCE. I don't want to be the group artist.

DR S: But I was saying what my perception was of you. You didn't say that you didn't want to be that or what you did want to be or anything. You winced and looked angry.

BRUCE Yeah, man, you know, you can just go on saying whatever you want to say, it's fine.

DR S: I don't say whatever I want to say.

BRUCE: Maybe you should.

DR S: Maybe I should? No, I try to think about what I say. There is a job we are trying to do here. Some things I think don't have anything to do with that and I wouldn't say them.

ARNOLD: Must we have such areas of controversy? There probably could be things we could talk about going on outside of the unit.

DR S: Outside of the unit.

ARNOLD: Of course, it's probably too irrelevant to what's happening. I think it's a better idea than sitting around here sighing and being afraid to talk.

DR R: It sounds like you're on to the drama going on right in here.

ARNOLD: How so?

DR R: Malcolm X comes to mind ....

ARNOLD: Well, it's just, just that I happened to be reading it.

DR R: It seems apropos.

ARNOLD: Well, it's like ... I mean he, he thought that the audience was reacting strictly to him. He didn't realize that the audience, people who were watching him, were trying to impress something upon his mind also. By the way the audience as a whole was reacting. He never considered this, how his policies were changed by the people he talked to. You know, the reception he got influenced his mind and his actions.

In this excerpt Bruce is manifesting new behaviour in transactions with authority figures. The excerpt starts with Bruce stating that the patients are responsible for defining and articulating the boundaries of their individuality. They are the authorities on who they are and what their problems are. There is clear recognition that unless they let staff authority figures know how they think and feel, the staff are unable to do their job. However, feelings of being imposed upon and anger at being imposed upon lead to concern over differentiation and a continuing tendency of the patients to keep themselves anonymous. Ann adds to the understanding of patient anonymity. She says she is too preoccupied with establishing her individual boundaries to be able to deal with the group at all at this time. Arnold says leaders can tell from the way the group is behaving what the group needs and wants. He implies that the group's behaviour is motivated and that it represents an effort to get something from the leaders and to control them. This is more important than defining the boundaries of the self. He is disturbed by Bruce's fight with Dr S and Dr R and wants to lead the group away from internal areas of controversy. He protests about the doctors' refusal to accept the patients' messages that they are helpless and must be cared for.

What dynamics of the group as a whole may be inferred from this excerpt? The group appears to be dominated by a covert (and often overt) assumption of dependency upon the professional staff members. This is the pervasive dynamic to which the patients relate in a variety of ways. They all appear to feel needful and dependent. This results in their feeling highly vulnerable to authority figures, perceiving them as extremely coercive. In this excerpt there is some shift in Bruce, who is manifesting new role behaviour in his assertion of the authority of the patient role in the group if it is to be a work group. This is fragile leadership and exemplifies the kind of transaction on the boundary between the individual adolescent and figures in authority upon which we focus.

Arnold is an articulate spokesman for the usual patient position of basic assumption dependency. He emphasizes the patients' covert communications which in this group seem to express a need for protection and care from authority figures demonstrated through acting helpless and fearful. His contributions define the boundary between patients and staff as an area of struggle in which patients repeatedly attempt to evoke from the staff a basic assumption dependency leadership. This takes precedence over self-definition as the patients' task in the group.

How do we accomplish work in this group situation with the powerful basic assumption dynamics which exist in it? Work is promoted through our position that the patients are responsible for their participation and contribution in the group as they are responsible for their behaviour in the hospital. Their participation in our programme is voluntary and represents a choice which they have made for which they are responsible. The patients often want to deny this responsibility and to put it on their parents or on us. They often want to insist upon their helplessness and their inability to behave responsibly and at the same time to express hatred towards the professional staff for exercising control over them. They want to deny that they themselves have any role in giving away their own controls and their own responsibility. Margaret Rioch discussed the central importance of dynamics similar to these in educational situations (Rioch, 1971). These are clearly not group dynamics which are seen only in a psychiatric unit.

The patients tend to repeat in the unit study group roles they have taken and are taking in their families. The ongoing tasks of the group is to work interpretatively on these roles in the many ways that they are manifested. This facilitates the adolescent's conscious experience of new possibilities in role behaviour in relation to peers and authority figures in a social organization away from his family. In this way his group experience helps him resume the task, interrupted in the period of identity confusion, of learning and integrating appropriate, mature, and responsible social roles.

In summary, we have described a programme of research and treatment studying changes which occur in the adolescent's internal psychological boundaries, and in the characteristics of the boundaries between the individual adolescent, his family, his peers, and social institutions. These changes are initiated by the psychological maturation of puberty with ensuing reorganization of the individual's internal psychological boundaries. They are also determined by experiences which occur within the boundary areas between the individual adolescent, his family, and his social groups. We have discussed a programme of research and treatment of disturbed adolescents and their families which is designed to help the adolescent articulate and integrate his experience at significant social boundaries and relate this to confusion within his own self boundaries. This allows progression in the development of ego autonomy and individuation in the adolescent with increasing coherence of his self-identity and integrity of his self boundaries.

References

Bion, W. R. (1961) *Experiences in Groups*. London: Tavistock Publications.

Edelson, M. (1970) *Sociotherapy and Psychotherapy*. University of Chicago Press.

Erikson, E. H. (1956) 'The problem of ego identity'. *Journal of the American Psychoanalytic Association*, **4**, 56–121.

Erikson, E. H. (1958) *Young Man Luther: A Study in Psychoanalysis and History*. New York: Norton.

Erikson, E. H. (1962) 'Reality and actuality'. *Journal of the American Psychoanalytic Association*, **10**, 451–474.

Freud, A. (1936) *The Ego and the Mechanisms of Defense*. New York: International Universities Press, 1967 (Revised Edition).

Freud, A. (1958) 'Adolescence'. *Psychoanalytic Study of the Child*, **13**, 255–278.

168

Freud, S. (1923) 'The ego and the id'. *Standard Edition of the Complete Psychological Works of Sigmund Freud*, nt. 19. London: Hogarth Press, 1961, pp. 3–66.

Hartmann, H. (1950) 'Comments on the psychoanalytic theory of the ego'. Reprinted in *Essays on Ego Psychology*. New York: International Universities Press, 1964.

Inhelder, B., and Piaget, J. (1958) *The Growth of Logical Thinking from Childhood to Adolescence*. New York: Basic Books.

Jacobson, E. (1964) *The Self and the Object World*. New York: International Universities Press.

Landis, B. (1970) 'Ego boundaries'. *Psychological Issues Monograph*, No. 24, Vol. VI, No. 4. International Universities Press.

Miller, E. J., and Rice, A. K. (1963) *Systems of Organization*. London: Tavistock Publications.

Rice, A. K. (1967) *Learning for Leadership: Interpersonal and Intergroup Relations*. London: Tavistock Publications.

Rice, A. K. (1969) 'Individual, group and intergroup processes'. *Human Relations*, **22**, 6, 565–584.

Rioch, M. J. (1971) ' "All we like sheep ..." ' (Isaiah 53 : 6); followers and leaders'. *Psychiatry*, **34**, 258–273.

Schafer, R. (1968) *Aspects of Internalization*. New York: International Universities Press.

Shapiro, R. (1963) 'Adolescence and the psychology of the ego'. *Psychiatry*, **26**, 1, 77–87.

Shapiro, R. (1966) 'Identity and ego autonomy in adolescence'. In J. H. Masserman (ed.) *Science and Psychoanalysis*. New York: Grune Stratton.

Shapiro, R. (1967) 'The origin of adolescent disturbances in the family: Some considerations in theory and implications for therapy. In G. H. Zuk and I. Boszormenyi-Nagy (ed.) *Family Therapy and Disturbed Families*. Palo Alto, Calif.: Science and Behavior Books.

Shapiro, R. (1968) 'Action and family interaction in adolescence'. In J. Marmor (ed.) *Modern Psychoanalysis*. New York: Basic Books.

Shapiro, R. (1969) 'Adolescent ego autonomy and the family'. In G. Caplan and S. Leborici (eds) *Psychological Perspectives*. New York: Basic Books.

Shapiro, R., and Zinner, J. (1976) 'Family organization and adolescent development'. In E. Miller (ed.) *Task and Organization*. London and New York: Wiley, 289–308.

Shapiro, R., Zinner, J., Berkowitz, D., and Shapiro, E. (1975) 'The impact of group experiences on adolescent development'. In M. Sugar (ed.) *The Adolescent in Group and Family Therapy*. New York: Brunner/Mazel, 87–104.

Turquet, P. M. (1971) 'The Bion hypothesis: The work group and the basic assumption group'. Four lectures given at the National Institute of Mental Health, 26 May, 28 May, 2 June, 6 June.

Turquet, P. M. (1974) 'Leadership, the individual and the group'. In G. S. Gibbard, J. J. Hartman, R. D. Mann (eds) *Analysis of Groups*. San Francisco: Jossey-Bass, 337–371.

Zinner, J., and Shapiro, R. (1971) 'Projective identification as a mode of perception and behavior in families of adolescents'. Presented at the 58th Annual Meeting of the American Psychoanalytic Association, Panel on Adolescent Development from the Perspective of Family Studies, Washington, DC, 29 April–3 May.

Zinner, J., and Shapiro, R. (1972) 'Projective identification as a mode of perception and behavior in families of adolescents. *International Journal of Psychoanalysis*, **53**, 523–529.

Chapter 12

Learning and the Group Experience

Barry Palmer

In 1976 I took part in a one-day seminar on a particular approach to management development. My own contribution to the seminar was a lecture on learning. At the end of the day one of the participants commented that he assumed the two main influences on the approach presented at the seminar were Wilfred Bion and Gregory Bateson. The indebtedness to Bion had been made clear in my lecture, but his reference to Bateson was a surprise to me, since I knew nothing of his work. I obtained a copy of his collected papers (Bateson, 1973), and found that, although some of his terminology was unfamiliar, his ideas had considerable relevance to my current thinking about learning, to management development, and to the working conferences on group relations (Rice, 1964) in which I had been involved since 1963. The book generated new lines of thought by forcing me to think about familiar experiences in unfamiliar categories, and brought into prominence issues of which I had previously been only peripherally aware. At the time of writing I have not yet put them down.

One of Bateson's interests is in our apperceptive habits, how we acquire them, and how we modify them. (To apperceive means 'to unite and assimilate a perception to ideas already possessed, and so comprehend and interpret'; Concise Oxford Dictionary, 6th edition, 1976. In these terms, the group relations conferences are concerned with how we apperceive the situations in which we find ourselves in groups and organizations.) Our behaviour manifests not only the specific skills we have learned, the specific knowledge we have built up, and the specific conventional actions we have been trained to perform. It also manifests pervasive assumptions about what reality, physical and social, is like, and what is to be expected from it. The words we use to describe people—optimistic, pessimistic, dependent, caring, ruthless, feckless, idealistic—pick out, from the totality of their behaviour, a characteristic set or orientation towards the world:

> Two men look out through the same bars:
> One sees the mud, and one the stars.

The value of Bateson's theory of learning is that he brings together in a single scheme the processes of learning which give rise to the complexities of our apperceptive habits, and the more simple learning processes which have been described by experimental psychologists. He therefore helps us to recognize

169

and distinguish between the different types of learning which take place through our educational activities—for example, between learning which is a form of involuntary conditioning and learning through intentional exploration and insight.

In this paper I propose, therefore, to expound some of Bateson's leading ideas, and then use them to examine the nature of the learning process in group relations conferences, what participants may be expected to derive from them, and the inherent demands of the staff role in such events. It is hoped that this will throw light not only upon the conferences themselves, but upon learning and teaching in a wide range of contexts. I shall suggest that Bateson's concepts, as presented in his collected papers, do not adequately describe the processes we encounter in experience, and work towards a tentative model which seems to place his insights in a more adequate frame.

Other writers have had a major influence on the paper, some of whom figured more explicitly in previous drafts than they do now, and cannot always be acknowledged in specific references. These include Wilfred Bion (1962, 1963), Michael Polanyi (1973), Liam Hudson (1972, 1975), and in another mode, T. S. Eliot (1963). It is also impossible to acknowledge adequately what I have learned from those with whom I have worked in the Grubb Institute and in the group relations conferences, including Pierre Turquet, with whom I had the privilege of working from 1963 until his death.

Levels of learning

We shall begin by considering the theory of learning developed by Bateson. He proposes first that the simplest level of learning, and that which has been almost exclusively studied in the psychological laboratory, is a trial and error process by which the human or animal subject develops a new response or set of responses to a specific stimulus or problem. A dog learns to associate the sound of a buzzer with the imminence of food, and so becomes conditioned to salivate when the buzzer sounds. A child repeats a poem he is told to learn by heart, until the stimulus of each word or phrase triggers off a memory of the word or phrase which follows, and he is able to recite the poem right through (even if he has little idea what it means). There are many different ways of structuring the learning process, as the different approaches to teaching children to read, in use in our primary schools, show. Bateson identifies a number of distinct learning contexts which have been studied in the laboratory (Bateson, 1973, pp. 258 ff.), and shows that in each case the learning observed is 'a *change in specificity of response* by correction of errors within a set of alternatives' (Bateson, 1973, p. 264). By this process a child learns to walk, play the piano, recite multiplication tables, look both ways before crossing the road, or wash his hands before meals. Bateson refers to this level of learning as Learning I (or proto-learning). He also points out that Learning I can continue until the learned response becomes automatic, or the skill is exercised at the level of reliability demanded by the task. The child no longer has to give attention to walking, and washes its hands as a matter of routine. His response to particular situations has become, to use Bateson's term, 'soldered in'. Learning I has tailed off to a state of Learning O or zero-learning. This expression is not as equivocal as it looks. In some circumstances we use the word 'learn' to refer simply to receiving a signal: I 'learn' that there is a strike on the railway, and travel to work by bus. The first time there was a strike, I had to find out the best way to get to work by trial and error (Learning I). Now my response is soldered in: if strike, then bus.

This last example leads into a further issue, that of the *context* in which Learning I takes place. There would be no possibility of my learning what to do about strikes if I could not assume that other conditions remained more or less the same from one strike to the next. If the bus routes, and the days and times on which the buses ran, were chosen at random by the drivers, so that they were wholly unpredictable, then learning would be impossible for me as far as travelling by bus was concerned; every strike would present me with a new situation. I might then learn that the best solution was to walk to the office; but this would presuppose that the same routes could be followed on any day— that streets were not liable to be blocked off in the night, or the streets of London rebuilt on a new plan every morning.

Learning I therefore presupposes a recurring context, such that the second context in which the stimulus is encountered or the problem is tackled may be construed, when compared with the first, to be 'the same'. This has farreaching consequences, because in life outside the laboratory, and, strictly, within the laboratory too, no two situations are ever exactly the same. No patient has exactly the same symptoms as the last, though the general practitioner would require more than seven minutes for each patient if he could not assume that most of the complaints he encountered were the same as those he had encountered before. No client has exactly the same problems as any the solicitor, social worker, or management consultant has seen before; no conference small group follows exactly the same course as any which have taken place before. Yet unless we can construe them as in some way 'the same', we can transfer nothing we have discovered in the past to the new situation; and we are helpless. In East Coker, reflecting on writing poetry, Eliot depicts a situation in which nothing which has been learned about this task in the past is adequate to the demands of the new experience:

> Trying to learn to use words, and every attempt
> Is a wholly new start, and a different kind of failure
> Because one has only learnt to get the better of words
> For the thing one no longer has to say, or the way in which
> One is no longer disposed to say it. And so each venture
> Is a new beginning, a raid on the inarticulate
> With shabby equipment always deteriorating ... (Eliot, 1963, p. 202)

Bateson's thesis is that, whatever we learn at the level of Learning I, we are also learning to recognize and inhabit a context. This latter process he calls Learning II (or deutero-learning). Learning II has effects which extend beyond the original learning situation. If a child is taught to spy on his parents (Bateson's example), he not only learns a skill (Learning I), he may also build this experience into his whole philosophy of life. It is likely to colour his whole attitude to the family and to authority, and thus influence his behaviour in many other situations which he construes as in some way 'the same'. What did the subjects learn in the famous Milgram experiments on obedience to authority (1963)? At the level of Learning I, perhaps, to respond less compliantly to the orders of people in authority. But at the level of Learning II, their expectations of the world may have been altered in a more comprehensive way. They now live in a world in which polite people in white coats from reputable institutions may seek to persuade them to take part in personally stressful experiments, without disclosing their true reasons.

The effects of Learning II in the development of character become evident, in psychotherapy and elsewhere, in the phenomenon of transference (Bateson, 1973, p. 271). The patient construes his situation *vis-à-vis* the analyst as in some way 'the same' as his position *vis-à-vis* some other important person, usually a parent, in the past. He therefore responds to the analyst in the way he learned to respond to his parent in the past (Learning I), and in so doing invites the analyst to construe their relationship in the way he, the patient, has learned (Learning II) to construe it.

Bateson concludes that Learning II determines a large part of the relational life of all human beings, and is a major factor in shaping what we think of as the character of the person—whether his is, say, optimistic, fatalistic, suspicious, or trusting.

Learning II may thus be defined as a process through which the ways in which we read or perceive situations are changed, and hence through which the sets of alternative courses of action from which we choose are changed. The doctor learns to interpret a number of recurring symptoms—temperature, vomiting, spots, pain in various places—according to the syndromes or combinations in which they occur. Having identified the syndrome, which may be labelled 'influenza', 'measles', or 'lead poisoning', he is then presented with choices between alternative approaches to treatment. He is not in a position to apply what he has learned about drugs, diet, or surgery (Learning I) until he has arrived at an interpretation of the symptoms with which he is presented (cf. Polanyi, 1973, pp. 49 ff.).

Bateson also defines Learning II as 'a change in how the sequence of experience is punctuated' (p. 264). He continues:

We suggest that *what* is learned in Learning II is a way of *punctuating events*. But a way of punctuating is not true or false. There is nothing contained in the propositions of this learning that can be tested against reality. It is like a picture seen in an inkblot; it has neither correctness nor incorrectness. It is only a way of seeing the inkblot. (p. 271)

It may be objected that a doctor's diagnosis is very different from a picture seen in an inkblot, and that the patient's deterioration or recovery provides a practical test of its truth or falsity. I shall in fact go on to draw a distinction, which Bateson does not explicitly make, between our automatic apperceptive habits and more deliberate processes of diagnosis and interpretation. Nevertheless, the connection between the diagnosis and the outcome of the treatment is never wholly certain and sometimes very obscure.

Bateson is thinking primarily about apperceptive habits and about character. We may think, for example, of someone whose life experiences, coupled perhaps with physiological factors, have led him to construe his relationships in what others might regard as a paranoid frame of mind. In response to certain cues, which may be highly specific or may be as generalized as the presence of other people, he construes those around him as hostile and responds accordingly. Now others may observe him and say: 'His way of seeing the world is wrong; he misjudges other people's attitudes towards him.' But this is simplistic, as those whose business is with personality change will know. I have a friend who has moved from job to job over the years, and who rings me up periodically to tell me how his latest group of colleagues have snubbed him, ridiculed him, told lies about him, and eventually conspired to get him the sack; and I believe him. The construction he places upon what happens is self-consistent. I find myself not returning his calls when he rings and I am out, and when he is speaking on the phone I become testy and exasperated and pull wry faces at other people in the room. So I know that when I am in his world I am hostile to him too.

What I am unable to do is to enable him to step outside this world-view, this way of punctuating events, and see his own character as factitious rather than given—the way a trip to France or New Guinea causes us to see how people behave in Britain as just one way of behaving. This change of perspective, which is a change from being immersed in one's world to being able to see it whole, is referred to by Bateson as Learning III. He adds that 'to demand this level of performance from some men and some mammals is sometimes pathological'.

Learning III, then, is a process by which we learn to recognize and gain control of our own apperceptive habits. Since, as the illustration of my persecuted friend shows, the premises on which we base our relations with others tend to be self-validating, Learning III entails discovering a capacity to doubt the validity of perceptions which seem unquestionably true. In psychotherapy, the therapist seeks to achieve 'a confrontation between the premises of the patient and those of the therapist, who is carefully trained not to fall into the trap of validating the old premises' (Bateson, 1973, p. 273). This is something different from merely replacing one apperceptive habit by another, as might be the objective of behaviour therapy—though this itself is, as Bateson says, no mean feat. It is also something different from being knowledgeable about one's own character, in the manner of those who justify their behaviour with statements like: 'Well, you see, I am a very dependent [obsessional, paranoid, untidy] person.' The experience of Learning III is the experience of becoming responsible for one's dependence (obsessiveness, paranoia, untidiness) as something one *is*, and *is doing*.

Bateson's analysis leads him, not surprisingly, into references to religious conversion and Zen Buddhism. Traditional Christian language describes conversion in terms close to this description of Learning III. The convert is extricated from his former ingrained manner of experiencing the world, and everything is transformed: 'When anyone is united to Christ, there is a new world (*ktisis*, creation); the old order has gone, and a new order has already begun' (II Corinthians 5 : 17). The Zen experience of *satori*, or awakening, takes place, it appears, when the individual has a glimpse of reality unpunctuated into subject and objects by his own ego, when there is simply 'a continuous, self-moving stream of experiencing, without the sense either of an active subject who controls it or of a passive subject who suffers it' (Watts, 1973).

The wider movement of which the Tavistock and Grubb Institute conferences are a part has evolved to embrace radical therapies and religious activities, and it is evident that some people come to our more employment-oriented events with hopes of transformation and fears of breakdown. Those who take consultant roles in these events are continually faced with the problem of extricating themselves from the habitual ways of reading group situations which they have learned through previous experience. Bateson's concept of Learning III therefore promises to throw light upon some of the most demanding aspects of group relations conferences.

Before discussing the relevance and limitations of these concepts when applied to these activities, it may be useful to summarize them. Bateson draws attention to the following hierarchy of levels or orders of learning (cf. Bateson, 1973, pp. 263 f.):

Zero-learning: a condition in which the individual makes specific responses to specific stimuli or situations. Right or wrong, these responses are not subject to correction; they are 'soldered in', or habitual.

Learning I: a trial and error process through which the individual adapts to his environment, finding a new response or pattern of responses to a given situation or stimulus. The process is one of correcting errors of choice within a set of alternatives.

Learning II: a process of corrective change in the set of alternatives from which choices are made; change in the way the individual construes his circumstances or punctuates his experience, and therefore in the knowledge and skill derived from Learning I which is brought to bear.

Learning III: a process of gaining control of, and hence changing, the habitual ways of construing situations which are the outcome of Learning II.

The aims of group relations conferences

It is not my intention to describe the rationale and method of the group relations model as developed originally by Rice, Trist, Turquet, and their colleagues at the Tavistock Institute, and subsequently by a number of other institutions including my own. They have been described by Trist and Sofer (1959) and Rice (1964), and in a number of more recent volumes and articles (Rioch, 1970; Colman and Bexton, 1975; Miller, 1976a; Rioch, 1977; Palmer, 1978).

The learning process which the conferences are intended to promote has been described in various ways over the years. As I see it, it can be analysed into a number of associated changes in the participant's focus of attention and in the way he or she construes social and institutional situations. These are:

(1) *Developing a habit of attention to his own ongoing experience.* This aim finds expression in the model provided by consultants (as staff assigned to group sessions are called) in basing their interpretations upon what is happening, and happening to them, in the 'here and now'. It is assumed that an effective interpretation is one which brings the individual to himself, alive and engaged with other persons and objects, here and now, at least momentarily defeating the strategies through which he avoids this recognition (cf. Strachey, 1934, on the 'mutative' interpretation).

(2) *Learning to recognize fantasy as a mode of experience,* and to distinguish between fantasy and reality. The word 'fantasy' is used here, not in the colloquial sense of an idea about reality which may or may not be true, but to refer to a mode of experiencing relations with objects which is usually unconscious. The phenomenology of fantasy has been described very usefully by Laing (1961). The conferences are not distinctive in focusing attention upon fantasy; this is an integral part of many group activities intended to develop self-awareness.

The distinctive orientation of the conferences we are discussing is towards the influence of fantasy in working groups and institutions; that is, in contexts where survival and achievement depend upon interpreting, intervening in, and adapting to the realities of the environment of the group or institution. There is therefore a drive beyond identifying fantasies, with the inherent fascination of doing that, towards understanding the obstructive or vitalizing influence of fantasy upon adaptive work.

(3) *Learning to recognize the influence of shared fantasy in groups and organizations.* One of the most farreaching hypotheses arising from Bion's original work on the behaviour of small groups, was that the behaviour of individuals who have come together as a group may be viewed as their personal and distinctive responses to a shared fantasy of the world of the group and figures within it (Bion, 1961; see also Ezriel, 1950). This is one of the basic working hypotheses of the conferences. By processes which we shall consider later, it has tended over the years to become an item of orthodox belief, with consequent impoverishment of the conference as an exploratory situation.

(4) *Becoming alert to the influence of fantasy in relations between leaders and followers,* between those who depend and those who are depended upon. This element in the learning process was identified retrospectively, rather than constituting an explicit aim from the beginning. Through working on this paper I have come to the conclusion that this emphasis arises as a result of assumptions about learning on which the conferences are based. It is assumed that members can derive little of practical value from the conference unless they learn to learn by analysing their own experience. Staff therefore resist being made into teachers or experts who would accept responsibility for imprinting new knowledge and skills in passive students. This stance plunges staff and members into all the tensions and ambiguities of insecure, dependent relationships.

(5) *Gaining facility in the use of a number of key theoretical concepts* for describing the unconscious structuring and conscious organization of working groups. It is the belief of the writer that without such concepts the participant is ill-equipped to make use of the conference in interpreting behaviour in his organization, and that conferences which do not assist participants in mastering these concepts, for example through lectures, deprive them of one means of directing their own learning.

Levels of learning in conferences

When Bateson's concepts are used to reinterpret what happens in conferences, they illuminate a number of significant features.

First they draw attention to a level of learning prior to that with which we are usually concerned. At the level of Learning I, the participants find their way around the physical and social environment of the conference. In a way analogous to that of rats in a maze, they learn to locate where their various needs can be met, within the conference centre and within the timetable of meals and sessions. If the geography of the centre is difficult to master, attention is diverted to this problem from that presented by the sessions themselves, and the confusion may infect (Learning II) boundaries which are not geographical—boundaries of time, task, and role.

Within the formal sessions a similar process takes place. A member discovers that a consultant does not answer his questions in the way he expected, or does not answer at all. This is a shock. He may try again, or he may watch how other people fare when they ask questions. Progressively he may learn to avoid exposing himself to the discomfort of the consultant's responses. He may thus react similarly to a rat which learns to avoid receiving an electric shock. Alternatively, of course, he may reappraise the context in which members and consultant meet, in which case we move into the realm of Learning II.

Learning I also influences group behaviour, and the behaviour of individuals in a group can sometimes be interpreted as a manifestation of what they have learned, at this level, in their role as group members. I took part with a colleague in a median group event (21 members and two consultants), in which the members quickly broke up the initial configuration of chairs, which had comprised one complete circle and two outer arcs on opposite sides, to sit in one large circle. In a subsequent session, however, a few members took the risk of sitting with one of the consultants in a smaller knot in the middle of the customary large ring. Almost immediately discussion developed into fierce criticism of the behaviour of one of the members in the centre, leading into a series of verbal attacks on Catholics, social workers, the upper classes, and other groupings who were seen as represented within the room. Many people were quite shaken by the violence of the session, particularly those in the centre who tended to become the focus of attention. The consultants made attempts to interpret this behaviour, but felt at the end that they had not succeeded in enabling members to discern the fantasy element in the objects they were attacking, and why the culture of fight and flight had become dominant in the session. In no subsequent session did more than one member sit in the centre, and the group appeared to be dominated by the belief that one circle meant safety, and two circles meant destructive conflict.

We may discern here two elements: (1) a learned pattern of behaviour (Learning I), that of sitting in one large circle; and (2) a view, rooted in unconscious fantasy, of the situation in which members found themselves—that is, one in which complex seating arrangements caused pain—which gave rise to the learned response. The development of this view (Learning II) modified the alternative behaviours open to group members (cf. definition on p. 174). It was sufficiently powerfully ingrained to cause group members to construe subsequent sessions as 'the same' as that in which the conflict was experienced.

This incident illustrates the equivocal nature of learning in group relations conferences. What is transferred from one session to the next within a conference may also be transferred to external situations subsequently, and indeed few organizations would back the applications of their staff to take part unless there was some such expectation. Yet, as Bateson points out, the ways of reading social situations which arise through Learning II tend to be self-validating. They are not right or wrong, only different. Thus the behaviour of members returning to their own institutions from conferences is frequently reported, by themselves and by others, to have changed in various ways: they have discontinued large gatherings of staff in favour of meetings of smaller subgroups; they are more ready to challenge the judgements of their bosses or colleagues; they are generally more disposed to aggression and anger; they are more able to keep their cool in confusing situations and take time to work out what to do. All these observable changes imply other, unobservable, changes in the way the individual construes the situations in which he finds himself, including his own position in it. And none can be declared changes for the better, or for the worse, without qualification. Large gatherings are suitable for the performance of some tasks and not others. There are circumstances in which it is constructive to challenge decisions, or express anger, or pause for thought in the midst of confusion, and circumstances in which it is not. Much depends, therefore, on the individual's capacity to interpret the circumstances in which he acts, rather than carry over patterns of behaviour unreflectingly from one situation to another. This capacity is not called into play at the level of Learning II as Bateson has described it.

The position reached

At this point the argument comes to a fork in the road. Within Bateson's scheme, it is illuminating to consider how awareness of the limiting effect of mental constructs built up through Learning II has led to activities aimed at providing conditions for Learning III, and to preoccupation with this level of learning. This I shall discuss in the following section. Our examination of Learning I and Learning II in the conference context has, however, already begun to indicate that these concepts require further development. In order to construct a theory of learning which integrates the conclusions of, on the one hand, experimental psychologists working with animals and human beings engaged in simple tasks like rote learning, and, on the other hand, psycho-analysts, therapists, and religious teachers concerned with profound changes in personality and world-view, Bateson has taken the former as his baseline and built upon that, applying the theory of logical types of Whitehead and Russell (1910). His implicit model of the learning situation is therefore one in which a subject learns to solve a problem, or to adapt to conditions, set up by someone else; learning is conditioning. This is so not only when he is discussing work with animals or rote learning; it also applies to his consideration of the development of character, since he locates the learning processes which determine character in early infancy, when the child is largely dependent on the conditions created by parents. What is missing in his analysis of Learning I and Learning II is an examination of those circumstances in which the human subject, and perhaps the animal subject too, manages his own learning, or engages consciously and deliberately in experiment, diagnosis, and interpretation. (Bateson himself recognizes that his scheme cannot be rigorously applied to all learning contexts (Bateson, 1973, pp. 261 f., 278 f.).)

Before developing this branch of the argument further, we shall return to an account of the growth of preoccupation with Learning III in group relations activities.

Learning III

In the early days of the group dynamics movement it appeared that, if people made their own behaviour in group situations an object of study, they might learn to modify their automatic responses to other people, and hence change a condition of zero-learning into one in which they were able to continue to change their behaviour in the light of experience. A key element in T-groups was, and I presume still is, the giving and receiving of 'feedback', a term taken from cybernetics and used to refer to information given to an individual about the effects of his words, manner, and behaviour upon those at the receiving end. Conditions were thus created where, through receiving feedback, people might become aware of their behaviour and its effects and seek to change it (Learning I). The expression 'learning by experience' meant 'learning by discovery': it was a trial and error method, seen as a preferable alternative to academic learning, through which the individual absorbs concepts without becoming acquainted with what they refer to—like becoming an expert on maps without ever seeing the territory they represent (cf. Bateson, 1973, p. 423, quoting Korzybski).

In the line of development, on both sides of the Atlantic, which has been motivated by interests in the learning and growth of the individual, people were soon faced with the familiar fact that, while we can make some use of feedback in modifying our behaviour, few of us have so little interests in the continuity of our own character that we are willing or able to go on redefining it indefinitely, in response to each new situation. Openness to Learning I is restricted by the effects of past Learning II. The organization of the personality, like that of the social institution (cf. Miller, 1976a, pp. 19 f.), has two functions. It is a utilitarian device, evolved pragmatically to regulate relations with the environment. It is also a defence against anxiety, a device for imposing order and predictability on the flux of events which we do not lightly abandon or modify.

Recognition of this factor may be seen as a major influence in the development of all those techniques which attempt to outmanoeuvre or dismantle the defences of the ego, such as the techniques of the encounter or personal growth movement. Some of these are defined as therapeutic, others are derived from 'ways of liberation' originating in the East. Their goal, in the terms used here, is Learning III. They aim to discard or bypass the punctuating function of the ego, and with it the corresponding limited repertoire of responses available to the individual in any situation; or, more realistically, to bring about awareness of this function and accept, if need be, the inevitability of its persistence, but to see it purely as a phenomenon, not to be clung to or defended; to take note of our fantasies and impulses, and indeed the totality of our world-view, without being impelled to act upon them or defend them (e.g. Watts, 1962, pp. 135 ff.).

Within the Tavistock tradition we have arrived at similar preoccupations by a different route. By making the group, rather than the individual, the object of study, participants have become aware of the influence of fantasy, and in particular shared fantasy, upon behaviour. The temporary conference institution has made it possible, it appears, for a substantial proportion of participants to have a glimpse of fantasy from the outside. As Eric Miller has expressed it (1976b), they have had the experience of being immersed in basic assumption thinking, and of emerging from it.

The problem of utilizing this experience has been that these transitions are more difficult in the context of an ongoing institution and one's own role in it. The ongoing institution is not disposable like the conference, and we all need our roles in institutions to provide us with defences against anxiety. They provide us with settings in which we can not only work to achieve goals, but also regress periodically to a state of dependence, and feel renewed, through participation in shared, sacred ideas (cf. Reed and Palmer, 1972). Transfer of learning has therefore been least problematical for people whose work is most similar to the conference set-up: for those engaged in temporary series of sessions with clients, patients or pupils, or in short-term project groups.

In such settings the individual has least difficulty in distinguishing between the role he takes up in the group, and who he is outside it. Such disposable groupings do not become primary settings for meeting one's own dependent needs; these must be satisfied elsewhere.

There has been a trend, particularly in the longer conferences, for an increasing proportion of applicants to be engaged in group work, in this restricted sense. This suggests that the primary task of conferences—that is, the function which is enabling them to survive—may be to provide opportunities for learning to those who work professionally with specially constructed temporary groups. If this is so, the role of some other participants may be simply to make up the numbers and contribute fees.

Since the majority of participants, particularly in the shorter conferences, are not professionally engaged in group work, and the appeal of the prospectus is primarily to managers and administrators, we find there is a mismatch between the aim and clientele on the one hand, and the *de facto* process of learning and transfer of learning which takes place. Our diagnosis is that leaders of institutions and sections of institutions require the ability to look critically at the mythology of the unit for which they are responsible (including the function of fantasy in such work-oriented devices as policies, organizational charts, procedures, and job descriptions). If they fail to do this, they may be unable to perceive the misfit between these principles, through which the activities of the institution are regulated, and those which are required for the continuing survival and development of the institution in current conditions. Through the conferences, managers have the opportunity to learn to recognize the influence of fantasy and mythology on behaviour in groups and institutions. But, for the reasons given, this learning appears to be insufficient in itself to equip them to appraise the behaviour of their own institutions, and of themselves in their leadership roles, in the same way—unless they are heroes to begin with. (This recognition has led, in my own institute, to work on methods of enabling managers to become aware of the constructs by which they habitually construe their working environment, and their role in it, by studying their recollected working experience with a consultant (Reed, 1976; Mant, 1976).)

It may be evident that the level of learning which is sought here is Learning III, since we are endeavouring to enable managers to gain control of the habitual ways in which they construe situations. The target is not, however, the whole person, and the character he has built up in the course of his life, but the 'person-in-role', and the characteristic actions through which he does his job.

When we turn to the experience of staff in these conferences, a similar problem becomes evident. Indeed, for those whose professional work is based substantially on the assumptions, theory, and methods of the group relations conferences, it is the same problem. Our dilemma has been to develop professionalism, with its inherent standardization and routinization, in a field where the essence of the role is openness to what is new, to the unknown. We are faced continually with situations in conferences which are not wholly unfamiliar, and for which we have learned (Learning I) responses which seemed to be effective in the past; yet we know that if they cease to surprise and disturb us, we can no longer do our job.

In groups of staff the problem presents itself as one of character or personality —one's own and those of one's colleagues. For those of us who work together frequently, it is increasingly difficult to distinguish between the person and the role; that is, between behaviour manifesting personal values and constructs which have been built up over a lifetime (Learning II), and behaviour manifesting an idea of the staff role which is open to criticism in the light of an agreed task. We therefore tend to accommodate to each other's idiosyncracies respect to actions which impinge upon the effectiveness of the conference.

Thus, by various routes, the group dynamics movement has reached a position in which, if its leaders are to continue to pursue the goal of improving human performance and quality of living, they will have to continue to engage with highly intransigent problems of self-awareness, as persons and in their roles. In a perceptive article, Kurt Back (1973) suggests that the group dynamics movement has maintained its idealism and optimism by basing its conclusions on groups, laboratories, and conferences of extremely brief duration. The brevity of these events systematically excludes experience of the tragic dimension in human affairs. This dimension is now reasserting itself.

Learning to learn

We shall now return to the question of the incompleteness of Bateson's analysis of learning, when applied to the conference setting. Our thesis, as stated earlier, is that his analysis does not adequately describe how individuals, in various circumstances, manage their own learning—when they are not, or not only, the objects of the experiments, diagnoses, and interpretations of other people, but contribute to these processes themselves.

We will take as our starting-point the use of feedback in a T-group. In our earlier account of this the nature of the learner's response to feedback was left undefined. Clearly this *may* be analogous to that of a rat which touches some object and receives what some psychologists quaintly call a 'noxious stimulus', or punishment. Repetition of this experience eventually leads to a condition in which the rat avoids the object consistently; the avoidance response is 'soldered in'. Similarly a group member, who is told that his habit of telling other people what to do makes them furious, may eventually stop bossing them about, especially if he feels their fury. This kind of learning has its limitations. As Mark Twain is alleged to have said, a cat that sits on hot stove will not sit on another, but it will not sit on a cold one either. The group member may not only stop being bossy but may avoid giving leadership altogether. Furthermore, the habitual way in which he reads his relations with others, which gave rise to his bossiness, may remain unchanged, and find expression in other ways. Furthermore, he may have responded to feedback which was actually a manifestation of anger in the group towards someone else, displaced onto him as a safer target. Only if he can become aware of these additional factors, and take them into account in seeking to change his behaviour, will his learning be adaptive beyond enabling him to avoid hostility during a transitory phase in the life of a T-group.

Similar considerations apply to the members of the median group event described earlier. Their behaviour suggested that they remained unable to distinguish between a hot chair configuration and a cold one.

Looking back on my first experience of the group dynamics movement, as a participant in a T-group, I have little doubt that, whatever changes in my behaviour may have taken place through unreflective conditioning, I came away with the knowledge, derived from experience, that it is possible to regard every occasion as an opportunity for learning about social behaviour, and about one's own strategies for dealing with other people. Whatever you do, you can learn something from the consequences, even if they are disastrous. Moreover, I had understood that what is learned depends upon the work which is done upon the raw material of the experience, and that the outcome of this work is never absolute truth, but only provisional judgements which provide the tacit hypotheses for further experiment. (Participants were provided with duplicated handouts analysing the learning process in these terms.)

Experience of the group relations conferences shows more clearly the nature of the transition from learning by conditioning to self-directed learning. In his first small group, for example, the naïve participant finds nothing he can, as he sometimes says, 'get his teeth into'. While the word 'task' may be used in explaining the purpose of the event, he cannot identify any task which would enable him to transfer into the group knowledge and skills he has gained elsewhere. He feels, as he also sometimes says, that he is in a group which is being asked to contemplate its navel (an image not wholly unconnected with Learning III). If he recognizes that the method the consultant is employing is to seek to understand the behaviour of individuals as an expression of their relatedness to a group, he objects to this. He may propose that they should agree to discuss a particular issue, and then pause periodically to consider how they behaved as they discussed it. At this stage he cannot imagine himself monitoring his own ongoing experience, without some additional form of organization to support him.

Some participants never get beyond this state of perplexity. For some, however, either in the course of a session or in reflecting on a session afterwards, the penny drops. Analytically, I would describe this occasion as one in which the individual becomes aware, fleetingly or more consistently, of the influence of fantasy in the life of the group. He perceives the object of the group's conscious attention, the object with which they are preoccupied in fantasy, and the difference between the two (cf. Strachey, 1934). Laing, writing about unconscious fantasy ('phantasy'), describes this recognition in terms reminiscent of Bateson's account of Learning III:

Most people are unconscious of this mode of experience. This is not necessarily so. Phantasy can become conscious, in so far as a person can allow his own reflective awareness to be open to it. In becoming thoroughly and radically aware of phantasy both in terms of *content* and *modality*, the person is subject in his whole being to a re-valuation of himself and others. (Laing, 1961, p. 25)

I can still remember, and have described elsewhere (Palmer, 1978), the first occasion in a group when I became aware of 'phantasy' in this way. The members of the group, who came from one factory, were discussing the shortcomings of a chaplain whom they encountered from time to time at work. I suddenly recognized that what they were saying about him, and in particular the feelings they were expressing about him, also expressed very precisely their perceptions of, and relationship to, the colleague to whom I was acting as co-consultant in the group.

At that moment I was like a bewildered rat who accidently treads on a lever and a piece of cheese falls into his cage. I now knew the potentialities of the situation, and though it might be some time before I found the lever again, I was prepared to work for the reward. In my case, however, the reinforcement was intrinsic to the task, not a reward supplied by an external experimenter or teacher. Nor was I obliged to wait for it passively, or search for it haphazardly; however uncertainly and inefficiently, I could begin to manage my own exploration. I suggest that, in many areas of activity, learning a new skill or a new way of looking has this quality, and is quite different experientially from changing one's behaviour through being conditioned. The reader may reflect upon his experience of learning to listen to what there is to be heard in music, or of developing spontaneous proficiency and style in any sport.

Learning to interpret

Our discussion of self-directed learning has necessarily led us into an examination of the processes by which we construe the situations in which we seek to learn from experience. To backtrack for a moment, it will be recalled that, following Bateson, we said:

(1) that Learning I was only possible, and indeed only a meaningful concept, if the learning individual was assumed to construe successive situations as 'the same', so that, say, what I had learned about getting to the office during one rail strike could be used during the next strike;

(2) that individuals are observed, in the course of time, to change the way they construe successive situations, so that they subsequently select their responses from a new range of alternatives (Learning II).

It is now clearer that we should distinguish two elements in the process by which learning is transferred from one context to another. First, there is an automatic learned response to a specific stimulus or pattern of stimuli which acts as what Bateson calls a 'context-marker': it is taken by the individual as a signal that he is now in a situation which is the same as one in which he has experienced pain or arousal. The cat sees a stove, and refuses to sit on it; the group imagines a complex configuration of chairs, and avoids sitting in it; the patient, responding to less obvious context-markers, sees his therapist as like his father and responds accordingly. The capacity to learn in this way is necessary for survival, but, as these examples show, the response is not necessarily functional in the new situation.

Secondly, there may be activity, in imagination or practically, to find out the nature of the correspondences between the new situation and the previous one; or, since the previous one is often forgotten, to assess the degree of match and mismatch between the way the situation was initially and spontaneously construed, and the verifiable features of the new situation. At the risk of overestimating the sophistication of the cat, we may imagine it approaching the next stove warily, ready to recoil but suspecting that all stoves are not hot. The group member may arrive at the tentative conclusion that rearranging chairs does not automatically generate violence, and either experiment with sitting in different places himself, or turn his attention to the capacity of the consultants to discern and demonstrate the meaning of the violent behaviour, which he may suspect is the more basic question. The therapist may seek to mobilize the patient to consider the discrepancies between his expectations of the therapist and how the therapist is actually behaving.

This second operation may not take place. Automatic responses take place in a world where the meaning of context-markers is unequivocal. They may signal imminent danger, but at least the danger and the response required are not in doubt. 'Reality-testing' entails pausing to assess the fittingness of such impulses, and enduring uncertainty about what the context-marker portends, and what therefore the best response may be. In a group there is the additional problem that reality-testing may entail calling in question a shared view of the meaning of the context-marker, and hence jeopardizing one's own good standing in the group, with fantasies of rejection and isolation. Laing has described vividly the difficulty of the schizophrenic individual within the family, in finding a way of testing the validity of the way the world is seen within what he calls the 'nexus of phantasy':

The quality of reality experienced inside the nexus of phantasy is an enchanting spell. Outside, the world seems cold, empty, meaningless, unreal. . . . The way out is via the door. But within the phantasy of the nexus, to leave may be an act of ingratitude, of cruelty, of suicide, or murder. The first steps have to be taken still within the phantasy, before it can be apperceived as such from the outside. Herein is the risk of defeat or madness. (Laing, 1961, p. 24)

We have here arrived in well-trodden territory. The distinction between these two elements in the transfer of learning is related to that drawn by Freud between the pleasure principle (or pleasure–pain principle) and the reality principle, and between primary process and secondary process (Freud, 1958); by Bion, in the group setting, between the types of mental activity associated with the basic assumption group and the work group (Bion, 1961); and by the work of my own institute, between S-activity ('survival-activity') and W-activity ('work-activity') (Reed and Palmer, 1972). As Rycroft (1968, pp. 104 ff.) has pointed out with respect to Freud's concepts, it is false to regard these two types of mental activity as alternatives, or as in conflict in normal functioning. Only under stress, or in neurosis, do automatic responses, rooted in fantasy, obliterate reality-testing and the sophisticated operations of experiment, diagnosis, and interpretation. Both types of mental activity are essential to normal functioning, and under conditions of tolerable stress are inextricably bound together.*

(It is because of the untenable assumptions implicit in the Freudian terminology that we have in the Grubb Institute preferred our own coined terms, and it is these that I propose to use later in this paper.)

At this point we are in a position to reconsider the problem raised by Bateson about the validity of the ways of construing situations learned at the level of Learning II. He points out that a way of punctuating events is in itself no more true or false than a pattern perceived in inkblot. Similarly, if a conference member returns to his organization and begins to perceive the patterns of behaviour identified by Bion (dependence, fight/flight, pairing, or expectancy) in the committee meetings he attends, this may lighten the boredom of committee meetings, but hardly qualifies as knowledge. The meeting is his inkblot. However, if he exposes these private interpretations to testing, by acting upon them and thus, as it were, putting his money on them, he breaks out of a world of purely private meanings. Analysis of what exactly he finds out, and what is the status of that knowledge, would take us into epistemological problems beyond the scope of this paper. Instead I will illustrate the process I have in mind.

During a recent follow-up day to a short course for men and women in education, a schoolteacher described how he had handled an incident in his school. Certain boys had been given the opportunity to decorate a room for Christmas. Another boy, who was not included, had festooned another room with scraps of torn-up newspaper. He was a member of a group of boys well known to the staff, and frequently in trouble. Instead of tackling the boy himself, the master took the group to task, firmly but without rancour, for putting up the boy to express their jealousy of the boys doing the decorations, and leaving him, as in the past, to get into trouble for what he had done. To the master's surprise, apparently, several of the boys acknowledged that this was what they were doing. They accepted that they should tidy up the mess together, and there was a marked improvement in the scapegoat's behaviour.

The teacher who described this incident was a psychologist who had come to the course sceptical about the psychoanalytic approach to the study of group behaviour. It was clear that through the course he had begun to entertain the notion that groups make use of individuals to express the illegitimate wishes of other members, with sufficient conviction for him to be prepared to put the idea to the test in a situation where there was genuine risk if he misread what he was up against. If he continues to test out the idea in this kind of way, we may suppose that he will increase his understanding of the behaviour of groups of boys. This understanding will be capable of being stated in words and, though

*We should also note Peter McKellar's terms A-thinking ('autistic') and R-thinking ('reality') (1968). As his terms imply, he is closer to Freud than to Rycroft or ourselves, in his usage of these terms, since he restricts A-thinking to such phenomena as dreaming, day-dreaming, and hallucinations, and does not take account of the party played by S-activity in normal engagement with reality.

such statements will always be incomplete and provisional, maps of the territory rather than the territory itself, they will if all goes well be increasingly reliable as a basis for action. The same process of learning may contribute to the refinement or criticism of Bion's theory of group behaviour, though this refinement or criticism will not get beyond the teacher's own thinking unless he takes deliberate steps to communicate his conclusions.

The hierarchical promotion of knowledge

We have thus concluded that learning may be a reactive process by which we are conditioned to respond to certain situations in predictable ways; or it may be a proactive process by which we test out the match between our view of situations and what the situation proves to be when we take steps to probe it, in imagination and, more conclusively, in action. Through the latter, more complex, process, we arrive at working hypotheses, theories, and rules of thumb, which are in principle always open to modification in the light of new experience. As Popper (1968) has asserted, the essence of scientific enquiry is the search for the conditions in which current hypotheses break down. Nothing new is learned by repeating tests which confirm existing theories.

Bateson's analysis draws attention to the fact that, for various reasons, our working hypotheses have a tendency to lose this provisional quality and become reified as definitions of what the world is like—and if the facts do not fit, so much the worse for the facts. As we have said, the doctor, the solicitor, and the small group consultant tend, and must inevitably tend, to categorize the situations they encounter, and then to select their respective 'treatment' according to these categories. And there is no doubt that their clients are sensitive to this, resent being bulk-handled, and respond with disproportionate warmth to the representative of any profession who confirms their sense of being a unique individual.

This transformation of provisional judgements into habitual ways of categorizing situations has at least two functions. There is on the one hand a benefit in economy. It is impossible to envisage a mode of human life in which every moment is responded to as a wholly unique occasion. If we could not hand over some of the operations we have to perform to our automatic pilot, we would not be able to give our attention to the tasks which cannot be carried out without conscious attention. The second function is that of fending off fears of helplessness and resourceless dependence. As long as I can construe the situation I am facing as one of a kind with which I am already familiar, I can call upon existing knowledge and skill to deal with it. To the extent that I am faced with having to decide what to do about it from scratch. In small doses this is exciting, but if the dose is too large it may be frightening.

This is described by Main (1966) as follows:

The development of knowledge, concepts, theories and techniques, represents man's attempts at mental mastery of his environment by ego processes. Ego mastery gives a certain kind of pleasure which comes, in part, from the replacement of feelings of helplessness in the face of a mysterious reality by feelings of *power* over it and competence in dealing with it . . . .

He goes on to describe a process, akin to that we are considering here, which he calls the 'hierarchical promotion of ideas'. This is a process by which an idea 'can change its mental residence, moving from the experimental and thinking areas of the ego one generation into the fixed morality areas, the ego ideal and the super-ego, of the next'. The reality principle is replaced by the morality principle. He goes on:

From their early regard as interesting mental tools to be taken up or discarded according to their usefulness for the task in hand, ideas are liable to become, in their passage from one person to another, mere beliefs, sets of never-to-be-questioned, always-to-be-believed rules, which now handicap further thought.

He might have described the same process as it takes place in the course of the career of one individual. It is perhaps this phenomenon which leads to Eliot's pessimism about the value of the knowledge which is gained through experience: he speaks of the wisdom of the 'quiet-voiced elders', which turns out to be:

> ... Only the knowledge of dead secrets
> Useless in the darkness into which they peered
> Or from which they turned their eyes. There is, it seems to us,
> At best, only a limited value
> In the knowledge derived from experience.
> The knowledge imposes a pattern, and falsifies,
> For the pattern is new in every moment
> And every moment is a new and shocking
> Valuation of all we have been. (Eliot, 1963, p. 199)

Learning to revalue experience

Learning to interpret social situations is therefore a more complex and demanding task than, say, learning to interpret a foreign language. In the latter case the meaning of the words is unknown, and has to be discovered. In the former, we do not start with meaningless data, but with data to which we have already attributed meaning, automatically and unconsciously. Learning to interpret is therefore, in this context, learning to unlearn and relearn; or to revalue experience to which we have already ascribed a value. (I use the word 'value' here, since interpreting entails selecting certain data from the total flux of experience and thus ascribing value to them.) The experience is like that of the self-taught pianist or golfer, who is faced with the necessity of developing a more sound technique. His greatest problem is not that he does not know how to play a sonata or strike a ball onto a green and into a hole, but that he does.

The manager who seeks to reappraise the total pattern of his role performance within his institution is faced with a similar problem. So is the staff member in a group relations conference who acts as consultant in a small group, large group, or intergroup session. I shall outline what I see to be the demands of this aspect of his role, with its associations with Learning III.

The essence of the consultant's role is to make contact with the shared fantasy world of the group with which he is working, to experience his own responses as a person to that world, and then to bring into focus and articulate its core assumptions and images. That description, however, misrepresents the demands of the role. He aims to be 'in the world, but not of it', and when he has achieved that psychological stance he may be able to make interpretations which catch hold of what it is like to be a member of the group at that moment, and at the same time enable people to distance themselves from the emotions in which they were until that moment immersed.

This description, however, leaves out the fact that for much of the time the consultant does not sustain that stance. Bion speaks of the 'temporary loss of insight' (1961, p. 149) which prevents the analyst in the therapeutic group from perceiving that he is being asked to play a part in someone else's fantasy. For long periods I feel either alienated from the shared preoccupations of group members, or else caught up with them in automatic attractions and antagonisms, hopes and dreads, without being able to place these in any context. It seems that Mr X just is intolerable, or Mrs Y just is fascinating, but I have no insight into what they symbolize to me. I believe that I am meeting Mr X and Mrs Y as they are in themselves, rather than as the selves which have been activated in this group by its current emotional and practical preoccupations.

At this moment I am faced with the problem of achieving a shift of focus of the Learning III type. My understanding of the situation is no longer provisional and open to testing, but an automatic way of reading it which is out of conscious control. Part of the evidence that this is what has happened is that I am acutely preoccupied with the influence of my own character on the situation. I believe that the state of the group reflects once again my own inveterate jealousy or sadism or sense of omnipotence. But I cannot use this awareness as a lever to extricate myself.

How does the consultant learn to extricate himself? This skill, like others, cannot be taught but only discovered, first almost by chance, then more frequently, then perhaps as a result of deliberate mental gestures. Retrospectively, the maxims through which supervisors, colleagues, and writers on the subject have communicated what they have discovered may be useful in holding onto one's own experience.

Bion (1970), following Freud, has described the discipline of entering each analytic session 'without memory and without desire', and it appears from his accounts of his work that he is actually able to meet a patient or a group without perceiving them as the patient or group he met yesterday. He is therefore able to discover the connection between the behaviour and feelings of today and those of yesterday, without imposing his suppositions about this on the material prematurely. Approaching a group without desire means, among other things, letting go of the sense of responsibility for the usefulness of the session or for what is learned from it.

Probably the most familiar maxim about the consultant role is that the consultant makes contact with his relatedness to the group in fantasy by being alert to his own feelings. To put this another way, we have an immediate awareness of being involved in a social system which we suppress and discount, either habitually or selectively, when we do not like what we are aware of. If we can dwell upon this awareness, we have a clue to the way we have already construed the social situation we are in. The difficulty of knowing and using what one feels may not be apparent to someone unfamiliar with taking this kind of role. At different times I feel elated, angry, impotent, empty, benevolent, attracted, attractive, evil or bored. Often I feel merely dull, to myself and to the group. It is rarely easy to catch hold of the dominant emotion and reflect on its origins. Bowlby (1969, p. 113 ff.) suggests that emotions are the subjective aspect of the 'behavioural systems' which are activated in us at any moment by the situation we perceive ourselves to be in; they indicate the way we have appraised our environment. But in the moment of such feelings I do not wish to doubt why I feel as I do. If I am elated, I already 'know' what I am elated about. If I feel useless, this is just as I always feared and there is nothing to be gained by dwelling on it. Only when I am prepared to contemplate my elation or sense of uselessness here and now as a feature of the subjective life of this group (or a subgroup within it), and not merely of my biography or biochemistry, have I begun to find a foothold outside that subjective life.

Marion Milner (1952) describes various 'gestures' with which she has experimented as means of opening herself to a picture, a view, or a piece of music. There may be similar gestures for making effective contact with the fantasy life of a group. I found that I frequently returned to the staffroom after a session and said with feeling what was really on my mind in the session. I have since sometimes made the gesture of asking myself, during a session, what I would say if I were transported to the staffroom now. Sometimes it works. As Marion Milner also says (1937), these gestures are probably ways of achieving the death of the ego, or of that part of the ego which clings to a fantasy of omnipotent control and knowledge of its world. Perhaps the essence of the learning process we are endeavouring to understand is one of gaining familiarity with the experience of the series of mental states which constitute the Learning III transition. We may come to recognize, however dimly, the feeling of 'reality' which betokens immersion in fantasy; the feeling of inner chaos which is different from pathological confusion and is the conscious mind's way of registering controlled engagement in primary process thinking or S-activity (cf. Milner, 1969, pp. 248–256); the sense of revelation, wholeness, and security which accompanies the crystallization of insight into the group situation; and the feelings of letdown, anger, and mourning which follow when it becomes evident, as sooner or later it must, that the insight, even if it explains a lot, is incomplete, partially articulated, and subject to revision. These states have been mapped by Ehrenzweig (1970), Jaques (1970), Bion (1970), Reed (in preparation) and others. As we gain familiarity with the mental 'territories' represented by these maps, we are less likely to lose our way in them, or withdraw in panic. As Orpheus discovered, however, we may succeed in descending into the underworld and returning to the light, without necessarily bringing with us the loved object we went to find.

Eliot draws upon the mystical writers for his account of what is entailed in escaping from the falsifying patterns imposed upon reality by past learning. He conveys something of the paradoxical nature of the Learning III transition:

> In order to arrive at what you do not know
>   You must go by a way which is the way of ignorance.
> In order to possess what you do not possess
>   You must go by the way of dispossession.
> In order to arrive at what you are not
>   You must go through the way in which you are not.
> And what you do not know is the only thing you know.... (Eliot, 1963, p. 201)

A tentative model

In conclusion, I wish to put together into a tentative model the key ideas which have been discussed in this analysis. This model incorporates the three levels of learning identified by Bateson, and also the distinction between reactive and proactive learning, conditioning, and self-directed learning, which it has seemed necessary to draw in describing what happens in group relations activities. I would now wish to distinguish between the following processes.

(1) Processes by which the individual evolves responses through which he reduces the tension between himself and his environment, reducing anxiety, excitement, or pain and recovering stability. One example is the process by which the individual participates in basic assumption activity in a group, which, in Bion's words, 'requires no training, experience or mental development. It is instantaneous, inevitable, and instinctive' (1961, p. 153). These are processes in which S-activity is dominant. W-activity is suppressed or dissociated; it may, for example, supply rationalizations for actions triggered by quite other motivating ideas. They comprise both learning to punctuate experience into specific contexts (Learning II), and learning to respond to these contexts in specific ways (Learning I). The products of such learning are conditioned responses, corresponding under at least some conditions to fixed beliefs and fantasies; they are 'soldered in'. Such learning might be referred to as *learning for survival*.

(2) Processes of observation, experiment, appraisal, and interpretation, through which the individual tests the match between his existing patterns of behaviour and the maps of the environment implied by them, and available indicators of the actual state of the environment. They are processes in which W-activity is dominant, monitoring and harnessing the responses of S-activity. They also comprise both Learning I and Learning II. The products of such learning are flexible patterns of activity, based on provisional hypotheses, interpretations, and forms of organization. Such learning might be referred to as *learning for development*.

The word 'training', whether applied to animals, children, or adults, might be most usefully reserved for activities directed predominantly towards learning for survival. Training, so understood, is designed to inculcate prescribed responses and prescribed ways of construing the world. As such it is an essential element in social life. Learning for development is essentially a self-directed process. This is why statements of aim and task, in the group relations conferences, refer not to teaching or training but to 'providing opportunities for learning'. It is also what Ezra Pound (1951, p. 84) was getting at when he wrote: 'Real education must ultimately be limited to men who INSIST on knowing, the rest is mere sheep-herding.'

The paper by Main discussed earlier highlights the fact that the products of learning for development do not necessarily remain flexible and open to revision. Even those who insist on knowing do not always insist on the provisional nature of their conclusions, and they cannot insist that their disciples regard them in this way. Through hierarchical promotion they are institutionalized and eventually soldered in. We should perhaps distinguish between the fantasies which are installed through learning for survival, and the beliefs which are installed through this extended process; but the consequences appear to be in many ways the same.

This brings into view a third type of process, described by Bateson and referred to as Learning III:

(3) These processes are those by which habitual responses, and the unconscious fantasies and beliefs on which they are based, are brought back within the domain of conscious scrutiny and criticism, and revalued. This is a reflexive activity: W-activity is brought to bear upon the operations of the ego itself. It is thus to be distinguished from learning for development, which knows the difference between reality and fantasy, but does not know that it makes this distinction, and does not need to. This type of learning, as we have seen, is, when the fantasy or belief is strongly held, revolutionary. It involves 'catastrophic change' (Bion, 1965), 'positive disintegration' (Dabrowski, source unknown). Its products are not specific patterns of behaviour, but modifications in the personality itself, either as a whole or with respect to particular roles. Bateson refers to 'a greater flexibility in the premises acquired by Learning II— a *freedom* from their bondage' (1973, p. 275, his italics). It is fitting that he should have the last word.

References

Back, K. W. (1973) 'The experiential group and society', *Journal of Applied Behavioural Science*, **9**, 1, 7ff.

Bateson, G. (1973) *Steps to an Ecology of Mind*. St Albans, Herts.: Paladin.

Bion, W. R. (1961) *Experiences in Groups*. London: Tavistock Publications.

Bion, W. R. (1962) *Learning from Experience*. London: Heinemann.

Bion, W. R. (1963) *Elements of Psychoanalysis*. London: Heinemann.

Bion, W. R. (1965) *Transformations*. London: Heinemann.

Bion, W. R. (1970) *Attention and Interpretation*. London: Tavistock Publications.

Bowlby, J. (1969) *Attachment and Loss*, vol. 1, *Attachment*. London: Hogarth Press and Institute of Psycho-Analysis.

Colman, A. D., and Bexton, W. H. (eds) (1975), *Group Relations Reader*. London: A. K. Rice Institute.

Ehrenzweig, A. (1970) *The Hidden Order of Art*. St Albans, Herts.: Paladin (first published 1967).

Eliot, T. S. (1963) 'East Coker'. In *Collected Poems, 1909–1962*. London: Faber (first published 1936).

Ezriel, H. (1950) 'A psychoanalytic approach to group treatment'. *British Journal of Medical Psychology*, **23**, 59.

Freud, S. (1958) *Formulations on the Two Principles of Mental Functioning*. Standard Edition, vol. 12, London: Hogarth Press and Institute of Psycho-Analysis (first published 1911).

Hudson, L. (1972) *The Cult of the Fact*. London: Cape (paperback 1976).

Hudson, L. (1975) *Human Beings*. London: Cape.

Jaques, E. (1970) *Work, Creativity and Social Justice*. London: Heinemann.

Laing, R. D. (1961) *The Self and Others*. London: Tavistock Publications.

McKellar, P. (1968) *Experience and Behavior*. Harmondsworth: Penguin.

Main, T. F. (1966) 'Knowledge, learning and freedom from thought'. Academic address to Australia/New Zealand Annual Congress (unpublished).

Mant, A. (1976) 'How to analyse management'. *Management Today*.

Milgram, S. (1963) 'Behavioral study of obedience'. *Journal of Abnormal and Social Psychology*, **67**, 4, 371–378. In R. H. Walters, J. A. Cheyne, and R. K. Banks (eds) (1972) *Punishment*. Harmondsworth: Penguin.

Miller, E. J. (ed.) (1976a) *Task and Organization*, London and New York: Wiley.

Miller, E. J. (1976b) Notes on design of working conference entitled 'Authority, leadership and organization (unpublished).

Milner, M. (1937) *An Experiment with Leisure* (pseudonym 'Joanna Field'). London: Chatto & Windus.

Milner, M. (1952) *A Life of One's Own* (pseudonym 'Joanna Field'). Harmondsworth: Penguin (first published 1934).

Milner, M. (1969) *The Hands of the Living God*. London: Hogarth Press and Institute of Psycho-Analysis.

Palmer, B. W. M. (1978) 'Fantasy and reality in group life: A model for learning by experience'. In N. McCaughan (ed.) *Group Work: Learning and Practice*. London: George Allen & Unwin.

Polanyi, M. (1973) *Personal Knowledge*. London: Routledge & Kegan Paul (first published 1958).

Popper, K. (1968) *The Logic of Scientific Discovery*. London: Hutchinson (first published 1934).

Pound, E. (1951) *ABC of Reading*. London: Faber.

Reed, B. D. (1976) 'Organizational role analysis'. In C. L. Cooper (ed.) *Developing Social Skills in Managers*. London: Macmillan.

Reed, B. D. (in preparation) *The Dynamics of the Local Church*.

Reed, B. D., and Palmer, B. W. M. (1972) *Introduction to Organizational Behaviour*. London: Grubb Institute (duplicated lectures).

Rice, A. K. (1964) *Learning for Leadership*. London: Tavistock Publications.

Rioch, M. J. (1970) 'Group relations: Rationale and techniques'. *International Journal of Group Psychotherapy*, **20**, 340–355.

Rioch, M. J. (1977) 'The A. K. Rice Group Relations Conference as a reflection of society'. *Journal of Personality and Social Systems*, **1**, 1, 1–16.

Rycroft, C. (1968) 'Beyond the reality principle'. In *Imagination and Reality*. London: Hogarth Press and Institute of Psycho-Analysis.

Strachey, J. (1934) 'The nature of the therapeutic action of psycho-analysis'. *International Journal of Psycho-Analysis*, **15**, 127ff. (reprinted **50**, 275ff.).

Trist, E. L., and Soffer, C. (1959) *Explorations in Group Relations*. Leicester University Press.

Watts, A. W. (1962) *The Way of Zen*. Harmondsworth: Penguin.

Watts, A. W. (1973) *Nature, Man and Woman*. London: Wildwood House (first published in Great Britain 1958).

Whitehead, A. N., and Russell, B. (1910) *Principia Mathematica*. Cambridge University Press.

Chapter 13

Darkness

John Broadbent

I offer some literary parallels to group phenomena. People in groups often say, 'It's not like that—we're not sitting in that order'; 'He didn't say that; or, if he did, it doesn't mean anything'. Yet the characters of high literature manifestly do sit like that and say things like that—very odd actions and speeches occur; and the artist must intend some meaning. What's more, these events are usually felt to be, as a whole, true to life. So my thesis is that as the artist stands to life so the interpretation stands to the group.

I was in a recent meeting of a mutual consultation group. Pierre Turquet had been its initiating consultant at the Leicester University's conference in 1973. Something like this passage occurred:

A. It's stifling.
B. Somebody ought to start getting us out of it.
C. It can't be me because it would mean going into the dark and that's dangerous.
D. When you said 'going into the dark' you were gazing at the table in the middle of us. Isn't the dark the task?

Heart of Darkness

Marlow

I was at the time teaching a freshman course in literature which included Conrad's short novel, *Heart of Darkness*. Conrad has the story told by Marlow, the blunt, puritanical skipper who survives several of these tales with characterless heroism. Marlow—Mr Moral?—might be seen, in terms of Tavistock conferences, as the novitiate who has the experience but never changes; or as the manager who manages his task or his role as if he himself were not involved.

In need of a job, Marlow is introduced by three women to a company, based in Brussels, that is exploiting the Belgian Congo. Historically there was such a company; and Belgium exploited the Congo with notorious rapacity until the rebellion of 1959–1960. The events of fiction are drawn from history; but they are an unreliable chronicle. In a conference, in the life of any institution, people behave in ways that reflects, or refract, the world outside.

The women who help Marlow get his job are also, of course, urging him towards the darkness. They are two secretaries, and an aunt—infinitely respectable in black dresses but presented as Fates, *tricoteuses*, midwives, implacable administrators, destructive do-gooders. The company doctor, on the other hand, tries to restrain Marlow. He thinks the experience will send him mad; he forecasts changes that will 'take place inside, you know': the friend warning one against experiential learning. In 1890 Conrad, not yet a novelist, still in the merchant navy, was given the job of piloting a steamer on the upper Congo. This is the job that Marlow gets. His journey is divided into three phases by the Company Station near the river mouth; the Central Station 200 miles upriver; and, 800 miles further into the interior, the Inner Station. We may see these as stations of the cross on a journey past 'falls' back to the beginning of the world; or back to the primordial in oneself under analysis perhaps; or as stages in the membership of an institution, a marriage, the life of a group. Conrad's language allows us to move among these possibilities in parallel:

We penetrated deeper and deeper into the heart of darkness. It was very quiet there.... We were wanderers on prehistoric earth.... We could have fancied ourselves the first of men taking possession of an accursed inheritance, to be subdued at the cost of profound anguish and of excessive toil.... We could not understand because we were too far and could not remember....

A major theme in the story is the splitting of utilitarian commercialism on the one hand from surrender to chaos on the other. Both are evil. The administrators in Brussels are presented as efficient but, in their mahogany and black wool, there is a savage darkness. Now as Marlow penetrates Africa he finds the managers and clerks and accountants of the Congo stations efficient too, but heartless, without entrails, 'making correct entries of perfectly correct transactions'. They are models of one response to threat and change. The manager defends himself by being 'sealed'; he will not admit stimuli, nor express himself. The accountant is obsessional. They are 'hollow men' who won't dare the dark. T. S. Eliot used a quotation from *Heart of Darkness* as epigraph for his poem, *The Hollow Men*, published 20 years later: 'Mistah Kurtz, he dead'. Most of us, says Marlow, are carefully hollow too, 'stepping delicately between the butcher and the policeman, in the holy terror of scandal and gallows and lunatic asylums'. He congratulates himself on having 'at least a choice of nightmares' between butcher and policeman. He seems to suppose that no one can embrace both: if you choose civilization you must ignore the savagery behind it, pretend it isn't there—'breathe dead hippo, so to speak, and not be contaminated' (some cannibal sailors eat rotting hippomeat *faûte de mieux*). You must pretend, even though all the signs in the story are that civilization is just as dark as savagery. On the other hand, if you choose savagery it seems from the story that you can't carry anything civil into it; and you won't come back.

Some kind of middle line is taken by the plain, practical men in the story—boilermakers, navigators, people like Marlow himself who just get on with the job. But they steer so carefully central a course that they blinker out the problems on either side. They are at least in the middle of the river, getting wet—here I think of doctors, higher civil servants, social workers with their 'skills',

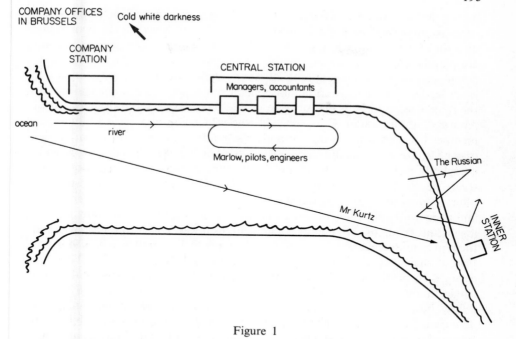

Figure 1

the helpful facilitators; but they are only, so to speak, the pilots and engineers trafficking up and down the river uncommitted to either end, and claiming a spurious independence of the commercials. It looks something like Figure 1.

Another response is embodied in a Russian dressed in patchwork who wanders like a Quixote of the jungle playing at exploration. His is the hippy solution, to accoutre himself with the castoffs of civilization, including an ancient textbook of navigation—a sort of *I Ching*. He plays with the wild and dark; he does not face it. He is the pseudo-Kurtz, the group maverick, the itinerant jester of the institutional event carrying the brochure, the party manifesto, the university calendar, from room to room.

Kurtz

The only person who does face the issue is Mr Kurtz. He is a brilliant entrepreneur but also 'chief of the Inner Station': manager and analyst combined. He lives and works at the Inner Station, with a black concubine and an entourage of cannibals; his garden fence is decorated with shrunk heads; he is known to engage in 'unspeakable rites' which, if spoken, would presumably be cannibalism and sexual orgy (*blow-up*, *blow-out*, blow-job, etc.).

The German word *kurtz* means short, but Mr Kurtz is abnormally tall: he is, so to speak, the long and the short of it. The managers lower down the river fear and conspire against him as a rival: he is astoundingly successful at acquiring ivory, he is notably efficient, he seems to be of a different class from them;

he may one day become general manager of the company and then woe betide them in their paltriness. So from one point of view Kurtz is the conference director in whom all meaning resides, all poles are reconciled; the staff group are plainly jealous of him but he may horrifyingly turn out to be one's own employer. From another point of view again, he is the alternative or rebel leader, for there is an actual general manager at the other end of the river, as it were, in Brussels; or is he in that case the dark-but-desired side of Ahura–Mazdah, Satan–God, the split leader? Or you may regard him as the member who is a work leader: nobody else really does very much; but in that case he is only superficially leading the work, for the effect he has is to provide everybody else with the mere fantasy that they could be like that too if they tried: he elicits hatred, and worship, not collaboration. In that respect he offers a basis for criticizing consultancy that pulls in strong transference and ambivalence. Even when you step outside the story and consider how readers (as distinct from his own members and staff, as it were) react to Kurtz, you find them in a muddle which often leads them to just throw up their hands in irritation at their own circling ambivalence—as my students and I did. They are easily then prevailed on by a no-nonsense leader such as a critic with but a single thought. Indeed, students tend to react to Kurtz moralistically: poor fellow, he should have been more careful not to get involved in those unspeakable rites. This comes of being taught for years that King Lear's trouble lay in being a bit peppery, and Macbeth's in ambition—nothing to do with *our* father or *our* daughter and what we feel about them, or with 'the affliction of these terrible dreams that shake *us* nightly'. Occasionally we have an educational experience that leads us on to the heath *with* Lear; or in a conference we really do experience what we feel about authority; how can these occasions survive the context in which they occur, the river's commerce? I doubt if they can; or, if they can, only by our providing more effective opportunities for implementation. But society affords mainly negative reinforcement for experiential learning: the textbook answer does get good marks, 'respect for authority' wins promotion.

What there can be no doubt about, though, is Kurtz's power. We might simplify our reading of him by saying that he shows us what we fear and what we adore in power, whether our own or others. It turns out not to be the efficiency, the profitability, or even the authority, so much as virility and expressiveness. Kurtz wields authority: he is described as king, idol, god; he is the company's agent in the darkness, the consultant in a distant room. But it is more important that he looks like a piece of ivory himself (for when Marlow reaches him he is already dying). He is then the omnipotent erection that survives the death of the elephant, the director's fantasied virility holding firm on our behalf. He is also a master of articulacy:

The man presented himself as a voice . . . of all his gifts the one that stood out preeminently, that carried with it a sense of real presence, was his ability to talk, his words—the gift of expression, the bewildering, the illuminating, the most exalted and the most contemptible, the pulsating stream of light, or the deceitful flow from the heart of an impenetrable darkness.

Witch and angel

The last clause provides him with menstrual flux, and leads us into another avatar of Kurtz: he is the only man in the story who has any trace of femininity in him; and the only person to have a sexual partner. Indeed he has two: his fiancée, whom he calls his 'Intended', back in Brussels; and his black concubine or witch at the Inner Station. Here again the interpretations proliferate embarrassingly. We have the figure of authority in the staffroom or the boardroom with his wife back home and his secretary here—but unable, in this story, to mobilize the others' sexuality. Kurtz has paired with 'the colossal body of . . . fecund and mysterious life': she is explicitly 'the image' of the jungle itself—implying that only through pairing can the task be done? or that the group/conference/institution is a womb to be impregnated by the leader? She is savagely virile, bedecked in metal rings and helmetlike hair (as Conrad's women often are): she, too, enjoys sexual ambivalence. Yet the urban Intended, with whom Kurtz has also paired, is a woman of pale-faced, muffled passivity, her hair an 'ashy halo'. Except that she looks rather like a gaslamp, the Intended is in no sense masculine.

Conrad lends himself to psychoanalytical interpretation: Kaplan and Kloss (1973) on *The Nigger of the 'Narcissus'* is best. And indeed it is easy enough at the level of individual psychology to see in these two women Freud's sensual and tender, which Kurtz has dissociated; but so far as we read Kurtz in group and institutional terms, what are we to think? What links the two women is death. When Marlow arrives at the Inner Station, Kurtz is already dying. Marlow, by his own lights, rescues Kurtz from the heart of darkness, carries him away downriver. As he steams off, the witch stages her grief on the bank with outstretched arms. But Kurtz soon dies on board. His last words are, 'The horror! the horror!' They bury him 'in a muddy hole'. When Marlow gets back to Brussels he breaks the news to the Intended. She grieves with an identical stretching of arms; but she is cheered because Marlow lies to her and says that Kurtz's last word was her name. What that is, the reader never knows. Let me offer a series of interpretations.

Interpretations

(1) First a pair of dismissive interpretations: either Kurtz himself is at fault in seeking his own soul, so he lost it; or Kurtz is merely our fantasy of what we would do if we sought our own souls—but we shan't. (The letter K, or X, recurs in ambivalent projections: see Kafka, and the sado-masochist Kai-Cay of Katy in Schneck (1965).)

(2) It is a case of pairing that is barren because it is basic assumption pairing, not workful. The pair are defied, seemingly omnipotent; Kurtz is voracious, he swallows the world. All others are impotent; they await the birth of the work from Kurtz and the witch. Marlow the midwife starts back down the birth canal to bring Kurtz into the world but the process is interrupted: Kurtz is not reborn

but suppressed back into the commercial anality of the muddy hole. Kurtz falls short. Marlow says that Kurtz, too, is 'hollow at the core'. He is not at all hollow in the way that the lower managers were; it can only mean that he is a voided tusk, an avoided task. Shifting about between the tale and its group avatar, I suggest that the pairing fails to work because it is not raised to consciousness but kept secret. We see the black concubine, we hear the words 'The horror!', but we never meet the horror or know what the rites were, just as we never know the name of either woman: each then is a fantasy, not a person. Even the witch's sexuality is all displaced on to metaphors used to describe other things—'brooding ... fringed draperies ... bared arms ... rigid'. Kurtz is said to have been able 'to penetrate all the hearts that beat in the darkness' and the story is full of metaphorical invasions but no actual coition occurs.

(3) That leads to a third field of interpretation, the disabling effect of the system as a whole. Of course there *is* invasion, all the time, but it is an imperialist, exploitative invasion of the Congo, rather than a piercing to the heart of darkness. Perhaps colonialism renders its beneficiaries impotent—as its victims suppose when blacks sneer at white sexuality; indeed it is one of the white beneficiaries' fantasies about themselves. With European imperialism at its height *c.* 1890, literature was populated by restless, angry women—Isben's Nora and Hedda Gabler, Froken Julie, Hardy's Tess and Sue, the heroines of *Howards End* and *Passage to India* who hear the darkness. Lowering the scale we note that both Kurtz's women are deprived of any share in management. The Intended lives in Brussels but she is quite separate from the *un*intended women who get Marlow the job. There is a confusing subplot about company secrets which ends in a manager actually stealing Kurtz's private papers from the Intended. She must be preserved intact. Sex and love must be kept apart; so must eros and work.

(4) Elaborating from there we can say that Marlow betrays Kurtz's achievement. Kurtz aims at the task: he tries to 'manage' the heart of darkness intimately instead of at an exploiting distance; he tries to marry the black concubine as well as the Belgian fiancée—sensuous and tender; he extracts the firm, white, potent order of ivory from the fecund chaos of the jungle. But moral Marlow pulls him back, aborts his task. In conference terms, Marlow is here a flight leader. He is the agent, however innocent he may claim to be, of the other kind of management: ultimately, of the whole system in which they live. It is capitalist imperialism but it could be any kind of total materialism. The system forbids self-development: 'there was nothing exactly profitable', Marlow notes, in cannibalism. Marlow also betrays himself. His return across the boundary into daily life is slow and painful:

A period of time which I remember mistily, with a shuddering wonder, like a passage through some inconceivable world that had no hope in it and no desire. I found myself back in the sepulchral city resenting the sight of people hurrying through the streets to filch a little money from each other .... They were intruders whose knowledge of life was to me an irritating pretence, because I felt so sure they could not possibly know the things I knew.

Yet he lies to the Intended about Kurtz's last words: not horror, but her name. In some sense she must as the Intended be the task; yet he lies, denying to her both his own learning, and what she might have learned. Here the collusion between commercial and sexual tyranny clarifies sharply: with the excuse of trade secrets she is denied Kurtz's papers; with the excuse of kindness she is denied Kurtz's horror. She is doubly castrated, of her potential roles both as manager and as sexual being. She is pushed back into the literal innocence of her self. Students tend not to see it like that: they accept Marlow's motive as 'caring' (their word); it would break her up to know the truth. The students are themselves victims, along with Kurtz and the Intended, of Marlow's priggish meddling; it is Marlow, agent of the state, who teaches them how to avoid Macbeth's nightmares and Kurtz's passion; but who provides them at the same time with certificates and degrees. It is in real life as though the choice truly lay between material growth, or spiritual growth: one is the price of the other, they claim. As we dismantle the physical provisions of the welfare state, we make no move to unfetter minds.

The best critics, such as Leavis (1948), accuse Conrad of being misty at the centre, not articulating the horror, the darkness, not extricating himself from a boyish fantasy. But perhaps that is Conrad's point, whether he knew it or not; that the failed or betrayed task is as near as we can get within our system to a goal? Halfway through the story Marlow says: 'It is impossible to convey the life-sensation of any given epoch of one's existence—its subtle and penetrating essence. It is impossible. We live, as we dream—alone.'

Conrad himself says of Marlow, as a narrator, that 'to him the meaning of an episode was not inside like a kernel but outside, enveloping the tale which brought it out as a glow brings out a haze, in the likeness of one of those misty halos that sometimes are made visible by the spectral illumination of moon-shine'.

Those statements do not excuse his mistiness as a writer but they do sum up a difficulty that members have in a here-and-now group; and the difficulty of implementing conference experience. They also suggest something of the nature of interpretative remarks: that meaning is already latent among people, and may merely be brought out, made manifest, by the flow of the telling, the interpreting; yet all the interpreter's glow can do is reveal the meaning as hazy: and what he says may be moonshine.

Ocean and aquarium

I shall offer two other cases, more briefly, where the experiences of literature and of groups entwine. The first concerns the way in which a group experiences literature. During the course in which we were studying *Heart of Darkness*, we also read some American poetry. We focused on two difficult modern poems, 'The Idea of Order at Key West' by Wallace Stevens and 'For the Union Dead' by Robert Lowell. They relate to each other and to Conrad something as is shown in Table 1. I was not concerned consciously with those structures but

Table 1

	Conrad	Stevens	Lowell
Symbolizations of order:	Marlow, craft	Idea, art (a girl singing on the beach)	The glass boundaries of an aquarium in Boston, now destroyed; art
Symbolizations of disorder:	Jungle, black people, heart of darkness	Ocean	Released fish, which are mirrored in the radiators of cars driven by black people
Environment:	River	Beach	City, with aquarium site being excavated as a car park

merely with getting the students to see what it is to read a poem concretely, to 'realize' it fully; and how when it is read that way—brought into the here and now, so to speak—and only then, it will reveal itself as a statement of the poet's deepest self, as an apperception of the universe.

On the beach at Key West there are a poet, a foreign critic, and a girl whose singing counterpoints the waves' crash:

> She was the single artificer of the world
> In which she sang. And when she sang, the sea,
> Whatever self it had, became the self
> That was her song, for she was the maker.

We got stuck at first base because the students would not even envisage the scene and the characters, so I turned on one of them and pretended to be a coastguard suspicious of his behaviour: 'I saw you down there with that foreign fellow and a young lady with no clothes on yelling her head off.' The student tried to explain: the critic and the girl joined in. When we got back to the police station I interrogated the ghost of Wallace Stevens on, in effect, the *structure* of the poem (why a marginal environment, why two men and a girl, why song and sea, etc.); and at the same time on his *sensibility* ('But officer, I was down there trying to integrate my ideas of order with my experience of chaos!').

How quickly that interlude got us moving—the little burst of fantasy, the donning of roles, the playing out of my professorial authority in terms of coastguard and policeman, the students taking on the creativity, becoming the poem's trinity and so on. None of that emerged at the time but what I'm proffering is a model for what may sometimes be available between consultant and group.

After coffee we returned to the other poem. It starts with Lowell's persona remembering his childhood, gazing at the aquarium tanks, which are ruined and dry:

Once my nose crawled like a snail on the glass;
my hand tingled
to burst the bubbles
drifted from the noses of the cowed, compliant fish.

A student turned to me and said, 'Now Mr Lowell, why don't you just lie back and tell me a little more about your childhood? How you felt about fishes, for instance? And did you have a black nanny?' I took my dose of analysis and we rapidly 'solved' the poem together at a level more sophisticated and more succinct than any published versions that I know of. Role reversal took the students into consultancy and hence into interpretation.

The Blacks: A Clown Show

My final example is Jean Genet's play, *Les Nègres: clownerie*. It comprises three groups: Audience, Blacks, Court. The Audience is specified: they must be white, or at the very least blacks disguised as whites. In other words, the economic basis of this institution is that the ruling class of the society it exists in as the ultimate employer, perhaps the consumer of both members and staff, Blacks and Court. Whatever we say in the conference, the university, the church, that institution is owned by our rulers. Blacks occupy the main part of the stage; they can be regarded as the members of a Tavistock conference, the social workers of a local authority. They are real black actors dressed up as parodies of the way whites see blacks—nigger minstrels. 'On the stage', one of them says, 'we are what they want us to be.' The Court occupy an upper stage at the rear. They, too, are black actors, but dressed up as parodies of the way blacks see whites—white masks, beaky noses, stiff uniforms, all role and no body. The staff of an institution, the County Council's committee for social services, are workers in disguise? Blacks and Court are also to some degree mirrors of each other:

Blacks	*Court*
'Queen' Felicity	The Queen
Diouf, a transvestite minister who later mimes the part of White Mother	The Missionary, later castrated
and so on	Governor-General
	Judge
	Valet

There are three salient events. First, the Blacks mime the rape and murder of a white woman. They do this to 'deserve the reprobation' of the Whites—to live down to their reputation. They have violence and extreme sexuality projected on to them—and enact it. Second, the Court sets out on a punitive expedition. They leave behind them a set of dolls, mannikins of themselves, on the upper stage. This is a fascinating version of the power of merely symbolic, disembo-died government; and of 'management in the mind'—management as fantasied when it cannot be seen: it is fantasied as puppets. During the trek they parody their own leadership roles as irremediably neurotic. The Judge is an obses-sional. The Governor-General cries out speeches such as, 'Tar and feathers, died like a rat, died like a dog, dyed in the wool, died in battle, hit the bottle, died in bed, cock-o'-the-walk. Hemlock'—authority by verbal tradition merely, the consultant in glossolalia. 'Madame,' he says later to the Queen, 'derrière vous, la jungle s'est refermée.' The Queen is frightened: 'Mais, nous sommes bien en France?' No: they have gone into the heart of darkness.

Thirdly, they confront the Blacks. At this culmination of the institutional event the Blacks seize power and kill the Court one by one. The reversal of power is triggered by the sound of gunfire offstage. News is brought that it marked the execution of a black traitor, in real life; so the Court take off their white masks for this section and join in with the others to discuss the real offstage issue: that is, that they are taking responsibility for their own blood, their own justice—their own group. Then they remask as the white Court, are judged, and executed.

J. P. Ward's brilliant essay (1974) on parallels between experiential learning and the drama of the absurd does not deal with Genet, who belongs rather to the theatre of cruelty. Parallels glare, yet I am left unsure how to relate my reading of *The Blacks* either to conference experience, or to experience of other institu-tions. Part of the confusion comes, I think, from Genet himself fudging the idea of role with his atavistic masks. The masks blur the difference between stereo-type—mere parody—and performance in a task-directed role. Another part of the confusion comes from trying to learn from a play what can only be learned from participation in an experienced event. This brings the theatre under Plato's condemnation, that it is a way of not working in reality but only of watching its imitation. You do not have to explore the boundary round your-self when they are doing it for you up there on the stage.

What provisionally I sense most strongly is the way the play as a whole relates to what is outside it. When the news is brought of the traitor's execution, and the entire cast, unmasked, engage in discussion, we have the model of an institution whose boundary has been breached in a way that has value for its members: they become more 'true', more united. It is a model obviously of the effect of war on a society or an institution. It suggests to me also the value in, say, a learning conference, or a university, or a factory, of built-in and regular opportunities for exploring the external boundary, for thinking about the relationship between external and internal roles, for considering the function of this institution in society at large or in the local community: that is, for studying the possible implementation and hence the meaningfulness of one's work. Then one ceases to be a cog, a black.

References

Conrad, Joseph (1897) *The Nigger of the 'Narcissus'*. London: Heinemann.
Conrad, Joseph (1902) *Heart of Darkness*. London: Blackwood.

Genet, Jean (1959) *Les Nègres: clownerie* performed. Published (1963) Marc Barbezat. Trans. Bernard Frechtman (1960) as *The Blacks*, London: Faber.

Kaplan, Morton, and Kloss, Robert (1973) *The Unspoken Motive: A Guide to Psychoanalytic Literary Criticism*. New York: Free Press.

Leavis, F. R. (1948) *The Great Tradition*. London: Chatto.

Meyer, Bernard C. (1967) *Joseph Conrad: A Psychoanalytical Biography*. Princeton University Press.

Schneck, Stephen (1965) *The Nightclerk*. London: Weidenfeld & Nicolson.

Ward, J. P. (1974) 'The T-group: authority and the consequences'. *Encounter*, **XLII**, 3, 30–40.

Chapter **14**

The Psychology of Innovation in an Industrial Setting

James C. Miller

The research reported on in this paper is the result of an interdisciplinary project of six social scientists* who shared an interest in organizations, but who differed widely in their theoretical orientations and their approach to organizational consultation. We acted as consultants to a small, innovative, technologically based factory in a middle-sized community in upstate New York. For those of us more familiar with governmental, education, and mental health institutions, it provided an opportunity to contrast the unclarities and uncertainties which characterize these systems with a greater potential for articulation and direction in a relatively isolated industrial operation. For those of us more familiar with business consultation, it presented an opportunity to study a small industrial unit in a larger corporate enterprise which was relatively distant from corporate management, and thus from the usual kinds of corporate training enterprises.

The plant was presented to us as a success story within the larger corporate organization. Since for most industrial organizations the primary task revolves, in one way or another, around making a profit, we doubted that the plant would have been presented to us as a success had it not been an economic success. As we learned more, we discovered that indeed by most standards it was an economic success, having developed production technologies that allowed the product to be produced at a lower cost than at other, similar plants without lowering the socio-economic status of its workers compared with those employed at other plants in the area. Moreover, it became clear that the plant was seen as a success in still another way. Labour–management relations were seen as having been maintained at a consistently high level of collaboration and satisfaction from the inception of the plant down to the present, such that turnover and absenteeism were low, job satisfaction was high, and workers generally saw it as possible to 'progress' within the system. To put it another way, the 'quality of life' within the organization was seen as more than acceptable, and as setting a standard for the corporate organization.

One possibility was that somehow, in contrast to the organizations with which we were more familiar, this organization seemed to have successfully utilized social, structural, and emotional factors in the service of the task that in other settings were disruptive of the task. Thus, while the usual difficulties in clarifying

*C. P. Alderfer, B. A. Astrachan, P. Bowers, A. Fitz, E. B. Klein, and J. C. Miller.

and achieving the primary task of human service organizations make them a valuable source for the study of task-disruptive structures and processes, this system seemed equally valuable as an object for study where the primary mandated task was in fact being effectively accomplished, and organizational structures and processes were apparently being effectively related to it. It seemed intriguing to try to find out if some of the organizational conflicts and deficiencies with which we were familiar were present in this organization, but had a different life history, i.e. were often channelled in the service of work.

The overall hypothesis is that innovative organizations frequently originate out of conflicts among organizational tasks or structures in established settings. If the innovators develop adequate techniques for changing the situation that they are mandated to change, they will be viable and will survive. The organizational settings from which they develop are usually identified as 'traditional' ways of dealing with problems, and are thought by the managers of innovative organizations to be inadequate. Thus, one of the first tasks of a new organization is to identify itself in some special way, either consciously or unconsciously. This implies a psychological constellation both in relating the organization to the outside world and in establishing structures and processes internal to the organization. The allegedly 'new' ways of doing things may relate to the development of new technology, new social and organizational arrangements concerning work, or whatever. Part of the psychology of such a venture will be to harness shared social fantasies around the nature of this 'new' work. We have elsewhere called the constellation of fantasies concerning innovation *utopian* fantasies (Miller *et al.*, 1977). The organizers of such a venture are not likely to see themselves as establishing just another plant, but to see it as an improvement on all existing arrangements and a primary source of hope for the future (Miller *et al.*, 1977).

Social defences

Decisions concerning role and skill discriminations for employees are central to the functioning of any organization. Such discriminations are always difficult because they involve evaluation and change for both the system and the individual. They are made even more difficult, however, by their tendency to arouse anxiety and fantasies of still greater, more fundamental personal change. The implications of group membership appear to be such that they tend to evoke a central fantasy: that of total care of abandonment, or total fusion or separation. Since one's livelihood usually depends on a stable relationship to one type of group or organization, work systems provide adequate reality to collude with such fantasies. The anxiety or guilt aroused by potential or actual change must be dealt with by the individual or by the system.

Social systems, as well as the individuals within them, normally have a wide variety of structures to rely upon in limiting anxiety and guilt (Jacques, 1955). The more common ones involve the pursuit, achievement, and maintenance of other values in viable group and intergroup structures. A group or a system, out of a threat to its members' well-being, may employ a variety of social defences as a means of dealing with conflict, anxiety, and guilt. In natural settings, it is often difficult to separate out relatively conflict-free functioning in the pursuit of values as opposed to system-defensive conflict resolution. Examples are given by Menzies (1970) in her analysis of hospital nursing practices. Nursing duties frequently involve anxiety-arousing situations. They require constant contact with physically diseased or injured persons who are frequently in pain, unable to care for themselves, and often in imminent danger of dying. There can be many conflicting feelings about the patient: of concern, of guilt, of resentment at the patient's dependent state, or of envy of the attention given the patient. To defend against these conflicts, nursing organizations establish a variety of compensatory goals and practices. These include frequent shifts of personnel, rotating assignment of nurses to patients, routinization of the relationship of the nurse to the patient, training in denying the significance of the individual, diffusion of task responsibility, and obscuring of authority structure. Even though these practices may interfere with the goals of patient care, they bind conflicts at a minimal level sufficient to allow the provision of the service, however impaired, to continue.

Other measures of social defence involve the degree to which attempts are made to establish levels of security around personal needs. The most general form is the provision of security around the work position. This involves systems of seniority, tenure, guaranteed wage, and the like. Programme specifications may carry the same security arrangement, whereby funds are guaranteed for projects on a term basis or for duration; space is guaranteed; and overriding goals are clarified and stated to place a high value on the programme in the future plans of the organization.

Whether such practices are adaptive or disruptive will of course vary with the situation being studied. Disruptive aspects of security arrangements regarding job positions and job programmes are perhaps the most frequent examples cited. The plight of the nonproductive employee, the outdated policy-maker, or the archaic job specification is a fixed part of our organizational lore. It is perhaps more characteristic of human service organizations that such defences tend to be disruptive because of the complexity and difficulty of the mandated task. Social defences also tend to be most disruptive in periods of rapid transition within a social system where the anxieties stemming from fantasies of abandonment or statelessness may be provided with greater reality.

Observations of organizational life from the point of view of social conflict and defence have had at least two characteristics that have made them partial preparation at best for the present consultation. One result of looking at the function of organizational structure in the reduction of anxiety has been to focus on role anxiety, i.e. anxiety due to particular constellations among positions and roles in organizations which lead to intergroup rivalries, scapegoating, and the like. Menzies' (1970) study of task activity is an exception, though focused on the delivery of health services. Miller and Rice (1967) make passing reference to task anxieties of airline staffs in offering services dangerous to their clients, but do little work in conceptualizing their findings from the point of view of conflict and defence. To date, therefore, very little theoretical work has been done on the analysis of conflict and defence in an industrial organization.

One can easily imagine the nature of the problem by attempting to analogize Menzies' observations on the task anxiety of nurses with comparable task anxieties among workers in the process of assembling a product. On the surface, the analogy does not appear to be very promising. Menzies' picture of nurses involved with various exaggerated personal needs of the individual does not at first glance seem to have much in common with the worker who runs a machine eight hours a day. Indeed, Miller and Rice (1967) seem to confirm this view by making explicit use of the conflict-defence model only in their analysis of an airline management and not in analysing industrial firms. On the other hand, little more than casual acquaintance with work positions in highly technologized industries makes it clear that there are equally impressive anxieties associated with these tasks. The least of the problem is that there are very frequently issues of personal safety involved. More importantly, there is usually an impressive accountability in the situation where an incompetently performed task may have considerable disruptive potential for the operation as a whole (e.g. the assembly line). Finally, there is the issue of the dehumanization of the work process itself, where a worker may spend the majority of his waking hours relatively divorced from human contact in the service of one or another technology. In many industries there is a distinct possibility of various kinds of stimulus overload, particularly noise overload, in the latent crowdlike atmosphere of large work areas. These anxieties, together with the numerous role anxieties that exist for the average worker (issues such as job security, status, and the like), must, in some sense, be responsible for the pervasive distancing and alienation which become a central feature of the worker's existence. One hypothesis in the present study would thus be that underlying task and role anxieties of the industrial worker, with concomitant defences of withdrawal, alienation, etc., will be a pervasive reality with which any management must attempt to cope. Such conflicts in the workers will form part of the underlying conflict for their managers.

The setting

We know very little about the thinking that went into the establishment of the plant where we acted as consultants. We do know that it was seen as a satellite operation, lauched from the central industrial location in the organization. Its mandate was to manufacture cartons and containers for the company's product, an expansion of the central plant's carton and container operations. It would, however, be located in a different part of the country, with a different workforce, an opportunity to employ newer technology, and with a different distribution area. In short, it would duplicate a manufacturing process for a different labour and consumer force.

The employees of the central plant chosen to establish the new plant were apparently seen as young, aggressive, technology-minded, 'whiz-kid' middle managers who wanted an opportunity to have more responsibility and greater opportunity to introduce innovative procedures into the manufacture of the product. The plant manager once jokingly referred to the managers who were asked to establish the plant as 'hard cases', which the consultants were left to interpret as meaning that they were somewhat difficult employees in the central plant, with special ambitions as well as technological and managerial visions that could not be realized in the older setting.

The personal qualities of the employees chosen as plant manager and production manager were important. The plant manager was a warm, somewhat reserved, paternalistic individual, with two work interests that made him an ideal candidate for a plant manager: (1) he had a knack for pursuing work-related technological innovations; (2) he had an abiding interest in developing more effective work-related plant social cultures. Thus, both on the technical and human side of the enterprise he was the man most interested in establishing the conditions under which effective and efficient work could be carried out. He appeared to be somewhat less interested in obtaining and maintaining power over individuals in everyday work relationships.

The production manager, on the other hand, was a very gregarious, aggressive, earthy individual who reminded one of an intelligent and effective military officer. He had an aggressive interest in 'making things happen', which made him a good candidate for the man on the job who would in a day-to-day sense run the plant.

Both men were interested in pursuing the benefits of modern technology and modern management techniques in the interests of creating an efficient organization. Both could remain committed, perhaps for the rest of their work career, to the goal of building such an organization. Neither was particularly fond of, or experienced in, the more cosmopolitan behaviour patterns of higher-level, urban-based management. They could in good conscience commit a major portion of the most productive years of their management careers to a provincial town, working at developing an innovative plant.

According to a company memo of this period:

When the development of the idea of a second plant ... started several years ago, it took many forms. One was buying an existing plant and re-equipping it. Another was building a new one ... and still another of building a plant on the West Coast. ... In the months from the time we knew the Central City plant was going to be built and when we started up ... the whole carton and container management team concentrated on plans for the new plant .... We talked of communications, of what people expect from their job, of what they don't like, of what they do like, of achievement, recognition of work itself, responsibility, advancement, salary structures, growth, etc. ... We were looking for a little bit better way to operate a carton plant. We finally came to the conclusion that we had done rather well in the development of machines, products and material, but that most of the things we were doing with people either were not helping to support our objectives, or were only slightly beneficial.

The plant is located, as I indicated, in a middle-sized community in upper New York. It was the first major industrial organization in the community, a position it has retained until the present time. It is a town with a small black population and relatively undifferentiated ethnic minority subgroups. Because of the lack of industrialization in the town, unions are relatively weak. The town has a reputation as a summer resort area, and as such attracts large numbers of middle-class and upper-class summer residents. The principal industry of the town thus is tourism, and the economy and social life of the community are based on the dominance of a majority of white-collar families with a summer influx of even larger numbers of white upper-middle-class tourists.

Physically, the plant is a modern industrial structure which is cleancut and pleasant, though architecturally undistinguished. It is barely distinguishable from thousands of similar structures built in the 1950s and 1960s. The impression of neatness is also preserved inside. Aside from management offices, which are located in a small wing as one enters, the entire work space is located under one very large, steel-beamed, concrete-floored area. The factory proper is well lighted and heated, and kept extraordinarily neat despite the fact that the ubiquitous need for paper, cardboard, ink, and glue provide certain stresses on tidiness. The work space appears to be organized by sub-areas, demarcated by different types of technologies primarily addressed to printing, cutting, and finishing containers.

The visit

As we began to interact with managers and employees, we were immediately made aware of two paradoxical aspects of plant behaviour. On the one hand, we were treated to a nearly flawless managerial handling of our visit, in which employees and programmes alike appeared before our eyes with efficiency, courtesy, flexibility, and enthusiasm. We were initially consulted about what we wanted to observe, and a programme was immediately galvanized into action in which all of our requests were met. Managers went out of their way to be available, and generously gave their time to entertain us during lunch and dinner breaks. Arrangements were made to excuse workers from jobs and to find replacements when necessary so we could interview them. We were given several opportunities to tour various parts of the plant, and given samples. We sought and obtained ample organizational literature.

On the other hand, in the midst of this managerial *tour de force* we were presented with an antithesis: virtually everything about the social and work life of the plant appeared to be informal. Employees did not have to use timeclocks and could come and leave in any way consistent with their work obligations. All employees referred to other employees by their first names. No one, not even the plant manager or production manager, was an exception. All employees saw the plant manager as accessible to them and enough interested in them to have almost daily contact. Each employee had a remarkably company-wide picture of the plant, and could talk intelligently about its goals and processes in almost any area. Virtually everyone, management and worker alike, was enthusiastic about working in the plant. For a time we thought it might be impossible to pry a complaint out of anyone. People were happy with wages and working conditions, with advancement, and with job security. There was very little turnover, and virtually everyone was willing to compare this plant favourably with any other place where he or she had ever worked. Many comparisons were made with the 'home' plant, picturing it as less effective and a less satisfactory place to work. Were it not for the obvious sincerity and enthusiasm of the people to whom we were talking, the unrelenting stream of slogans and truisms might have become a strain. The plant was seen as 'a good place to work, with good pay'; employees were 'gung-ho' for the company; there was high *esprit de corps*; workers were said to be 'loyal and hard-working'. Productivity and profits were pictured as higher than those of any comparable plant in the country; management was pictured as responsible and responsive; e.g. 'John's [the manager's] door is always open'.

Surrounding this enthusiasm, there appeared to be a well-conceived and well-implemented philosophy of work at the plant. They were well-articulated in company policy statements. The following are edited for brevity:

(1) If a person helps in making decisions and developing an idea or improvement, he will probably work harder to carry it out. All employees are capable of seeing the broad picture and supporting broad objectives, if they have sufficient knowledge and can see that the objective can eventually help them in achieving their personal goal.
(2) The broader an individual's knowledge and training, and the more skills he has, the greater his security. Mastery of several skills and some knowledge of many jobs make for a flexible, confident, secure worker.
(3) The most satisfied and productive people are those who feel they are achieving something worthwhile and are involved in the decision-making process, feel that they get recognition for the job well done, and are given responsibility.
(4) Most people today don't like rules and regulations unless the reason for them is obvious ... we have no timeclocks, no scheduled breaks where possible, and a minimum of restrictive rules.
(5) We believe in letting machines do the hard work and thereby reserving our energies for that part of the job that requires skills and brain power.

In order to achieve these objectives, a variety of procedures were employed, including considerable reliance on a worker advisory board, a suggestion box system, continuous job-bidding, and extensive interposition training programmes. In addition, strong emphasis was placed on unit responsibility for ordinary maintenance and housekeeping: 'we have a fine building designed to stay newlooking .... . Every employee is on a committee to clean the "corner" where he works'. Much use is made of an employee performance appraisal system, where employees appraise their own performance and that of other employees. An attempt was made to give an employee a picture of the relationship of his job to the total enterprise, and cost–benefit data is made available to him in order to understand in a rudimentary way some of the economics of productivity in his position.

These proposed solutions and their implementation in the plant are so impressive that one might be inclined to overlook the problems they are designed to solve. Concern over both the social and technical aspects of the production line were present from the beginning. One early memo concludes that 'the assembly line concept has resulted in limited job satisfaction and productivity at a fixed level'. But the problems are pictured as solved by production unit teams, interposition training, and frequent rotation of employees among both teams and positions. In all of the plant literature and in our discussions, there was but one brief mention of the issues connected with alienation of the workers from involvement in or responsibility for the enterprise. In this plant the traditional source of protection from or management of alienation—the labour union—is thought to be dysfunctional or superfluous. It is replaced by the offer of involvement in the industrial family. This is, in my view, a crucial organizational feature of the plant, involving strong efforts to maintain a unitary authority structure in which the workers are seen as members of a family where management takes on the responsibility of allowing the children to 'grow up' in the factory. The commitment is to producing better and better jobs for employees as they grow older in the institution. If a union were present, a more complex authority structure would be established, with a more or less continuous offer to the worker of reliance and dependence on the labour union in its fight with management for higher wages and better working conditions. The social defences which would parallel this organizational structure also shift from a focus on the development and use of utopian fantasies (in the unitary model) to the offer of fighting for security and well-being with the union *vis-à-vis* management.

One question we raised was: what are the structural advantages and disadvantages of 'unitary' authority, and how well can it be implemented in this plant? All of the major task and sentient systems have been developed on the assumption that there will be no labour unions. At the task level, the policy of training for many jobs and mastering several in the course of a career at the plant would be more difficult if a labour union were guarding job description changes as well as hiring and firing practices around such changes. Without a labour union, management has greater freedom to innovate and to adapt to a new technology. Fluctuation of positions and bidding for jobs are central features of the motivational system regarding positions at the plant, a part of the 'progress' or 'opportunity' mythology of the plant. Beyond myth, however, the policy of multiple skill training does appear to have major advantages to the worker. It is, on the one hand, management's version of job security; if a worker learns several skills at the plant he is less likely to be laid off by production changes. He is also more likely to progress through a series of increasingly more complex skill positions and is therefore less likely to stagnate in a single position.

At the socio-emotional level, it was clear to us that a well-established pattern of social fantasy had assembled around the unitary authority structure. The plant manager, John Frank, was seen as 'open', 'helpful', 'friendly', 'close', 'interested', and 'diplomatic'. At one point one of our interviewees, in a slip of the tongue, referred to him as *Mrs* Frank. The production manager, Tom Williams, was conversely said to be 'a take-charge guy', 'the man', 'a pusher'. We were told he 'gets the job done', and 'holds the reins', and 'is more the boss'. The two managers were frequently symbolized as parents of a 'big happy family': the plant's.

At an organizational level, we were interested in the link between these various symbolizations and the task structure of the plant. Any premonition that one can barely imagine a complex industrial organization of over 250 people constituting a 'big family' should be a good initial guide. Such a process of oversimplification should predictably yield some casualties. One would expect, among other things, that anyone mandated to maintain more task-related internal boundaries would have difficulty. This is indeed what we found, in the following ways:

(1) The delegation of authority to the three departments of the plant (printing, cutting, and finishing) has been ambiguous and has changed frequently. While we were visiting the plant, the cutting department superintendent was spending most of his time as the printing department superintendent; the head of that department was on a special assignment in the engineering branch of the plant; the number two person in the cutting department was on a special assignment doing computer programming work. These shifts were not identified by the people involved as being problematic. What was identified as problematic was the way that shift foremen were treated. All three shift foremen we interviewed had complaints about their position in the system. One of them summed it up: 'The foreman would like to see foremen backed up by management. Too many issues of people on the floor are acted on by management. They tend to please people on the floor rather than the foreman. The foreman is the middle man, not attended to quite as well. There is a gap between the front office and the foremen.' One foreman went so far as to suggest that 'maybe we don't need foremen'.

One way of characterizing this situation is to say that not much authority has been delegated either to middle management as a group, or to departments individually. The pairing of top management with the workers makes the task of maintaining boundaries between departments and between levels of authority difficult. The development of strong boundaries around departments would restrict the power of top management to control the everyday functioning of workers and to pair with them. Ironically, so would the introduction of labour unions. Paternalistic arrangements between top management and the worker preclude the delegation of authority either to middle management or to organized groups of workers.

(2) Further evidence of the paternalism of the system was provided by the plant manager's secretary. She commented that it was very difficult for manager's secretaries to mix socially or in any other way with women workers.

Our impression was that this was true for men as well. Indeed, the most pervasive spatial distancing in the plant was between management and workforce, symbolically separated by a long corridor. It was quite possible to remain in the management area of the plant and not be aware of the existence of the factory. It was our impression that the use of first names between top management and worker was an important screen for the underlying reality of the considerable distance that exists between them. Workers, while referring to top management as 'John' and 'Tom', treated them with considerable deference more appropriate to referring to them by their last names. One could argue that if management were serious about reducing distance between itself and the workers, the best way would be to delegate more authority to foremen or encourage the development of a company union. Then the most salient authorities would structurally be less distant.

(3) We sensed throughout our visit that the finishing department carried a special burden in the form of many of the functional difficulties of maintaining plant structure in its current form. Appropriately, a shift foreman for the finishing department was the most outspokenly critical employee to whom we spoke. His complaints were that his department mainly hired younger, lower-paid, less competent employees, that the work was more routine and needed to be more rigidly scheduled in assembly-line fashion. Most importantly, he felt that much of the localization of criticism for error in the plant was directed at the finishing department, where errors generated in other departments of the plant got 'dumped'. He said the finishing department was held responsible for about 2 to 4 per cent scrap, whereas 'actually only about 0.7 per cent of it is ours; it's really their responsibility'.

If one assumes that one corollary of paternalistic management will be a difficulty in maintaining internal boundaries, a complementary assumption would be that the organization would have a similar difficulty in maintaining task boundaries between the organization and the environment. That is to say, if there is a collusive arrangement between top management and worker in a familiar structure and in utopian fantasies regarding task, finer distinctions in relating subparts of either management or workforce to the outside world will be difficult to recognize. The strength of emotional ties to the overall reference group will make differentiated groups difficult to incorporate into the enterprise.

In the present instance, groups, such as hippies, women, blacks, ethnic minorities, and labour unionists all experienced difficulties in fitting into the modal image of the management–worker entente. Hippies were seen as alienated and disloyal, blacks were pictured as disruptive and irresponsible, women were typically given low status positions within the organization, and labour union leaders were pictured as disreputable psychopaths. It was not coincidental, therefore, that the most critical foreman of the finishing department was the only manager we met who was a member of an identifiable ethnic minority group. It was also not surprising to see the finishing and personnel department as being in greatest conflict about the current functioning of the plant. It would be the task of the personnel department to introduce and regulate the work contributions of 'special groups', and it was the current task of the finishing department to integrate such groups into the plant, since most of the lower-skill, introductory jobs were in the finishing department. The personnel and finishing departments could thus be seen as performing somewhat unrecognized total organizational functions. Between them, they were responsible for the input of most potentially disruptive groups into the system. During our visit, the only organization foul-up on our entire schedule had to do with the intersection between these departments. The personnel manager mismanaged our scheduled interview with the finishing department superintendent, and we were not able to see him.

Overview

Signs of what has recently been referred to as the 'new industrial revolution' are much more in evidence in this plant. It is small, and is located in a middle-sized community which has relatively little history of ethnic or class conflict. It is housed in new quarters with the latest technology. It has moved away from the assembly line where possible and towards the use of project teams organized around technological units. It has explored what is sometimes called 'participatory industrial democracy', which among other things has meant that employees can set their own work schedules, and worker's groups can set their own methods, suggest salaries, and guide production goals. According to management, the plant is moving towards a profit-sharing plan. It also appears to be moving towards a system in which the need for foremen and labour unions would be even further reduced.

In this paper, I have attempted to give one view of the psychology of this kind of innovative setting. It is a psychology based on the cultivation and use of a pattern of utopian fantasies about the nature of work in an industrial setting. These fantasies, centring as they do on bounty and unlimited potential, are particularly appropriate when the system is young and when it is growing and developing. On the other hand, if its product demand were substantially reduced, or if its technology or perhaps even its human participants begin to settle into patterns that appear to be relatively satisfactory solutions to the problems initially posed, utopian fantasies would become increasingly dissatisfying and irrelevant.

The present plant, in this view, may be entering upon just such an era. The next 15 years of the plant may be similar to the previous 15 years. Both the physical plant and its employees are becoming older. There are both technological and behavioural patterns that have become more widely fixed. For example, it is no longer a matter of seeing difficulties in the finishing department as the result of a technology with growing pains, or a work staffing pattern experiencing organizational pains. It now becomes a matter of seeking out someone to blame for 'errors'. As the median age of workers goes up, and the number of years on the job becomes longer, higher positions among the workforce become filled by 'veterans' of the plant. As we frequently heard, it becomes less possible to move up quickly within the organization. The sharing of utopian fantasies thus tends to be gradually replaced by the sharing of welfare fantasies: how am I seen by the organization? Is my job secure? Will I be protected against the influx of 'new' types like the young, the blacks, and other upwardly mobile minority groups? Particularly if these 'new' types enter with a different set of attitudes concerning the basic problems of isolation and alienation from work, they will come to represent past problems which were to a large extent 'solved' by the current organization of technology, work patterns, and sentience in the plant.

The consultation may have been welcomed into this plant in order to contribute in some minor way to the maintenance and development of the plant's utopian mythology. On the one hand, we could extol the successes of the plant in the service of expanding its discoveries to other plants; symbolically this plant could grow through the growth of similar industrial operations elsewhere. On the other hand, there seemed to be an awareness and concern about the gradual weakening of the utopian psychological assumptions of the plant. The plant manager indicated that he welcomed our efforts 'to stir things up a little bit'. There were two areas, however, which it was not seen as 'relevant' to explore: insurgent outgroups or minority groups (hippies, blacks, women, unions), and insurgent technologies. That we were not seen as technological consultants is understandable, but at no time were we encouraged to explore the relevance of technological change to the future of the plant's social system. The message was, 'We have done well with our machines, now we need to do better with our people.' What makes such a comparison salient is that it was just these two areas—insurgent technologies and employees—which gave the plant its distinctive formative character. We could only speculate that our 'irrelevance' in these two areas might signal the arrival of a new era in the history of the plant where welfare and well-being are scheduled to replace growth and progress as the dominant social myths.

References

Jaques, E. (1955) 'Social systems as a defense against persecutory and depressive anxiety'. In *New Directions in Psychoanalysis*. New York: Basic Books.

Menzies, I. E. P. (1970) *The Functioning of Social Systems as a Defence Against Anxiety. A Report on a Study of the Nursing Service of a General Hospital*. Tavistock Pamphlet No. 3.

Miller, E. J., and Rice, A. K. (1967) *Systems of Organization*. London: Tavistock Publications.

Miller, J. C., Rourke, P. D., David, G. H., Howenstine, R. A., Morrison, T. M., and Reed, H. D. (1977) *Reparation and Change: Psychological Aspects of Social Innovation*. New Haven, Conn.: CEGO.

Chapter 15

Open Systems Revisited: A Proposition about Development and Change

Eric J. Miller

Introduction

Reinventing the wheel is not always the profitless exercise it is made out to be. Familiar objects and ideas can be taken too much for granted: the wheel is just a wheel, and one tends to stop thinking about it in terms of a relationship between vehicle and surface. Conditions change, so that only through questioning that functional relationship does it become possible to confirm that the wheel really is the most appropriate solution. In this way better wheels are developed and very occasionally quite new relationships are conceived; so the tank or the hovercraft gets invented. Gosling (in press) has described his repeated experience as a psychoanalyst of discovering with surprise that the novel dynamic he has teased out with a patient turns out to be the classical Oedipus complex. But if he had identified and labelled it sooner, would the work have been so effective? Almost certainly not, because that construction might well have interposed a filter between what the patient said and what the analyst heard. Similarly, those of us who take staff roles in group relations conferences sometimes relearn unexpectedly what we thought we knew already, about groups and about ourselves. Yet what is relearned is never quite the same as what was learned before; and one of Pierre Turquet's contributions to staff groups was often to link that reexperience to the culture of that specific conference, in that specific environment, and in this way to generate new insights. As I see it, such a heightened capacity to listen to the data and to be surprised by them is the hallmark of the good therapist, the good educator and, indeed, the good scientist. Without making any such claim for myself, I intend to explore in this essay my own rediscovery of the open system.

The concept of the open system has been illuminating studies of group and organizational behaviour for a quarter of a century. Of my earlier colleagues at the Tavistock Institute, Rice in particular had seized upon it in the early 1950s.* 'Any industrial organization', he wrote, 'may be likened to an open

---

*I have written elsewhere about the development of organizational concepts at the Tavistock Institute in the 1940s and 1950s (Miller, 1976a, 1976b, 1977). Although the theory of open systems put forward by von Bertalanffy (1950a, 1950b) had a profound effect, thinking about groups and organizations as systems was already well established through the influence of Lewin (e.g. 1936, 1947, 1950). The Institute's early mining studies (Trist and Bamforth, 1951) had produced the concept of the *socio-technical system*, which provided a way of examining, and possibly reconciling,

217

system . . .' (Rice, 1958). Subsequently, he and others were to apply the open system model to analysis of the organization of enterprises of widely different kinds.

One fruitful proposition derived from the model is that a change in the relatedness of a system to its environment requires internal changes within the system: it must shift to a new steady state if it is to survive. A good deal of work has been done in this area, particularly with regard to the boundary conditions for effective work organizations. Rice's own experiments on work organization in weaving are a good example (Rice, 1958, 1963). These were among the earliest attempts to discover empirically the relationship between the internal characteristics of a socio-technical system and the variability of inputs that it could accommodate. A colleague and I were able to take this a little further in 1970, when we followed up Rice's original experiments after an interval of some 15 years: it proved possible to postulate why the original form of organization had survived in some areas and become diluted or disappeared in others (Miller, 1975). This study suggested that attempts to design systems to maximize productivity may well be precarious, and that our thinking about work organization should parallel that of modern ecologists, who are now saying that the appropriate 'conceptual framework for man's intervention into ecological systems . . . changes the emphasis from maximizing the probability of success to minimizing the chance of disaster' (Holling and Goldberg, 1971, p. 226). Working systems need to be robust and resilient enough to cope with considerable variation in environmental conditions without catastrophic breakdown. Emery and Trist have paid particular attention to the consequences for organizational systems of operating in a turbulent environment (Emery and Trist, 1965; Trist, 1976).

However, less attention has been given to a second proposition that is a corollary of the first: that significant internal changes within a system cannot be sustained unless consistent changes occur in the relatedness of the system to its environment. This is not to say that the idea of proactiveness has been neglected. As a colleague and I wrote recently:

We see much of our own work as directed towards helping individuals to discover their capacity for self-management, so that as they work in their various roles in various institutions, they are not merely reacting and adapting to environmental pressures but consciously acting upon their environment and shaping it into what they want it to be. (Lawrence and Miller, 1976, pp. 365–366)

And certainly this second proposition has been part of the conceptual baggage that I have carried with me into a number of interventions, including work on

---

the relationship between the psycho-social and the techno-economic elements of purposeful organizations. Von Bertalanffy was acknowledged in a paper on labour turnover by Rice and Trist in 1952; but the clear distinction between closed physical systems and open living systems was not yet fully recognized. Rice put the open system framework to practical use in his work with the Calico Mills in India, and by the time he finished writing *Productivity and Social Organization* in 1956, the distinction was explicit and beginning to be taken for granted.

rural development in Mexico that I shall be discussing below. However, much of one's time as a consultant is spent in engaging with the client system in the specific pressures of the 'here and now'. Theories, then, like Gosling's Oedipus complex, sometimes come back and surprise us, and perhaps take on new meanings. So it was only after more than two years of work in Mexico that I rediscovered the second proposition and saw in it implications that I had not fully recognized before.

The Mexican experience

Efforts at rural development in Third World countries have generally not been crowned with success. Indeed, for some 'beneficiaries' the results have been disastrous. For example, peasants who have been persuaded to abandon subsistence farming for a single cash-crop such as cotton may prosper for a while, but two or three successive years of infestation or depressed world prices can force them off the land. In many other cases the innovation just disappears and the peasants return to the *status quo ante*. Large numbers of rural drinking-water supplies, for example, which are proudly inaugurated as a contribution to villagers' health and welfare, are out of use within a couple of years, apparently because the local communities lack the skill or will to operate and maintain them. One response to these failures has been to move away from isolated crop improvement projects or health projects towards programmes of integrated agricultural development and, in a few countries, integrated rural development. Such a programme involves a wide range of interventions and investments, in farming technology, rural industry, credit, commercialization, road-building, transport, and other areas, designed to bring about economic advancement, and, alongside these, projects concerned with nutrition, health, housing, education, and so forth, intended to improve the quality of rural life. On paper, at least, this 'total system' strategy looks capable of bringing about the massive transformation that is required; and on paper, too, the achievements can seem impressive in terms of the numbers of wells dug, hectares irrigated, schools built, and so on. But all too often in the process of implementation the concept of integrated development gets lost. Objectives are confused; methods are inadequately worked out; government agencies find it easier to compete than to collaborate; officials are incompetent or corrupt. As a result, the experience of the recipients is often of isolated and even capricious actions, which seem unrelated to each other or to local needs. Programmes such as these therefore risk becoming more elaborate and costly mechanisms for producing the same failures as before.

The Government of Mexico introduced its integrated rural development programme in 1973. It was a large and ambitious undertaking, ultimately intended to reach some 20 000 rural communities in the population range of 300 to 3000. Between September 1973 and November 1976, I worked as a part-time consultant to the Directorate of Public Investments, which was the division within the Ministry of the Presidency responsible for establishing and administering the programme. Initially, the Directorate was seeking advice on the major organizational problems posed by the programme, which called for the coordinated intervention, at state and local levels, of many different federal ministries and agencies. Since organization is a means of carrying out a task, we had to consider what the task of the programme was. Each agency had its own specialized activity—road-building, rural electrification, irrigation, soil conservation, setting up village health centres, and so on—and all of these could be seen as potentially contributing to rural prosperity and welfare. But the critical word is 'potentially'. These new installations and projects were no doubt necessary conditions for development, but they were not sufficient conditions. They would contribute to development only if the rural communities themselves were able to use them and build on them. At that stage, therefore, I saw the task of the programme as 'to procure a self-sustaining process of rural development'. The problem was to identify the kind of relationship, at the interface between the 'developers' and their 'client systems', that would enable this to happen, and then to provide the conditions for the 'developers' to take up appropriate roles. This was my main preoccupation over the next three years.*

From my initial discussions in Mexico City and visits to the field, it rapidly became clear that, sometimes explicitly but often implicitly, two conflicting models of the development process were operating. These can be summed up as 'top-down' (Model A) and 'bottom-up' (Model B). Seldom in practice did they appear in a pure form, and indeed the same individual might seem to oscillate between them—perhaps voicing a Model B philosophy while acting on Model A assumptions. However, the confusion was not only his: he was expressing something of the multiple and conflicting objectives of the rural development programmes I am familiar with in Mexico and elsewhere. At the risk of stating the obvious, the distinctions nevertheless seem worth spelling out.

Model A: Top-down development

Increased agricultural production is a significant objective in all national programmes I know of. The document stating the objectives of the Mexican programme was careful to point out that this was a means of enhancing rural prosperity rather than an end in itself; but not all the participating agencies would regard this as a meaningful distinction. Increased production is certainly a national objective—in order to feed the growing urban population, to reduce imports, and to earn foreign exchange from exports—and it is an explicit part of the mandate of the Ministries of Agriculture and of Agrarian Reform. That, then, is the message that these ministries' officials, experts, and extensionists carry with them when they go into the field. They tend therefore to behave as if the primary task of the programme is 'to develop and organize rural communities so as to meet national production goals'. From this it follows that the local

*The evolution of the programme over the first two years, together with a preliminary model of the development process, is described (in Spanish) in Miller, 1976c.

community (or the population of peasant farmers within it)* is conceived as a subsystem within a national production system. There is a close analogy with a commercial holding company seeking a return from its investments in subsidiary companies. And indeed it is noticeable that this formulation of the objectives is associated with the application of principles of scientific management to community development: typically, attempts are made to organize each community according to a standard type of democratic, participative system that requires a collective structure, election of office-holders, division of labour, definition of functions, delegation of responsibilities and authority, and use of incentives. An underlying assumption of Model A is that there is a substantial consistency between governmental economic objectives and rural community needs. National programmes to achieve these objectives will benefit communities by increasing their prosperity. The orientation is technocratic: the experts know what needs to be done. Accordingly, any resistance displayed by the communities is irrational: with education and persuasion they will come to see that their own self-interest coincides with the national interest.

Model B: Bottom-up development

It is always a stated objective of rural development programmes to rectify gross inequalities of wealth; and one does not need to be a Marxist to recognize that much rural poverty (though by no means all) is a consequence of historical exploitation, which has generated not only physical impoverishment but demoralization, apathy, fatalism, and submissiveness. People are trapped in a cycle of deprivation from which they feel incapable of escaping and have given up trying: they do not perceive themselves as having any choices. Following from this diagnosis, the primary task of Model B can be stated in some such terms as these: 'to restore the self-confidence that will release energy and motivation for self-development'. The best-known exponent of this model is Freire (1972a, 1972b). His starting-point is a process of adult education which enables the peasants to examine and question the situation they are in. They learn that their impotence is a consequence not of inherent inferiority but of historical processes. These are reversible. Government aid is not a privilege that they should feel grateful to receive, but something they have a right to demand, even to fight for. In effect, the postulate is that they need to engage in something equivalent to revolutionary activity in order to regain a sense of potency and thereby to release energy for constructive self-development. Mobilizing as it does 'basic assumption fight/flight' (Bion, 1961), Model B slides imperceptibly into revolutionary activity for its own sake: the conflict of interests between the rural poor and Government is total; the primary task is to destroy the oppressors.

*To avoid complexity, I use the term 'community' throughout this chapter to describe any local 'client system' with which a development agency may engage. A settlement that has a collective identity and organization will be an appropriate client for a wide range of projects, and often it is useful to encourage such organization. Failing that, the boundaries of client groups may vary from project to project.

Neither Model A nor Model B was operating in a pure form within the programme. What I discovered from my discussions and field observations in 1973 and early 1974 was that there were more signs of the former model than of the latter, but that in fact one could identify the emergence of a third model, which was a kind of compromise between them.

Official programme policy listed the following criteria for selecting projects for investment:

1. Highest priority should be given to productive projects which guarantee large-scale permanent employment....
2. In the social field, the drinking water, health, education and housing projects should foster a positive change in way of life and, still more, a necessary change in attitudes.
3. Priority will be given to complementary projects which strengthen the profitability of investments already made.
4. In all cases an attempt will be made to satisfy the needs expressed by the people, and projects will be carried out only at the explicit request of the communities.

Elsewhere in this policy document, issued in April 1973, there was emphasis on promoting participation, 'so that a mechanism can be established which permits planning from the bottom up'. Community representatives were to be involved not simply in planning local developments but in design of regional strategies.

The intentions sounded admirable; but unfortunately a development programme is influenced less by good intentions than by the structure and culture of implementation. Usually there is strong pressure to act and to act quickly, as if inequities that have been condoned for generations should now be put right overnight. The dilemma of the Mexican programme, as of others, was that although the importance of inculcating an ethos of community self-development was recognized, the very process of undertaking a large and rapid investment in productive projects and amenities tends to put the community in a dependent posture, a posture which is antithetical to self-development. The model actually in operation can best be described as 'enlightened paternalism'.

Model C: Enlightened paternalism

The strategic unit of development was a 'microregion'. This would be identified on the basis of ecological and socio-economic uniformity and *prima facie* evidence of developmental potential. The average population was 75 000, and so it might contain 50–100 communities eligible for investments under the programme. An interdisciplinary team of some 20 members, drawn from the various agencies involved, would make an intensive tour of the microregion. Each community would be visited, perhaps for half a day, in order to survey its resources and needs and to identify possible projects. Towards the end of the visit all the men in the community would be assembled, and the team would outline the projects it had in mind and ask for comments and alternative suggestions. Essentially that was the moment of participation. The team would subsequently assemble all the data from the field visits, devise an overall strategy for the microregion, make preliminary estimates of sums to be spent for various types of investment (e.g. road-building, soil conservation, fruit-growing), and then select the most deserving projects under each heading from the total range of possible projects that had been listed originally. These recommendations then had to be approved both by the headquarters of their respective agencies in Mexico City and by the central organization of the programme itself. It would be at least six months later that the community would be told what projects, if any, had been earmarked for it. Sometimes the microregional strategy had a discernible coherence; but often it seemed more like an aggregate of projects. At the level of the community, any concept of a development plan was rare indeed: investments and interventions seemed arbitrary and often unrelated to each other or to priorities that the local population itself might have set. It could be said that the 'developers' were behaving as if the primary task of the programme was 'to demonstrate the Government's good intentions'. Their relationship to the communities was of benefactor to beneficiary. They came equipped with a 'gift-list' of projects that they could carry out, sometimes quite competently; and although they paid lip-service to the idea of 'bottom-up' planning, this was for the future: in this initial phase the recipients were perceived as incapable of assessing the options open to them or of choosing between them.

Such arguments had some validity. It takes time and skill to help a community to formulate its needs; and many peasants were distrustful of the Government: promises had been made in the past but never translated into action. Donation of, say, a drinking-water supply can give a community a feeling that it is being valued and help it to acquire some self-confidence. However, in some ways the 'integrated' programme was putting the beneficiaries into a more extreme position of passive dependence than some more conventional development projects that had been administered by individual agencies. Rural electrification schemes, for example, had required that part of the costs should be borne by the communities that benefited; and this encouraged each community to organize itself and to acquire some identity as a client system. Under the programme, such contributions were waived and hence an incentive to organize was removed. The benevolent paternalism of Model C was therefore tending to hold the communities in the passive-dependent posture and was doing little to encourage them to move into the more active, autonomous, entrepreneurial posture that was necessary if they were to become capable of self-sustaining development.

Model D: A negotiating model

My proposal was that the programme needed to move towards a 'negotiating model', which was in fact more consistent with its intentions. My thinking can be summarized as follows:

Essentially my argument is that the top-down Model A and the bottom-up Model B are both in a way right; that the search for areas of consensus and compromise between them, implied in the enlightened paternalism of Model C, while it may have been necessary to gain sanction for the Programme, was not the best solution for development; and that a Model D that overtly recognized divergences as well as commonalities of interest would be developmentally the most productive. The fact that a community comes up with an assessment of its own interests which does not match the assessment that a governmental agency has made does not mean that it has either to be blamed for its stubborn irrationality or praised for asserting its independence: it is simply a fact, and a predictable one at that. Correspondingly, the observation that the governmental agency is trying to implement policies that do not find local acceptance does not imply that one should either criticize it or sympathize with it: although the Federal Government acts with the ultimate authority of the people in the service of the people, it will not please all of the people all the time. These facts, then, are not to be swept under the carpet: they are matters for examination and for negotiation. It is through such a process at the interface of community and agency that the peasant begins to find the meaning of his role as a citizen of the Republic and begins genuinely to participate in planning for development; while the agency members for their part begin to question the relatedness of federal policies to local concerns. Both parties learn from the transaction. Assumptions get tested and modified. It is a process, in other words, that gives some reality to that over-used slogan, 'grass-roots democracy'. (Miller, 1976c, pp. 91–92)

The primary task of Model D could be defined as 'to provide resources to help each community to formulate, negotiate and implement its own community development programme'. The first element of the model, then, is a community development programme formulated by the community itself. This requires making available a consultancy resource through which the community can become aware of the possibilities of change. However, in designing a strategy for itself the community will need to take into account: the development programmes of neighbouring communities and of the administrative district of which it forms a part; and the policies and resources of relevant Government agencies. So we have as a second element the concept of conjoint planning and programming. These lead to, third, the negotiation of a contractual relationship between the programme and the community, in which each party undertakes to contribute resources to the community development programme that has been negotiated.

Much of my work as consultant to the programme from 1973 onwards was directed towards shifting from Model C to Model D. A fundamental change was required in the relationship between agency representatives in the field and the client communities. As I have indicated, these representatives were seen, and to some extent saw themselves, as benefactors; the community was the recipient of bounty. The agency representatives had the resources; the community had none. The representatives had the power to give or withhold projects according to their picture of whether the recipients could make effective use of the investment in them; the community had no control over this process. The transaction was one in which the situation was totally defined by the agency representatives; the community remained in a passive and dependent role. My observations revealed, however, that the authority and power of these officials in the field were mythical. The real power lay with their agency superiors in Mexico City. Indeed, the relationship between these superiors and their field representatives corresponded almost exactly to my description of the representative–community relationship. My proposition was that the administrative system, and the nature of these representatives' authority, or lack of authority, within it, had a determining influence on the nature of the development process through which the representatives related to the client communities. Unless the field representative could exercise authority in negotiation (instead of having to refer all decisions to his superiors), the community was unlikely to discover its own capacity to do so. The same applied to relations between agencies: to expect that the peasants would organize themselves for collaboration was hardly realistic so long as the participating agencies themselves had not learned to work together towards a shared objective.

Besides helping to introduce specific organizational and administrative changes that would push or pull authority outwards from the centre to the field, my role had an educational component: I was trying to teach my clients about systems. The task of the development process, as I saw it and still see it, is to produce robust self-managing systems. Any potential intervention has to be evaluated for its systemic consequences; and, as the negotiating model suggests, the nature of the relationship between development agency and client may be more significant for development in this sense than the content of specific projects. In this I was challenging the conventional wisdom not only of Mexican government agencies but international funding bodies, such as the World Bank and the Inter-American Development Bank, which, even in an 'integrated' rural development programme, call for an economic cost–benefit justification of each project and neglect effects on the process.*

With or without the benefit of my advice, the programme was expanding rapidly. By the end of 1975 about 5000 communities all over the country had received or were in the process of receiving investments under the programme, and with some there had now been contact for two and a half years. We had here a large-scale natural experiment in which it was possible to generate and begin to test hypotheses. As a start, I paid three short visits over the next few months to regions where the programme was said to be showing signs of 'success'. This was not precisely defined: the criterion I adopted was that there should be evidence of people beginning to manage their own development and, in particular, of reinvestment. For example, in one village, where a workshop provided employment and several cooperative poultry-keeping projects had been introduced, some of the income had been reinvested, but, more importantly, it was being used to finance new productive activities through purchase

---

*The following extract is indicative:

How does one assess whether the levels of services proposed are justified? In the first place, reference must be made to sector or national policies, which should preferably establish minimum standards criteria (e.g., so many health clinics of a certain standard per head of the population, possibly stratified by population density). Secondly, one should make certain that, within the national or regional minimum standards, the discounted total cost is the lowest . . . . (World Bank, 1975, p. 73)

Perhaps one should not be surprised at the number of rural health centres which look impressive in the statistics but remain unmanned or unused.

of cattle and of sewing-machines to make clothes for sale as well as for family use. In addition, a percentage of profits from poultry-keeping was paid into community funds, which were being applied to a children's playground and new public buildings. In another case, in order to provide permanent employment for landless labourers who had worked on road-building at the beginning of the programme, a small sawmill was built with a contract to supply posts for rural electrification. This generated a substantial surplus which, with the agreement of the workers, was used to seed further rural industries. A collective organization was formed and in little more than two years it had set up nearly 200 small enterprises providing about 1500 new jobs. Control of the individual enterprises and of the corporation as a whole was vested in the workers, who were mainly women and girls.

From these and other cases it was possible to identify some common factors. Characteristically, a representative of the programme had exercised leadership in getting a client group to visualize a desirable and attainable future state and to commit itself to taking the first steps towards achieving it. He had sufficient authority (sometimes reinforced by political power) to commit contributions from the programme, but these usually took the form of materials and technical assistance: the clients were expected to contribute labour to and often to manage construction and other activities. He and/or members of his team were in frequent contact with the client group; this seemed to have an important function in sustaining the vision of the future before there were any concrete achievements. Thus there was a good deal of dependency, even charisma, in the early phases, but this was not at the expense of self-depreciation of the clients: the leadership role had been so managed that the hope and potency invested in it had been re-routed back to the clients in the form of a growing belief in themselves and their own capacity to bring about changes. They themselves were taking initiatives—taking over the vision, as it were—to which the representative was able to respond flexibly on behalf of the programme. Explicitly or implicitly, the criterion he used was whether the proposal would enhance the clients' capacity for self-management; and so he might use programme resources to back projects that would not always stand up individually to a stringent cost–benefit analysis. (He seemed to have the freedom to do this partly because of the savings obtained through high participation of clients in earlier projects.) Management and initiation of projects had required a re-patterning of existing organizational arrangements in the client system or the emergence of new structures (such as the collective corporation). Finally—and this was my rediscovery—the changes in internal structuring seemed to be directly related to and contingent on changes in the relatedness of the client system to its external environment.

I found that these brief field studies had sharpened my insight into under-development and therefore the processes of development. Underdevelopment could be defined operationally as 'relative lack of control over relations with one's environment, where that includes both the local physical environment and the external environment that comprises the wider socio-economico-political system'. Specific aspects of these relations—economic and other—can be identified, analysed, and sometimes measured. Development, then, implies a change in such relationships in the direction of influencing and controlling the environment, instead of being controlled by it—a change from impotence towards potency. Following from this, I could assert much more unequivocally that *the primary task of a development programme is to help the client system to increase its control of its environment.* That furnishes the criteria for effectiveness; that is the task for which the development agency needs to organize itself.

Four aspects of this task may be identified. Two of these are familiar enough; but I suggest that the significance of the third and, in particular, the fourth is insufficiently recognized.

The first aspect is development of the human resources of the community. (I am continuing to assume here that the client system is a rural community.) Thus it is obvious that education can inculcate new techniques and skills; literacy gives access to alternative values and goals. Similarly, improved nutrition and health can release greater energy for existing and new activities.

The second aspect is enhancement of the physical resources of the community. This is the objective of many development agencies, which, as we have seen, often measure their performance by the number of wells dug, health centres constructed, households provided with electricity, etc.

However, as I illustrated with the example of drinking-water systems, installation is not synonymous with utilization. These projects, therefore, are to be regarded only as means, not as ends in themselves. The criterion of effectiveness lies in my third aspect: have they helped the community to extend its control over its physical environment? An extensionist may work hard and successfully to arouse enthusiasm for a new agricultural technique, which really seems to be moving the boundary between the farmers and their physical environment; but after two seasons of successful operation, with markedly higher yields, the farmers regress to previous methods. Sometimes this is simply because the extensionist has failed to ensure that supplies of the requisite seeds and fertilizers will be readily available. Sometimes it is because he has misjudged the 'goodness of fit' between the innovation and the prevailing culture. As Jennings (1976) points out, extensionists may also ignore the pragmatic wisdom of peasant communities that has enabled them to survive: they are not interested in crops that produce a very high yield in good years; the varieties they have learned to plant are those that will minimize the chances of a total crop failure in the bad years. But often the most plausible explanation in such cases is simply that the farmers have not acquired the skill to manage the new process themselves: they have been dependent on the extensionist, so that only his continuing presence has permitted the innovation to be sustained.*

---

*Sometimes, of course, the experts cannot bear to leave it to the farmers: to ensure 'success', as measured by output, they may take on more, rather than less, of the management of the project. Heckadon (1973) cites an excellent example from Panama. As he points out, this contributes nothing to the learning of the client system. Developers in general find it difficult to allow their protégés to make mistakes, even though mistakes can often teach the most valuable lessons.

So I come to the fourth aspect, and with it a reformulation of the second proposition stated in the introduction: that the community will not achieve greater control of its local physical environment, or the achievement will not be sustained, unless the change is also accompanied and reinforced by corresponding and more permanent changes in relations with the external environment: the community needs to become more autonomous and influential in managing these relationships also. Many of these changed relationships will be economic: for example, the community sells produce instead of exporting manual labour; it sells its produce in processed form instead of selling it unprocessed (for example, cheese instead of milk); it diversifies its products; it extends its control over distribution and so commands higher prices; and so on. Obvious though these points may seem, it is surprising how often they are missed, even in supposedly integrated development programmes. Extensionists promote higher yields without considering the process of commercialization: farmers have little incentive to increase output if all the extra profits go into the pocket of the traditional middleman. (Nor is a government purchasing agency always a viable alternative: Ackoff (1977), also writing on development planning in the Mexican context, cites cases of agency employees being bribed by the middlemen to reject farmers' offerings, which were then sold to the old buyers at depressed prices.) Farmers may therefore need to be helped to establish their own co-operative marketing arrangements, bypassing the middleman, if they are to get a proper return. Along with such economic gains, a less obvious, more subtle and more significant change seems to occur: a change in the community's identity and self-image.* As a result, for example, of bypassing the old channels and managing distribution themselves, the people acquire a different—more potent—image in the external environment, and this in turn reinforces an emerging image of themselves as more potent, both collectively and individually.† In this way, technical and structural changes become confirmed by a cultural transformation. The outcome, then, is a system that has discovered the possibilities of exercising autonomy and choice and has become capable of managing itself in a self-sustaining process of development.

Implications

In the introduction, I suggested that the second proposition derived from the open system model had not received nearly so much attention as the first.

*Or, as Pierre Turquet might have put it, a change in the 'community-in-the-mind'. He developed the heuristic concepts of 'management-in-the-mind' and 'institution-in-the-mind' as a means of exploring unstated and often unconscious assumptions that might explain the interrelatedness among a set of groups, which perceived themselves as subordinate to the same absent management or as parts of the same institution. Sometimes it is a shared fantasy; sometimes it contains divergent elements which different groups represent and express in their interrelations.

†In one of the villages mentioned above, several different family enterprises were engaged in poultry-keeping. Among themselves they organized their production cycles so as to maintain a steady overall output and in the market of a nearby town they manned a stall to sell the dressed chickens. The stall bore the name of the village and quickly acquired a reputation for quality and reliability. This in turn helped to sustain the collaborative arrangements and was quite evidently a source of pride and added self-confidence in the village as a whole.

My own experience in Mexico indicates why this may be. In its original and generalized formulation it appears relatively bland: 'that significant changes within a system cannot be sustained unless consistent changes occur in the relatedness of the system to its environment'. Applied in the context of rural development, however, the requisite change in relation to the environment is one of greater influence and control—a reversal of deprivation and often of exploitation. Inescapably, therefore, the second proposition takes us into uncomfortable issues of power and conflict; whereas the first proposition, in focusing on adaptation to a changing or turbulent environment, keeps our feet on much safer ground.

Although I say 'inescapably', it is tempting in fact—and a temptation to which I have at times unwittingly succumbed—to shy away from the implications by using a terminology that describes the state of the system without explicating the consequence for transactions across the boundary. So one speaks of 'moving from heteronomy towards autonomy', of 'self-management', or of 'managing one's own development'. The tacit hope perhaps is that power-holders in the environment affected by these changes will not actually notice them, or will adjust, or will even applaud and support them. Nor is this totally implausible. If a development programme brings to a region a significant increment of prosperity, the 'positive-sum' model may apply: economically every party gains. Relative losses by the existing power-holders in the 'zero-sum game' of power will be less noticeable, or at least less unacceptable. Ultimately, however, one cannot duck the reality that development is a political activity, concerned with the reallocation of power.

In fact, by instituting a rural development programme at all, a national government is committing itself to rectifying accumulated inequalities; hence the clients of development are the neglected districts in a state, the neglected villages in a district and, at the microlevel, the neglected subgroups in a village. Through its agencies the government needs to form coalitions with these clients, by means of which they become capable of acting back upon their environments and so rectifying the inequalities. It is by its willingness or otherwise in practice to implement such coalitions, of course, that a postrevolutionary government displays whether it is indeed continuing to pursue stated revolutionary aims or merely engaging in rhetoric. The government's development agent in the field therefore faces interesting dilemmas. His problems are least—indeed, he can gain a great deal of satisfaction—if he can see himself as championing the cause of a backward, homogeneous community and helping it to acquire independence of anonymous external exploiters. Perhaps for that reason he is inclined to perceive the local community as more cohesive than it actually is, to miss signs of internal factionalism, and to promote egalitarian, collective forms of community organization in settlements of small farmers whose culture values individualism. Once the exploiters become identifiable figures, especially if they live within the community, he is faced with awkward and contentious choices that he would prefer to sidestep. Co-option is one strategy to evade confrontation: that is to say, the development agent allies himself with the 'exploiter' and attempts to persuade him to make room for the development of the 'exploited'. He is likely to do this under two conditions: first, he perceives the political power of the government that employs him as being dependent more on the support of the 'exploiter' than of the 'exploited'; and the second and related condition is that he identifies the 'exploiter' as belonging to a social class from which government officials and experts, including the development agent himself, tend to be drawn. Co-option of this kind may have a marginal effect in mitigating inequalities; it will not procure any lasting change in the politico-economic structure. Other strategies may also be used, which come closer to, but nevertheless avoid, direct confrontation. Important here is the encouragement of cooperative interest groups that transcend village boundaries for purchase of supplies, credit, or marketing. The traditional power of rural landlords and merchants has relied on the absence of organization among the scattered, 'exploited' groups in different villages. Any change achieved through a coalition between the development agency and an exploited subgroup within one village is most unlikely to be sustained unless that subgroup has formed an effective alliance with similarly deprived subgroups in other villages. If it is to pursue its task, the development agency needs to promote such an alliance as its client system. Direct confrontation between the development agency and local 'exploiters' may not be necessary to bring about change. However, if I am right in postulating that development ultimately involves reallocation of power, then no significant change will in fact occur unless the agency itself feels powerful enough to risk such a confrontation. In Mexico, as a result of the programme, some state governors are now perceiving that their power-base is shifting: actual or potential coalitions between Federal development agencies and the rural poor mean that the old rural establishment can no longer be relied upon to control the votes; and so such governors find it useful to be perceived by the villagers as protagonists of development.

Although such a shift is encouraging evidence that development, as I have defined it, is actually happening, it raises further interesting problems. Certainly, many of the traditional local middlemen have been exploitative; but it does not follow that, if they are bypassed or eliminated, exploitation and inequality will vanish. Convenient though they may be as scapegoats, they are only one element in a distribution system through which the grower receives only a fraction of what the consumer pays for food.* Many power-holders are invisible. A fuller understanding of power requires scrutiny of the 'mobilization of bias' :† that is, who gains and who is handicapped by the dominant values, myths, established political procedures, and rules of the game. Such an analysis will show, of course, that the ultimate culprits are the rich industrialized countries; and my definitions of underdevelopment and of the task of development are as appli-

---

*A mark-up of 500–600 per cent is normal in Mexico. One writer reported that, in August 1971, growers in the Northern Sierra of Puebla were receiving the equivalent of $1\frac{1}{2}$ cents for a kilogram of avocados which sold for 1 dollar in the supermarkets of Mexico City—a margin of no less than 7200 per cent (Paré, 1975, p. 40, footnote).

†See Bacharch and Baratz, 1962, and Schattschneider, 1960.

cable to countries as to rural communities. However, to tackle underdevelopment as an international problem is not a substitute for action at local levels: elevation of a problem to huge and intractable proportions is a familiar justification for doing nothing.

What I want to suggest in conclusion, and briefly to illustrate, is that my rediscovered second proposition, along with its political implications, is relevant not only to rural development in the Third World but to other forms of development much nearer home: for example, organizational development, psychotherapy, and group relations training conferences.

Organizational development seems very often to assume a closed system model. Attempts are made through a team-building exercise, for example, to rearrange and 'improve' relationships within a group. Such an exercise is undertaken because the group is seen as less effective than it might be. 'Effectiveness' is here synonymous with capacity to influence the environment—with power. (One recalls that Bertrand Russell defined power as 'the production of intended effects'.) Our proposition tells us that unless there is change in the relatedness of the group to its environment—a change in the direction of greater potency—the internal improvements in relationships will not be sustained. If the group is a senior management team, the hoped-for outcome is greater potency in relation to customers, competitors, or suppliers. If, however, this outer boundary is intractable, then it is predictable that either the management team will redirect its energies into conflict with other groups within the enterprise—for example, trade unions—or it will regress. If on the other hand the group being 'developed' lies not on the boundary of the enterprise but inside it—for example, a production department—so that its environment consists of other departments, then 'successful' internal development will depend on changes in relationships with one or more of those departments. The resultant conflict may well be productive, though it is often unwelcome because it calls into question the established 'mobilization of bias'. My point is that, although many people may wish otherwise, organizational development cannot be effective without also being a political activity, involving changes in the distribution of power. Whether he is aware of it or not, the OD consultant is implicated in that activity. His intervention engages him in a coalition with a client system, which is normally a subgroup within a larger organization. Even though he may claim to be an uncommitted professional, he cannot escape external perceptions of that coalition and interpretations placed upon it. It is not surprising, therefore, that the casualty rate among OD change agents is high. To survive, the change agent must either help his client to become very successful—i.e. powerful—or else get out before the client begins to test his new-found muscle. If the client then discovers that either his spirit or his flesh is weak, the change agent is subject to violent extrusion.

Psychotherapy and group relations conferences are less risky for practitioners. Both invite the individual to reexamine and restructure aspects of his internal world and to reconsider person–role relationships in the light of new understanding. Our proposition suggests, however, that neither patient nor conference member will sustain the revised understanding and conception of self unless it can be implemented in revised role relationships. Like the OD change agent, the therapist or consultant is implicated in a political activity. To plead professionalism, and to claim that it is for the client/patient/member to decide what use, if any, to make of his insight and learning, is surely an evasion if one knows that persistence of the insight and learning is contingent on new role relationships that will reinforce the understanding that has been gained? I myself have written elsewhere that:

It is on [the member's] own authority to decide what to do with this understanding in his roles in other institutions, whether as manager or managed. However, I acknowledge that I personally hope that he will acquire greater potency to question and perhaps change his relationship with his working environment. (Miller, 1977, p. 44)

But is this good enough? If learning can be sustained only through change, do I not have to risk taking a moral stance in relation to possible changes? Pierre Turquet was more willing than most of us to accept the moral and political responsibilities of the professional role and to make his judgements overt.

References

Ackoff, R. (1977) 'National development planning revisited'. *Operations Research*, **25**, 207–218.

Bachrach, P., and Baratz, M. S. (1962) 'Two faces of power'. *American Political Science Review*, **56**, 947–952.

Bertalanffy, L. von (1950a) 'The theory of open systems in physics and biology'. *Science*, **3**, 23–29.

Bertalanffy, L. von (1950b) 'An outline of general systems theory'. *British Journal of the Philosophy of Science*, **1**, 134–165.

Bion, W. R. (1961) *Experiences in Groups*. London: Tavistock Publications.

Emery, F. E., and Trist, E. L. (1965) 'The causal texture of organizational environments'. *Human Relations*, **18**, 21–32.

Freire, P. (1972a) *The Pedagogy of the Oppressed*. London: Sheed & Ward.

Freire, P. (1972b) *Cultural Action for Freedom*. Harmondsworth: Penguin Books.

Gosling, R. (in press) 'A study of very small groups'. In J. Grotstein (ed.) (title not yet known). New York: Aronson.

Heckadon, S. (1973) *Los Asentamientos Campesinos: un experincia panamena en reforma agragia*. Guatemala: UNICEF.

Holling, C. S., and Goldberg, M. A. (1971) 'Ecology and planning'. *Journal of the American Institute of Planners*, **37**, 221–230.

Jennings, P. R. (1976) 'The amplification of agricultural production'. *Scientific American*, **253**, no. 3.

Lawrence, W. G., and Miller, E. J. (1976) 'Epilogue'. In E. J. Miller (ed.) *Task and Organization*. London: Wiley, 361–366.

Lewin, K. (1936) *Principles of Topological Psychology*. New York: McGraw-Hill.

Lewin, K. (1947) 'Frontiers in group dynamics: I. Concept, method and reality in social equilibria and social change'. *Human Relations*, **1**, 5–41.

Lewin, K. (1950) *Field Theory in Social Science*. New York: Harper Brothers.

Miller, E. J. (1975) 'Socio-technical systems in weaving, 1953–1970: a follow-up study'. *Human Relations*, **28**, 349–386.

Miller, E. J. (1976a) 'The open-system approach to organizational analysis, with specific reference to the work of A. K. Rice'. In G. Hofstede and M. Sami Kassem (eds) *European Contributions to Organizational Theory*. Assen: Van Gorcum, 43–61.

Miller, E. J. (ed.) (1976b) *Task and Organization*. London: Wiley.

Miller, E. J. (1976c) *Desarrollo integral del medio rural: un experimento en México* Mexico, DF: Fondo de Cultura Económica.

Miller, E. J. (1977) 'Organizational development and industrial democracy: a current case-study'. In C. Cooper (ed.) *Organizational Development in the UK and US: A Joint Evaluation*. London: Macmillan, pp. 31–63.

Paré, L. (1975) 'Caciquismo y estructura de poder en la Sierra Norte de Puebla'. In R. Bartra *et al.*, *Caciquismo y Poder Politico en el México Rural*, Mexico, DF: Siglo Veintiuno Editores, 31–61.

Rice, A. K. (1958) *Productivity and Social Organization: The Ahmedabad Experiment*. London: Tavistock Publications.

Rice, A. K. (1963) *The Enterprise and its Environment*. London: Tavistock Publications.

Rice, A. K., and Trist, E. L. (1952) 'Institutional and sub-institutional determinants of change in labour turnover'. *Human Relations*, **5**, 83–90.

Schattschneider, E. E. (1960) *The Semisovereign People*. New York: Holt, Reinhart, & Winston.

Trist, E. L. (1976) 'A concept of organizational ecology'. Address delivered in Melbourne, July.

Trist, E. L., and Bamforth, K. (1951) 'Some social and psychological consequences of the longwall method of coal-getting'. *Human Relations*, **4**, 3–38.

World Bank (1975) *Rural Development: Sector Policy Paper*. World Bank, Washington, DC: World Bank.

Chapter 16

A Concept for Today: The Management of Oneself in Role

W. Gordon Lawrence

The group relations training which continues to be developed and articulated through the Tavistock Model that this book explores is not an activity that is divorced from concerns about the larger society. Since these educational ventures began there have been shifts in the larger society and, for example, authority has become a 'bad object' even though, on the surface, it looks as if we are living in stable, rational enterprises and institutions. In much the same way that the development of psychoanalysis as a discipline of thought and practice has meant that an analysis takes longer as analysands become more defended simply because there are more insights publicly available, I guess that participants in group relations experiences, too, become defended. More positively, however, it can be said that having experienced, identified, and named particular social phenomena of an unconscious nature which can be rediscovered in each educational venture, hitherto unnamed phenomena begin to become apparent. Therefore I believe that there are two challenges before those who sponsor and take up consultant roles in such group relations ventures. The first task is to continue to identify unconscious social processes as manifested in group settings. The second task emerges from this and the history and traditions of the thinking and practice generated through this Tavistock Model: to make explicit and to realize the political value of this work. This is the concept of the management of oneself in role.

In an earlier paper the writer and a colleague attempted to put flesh on the bones of this notion. We wrote:

The self-managing individual ... is refusing to allow cultural assumptions to remain untested and he is disentangling the cobweb of myths and mysteries of our social institutions. He has to differentiate between what is conventionally agreed to be reality and what is reality for him. Thus, whereas it is widely accepted that the search for scientific objectivity requires the individual to suppress subjective judgement, we would turn this proposition on its head and postulate that objectivity is essentially the clarification of one's own subjectivity.

But as he examines more closely what is inside and what is outside and tries to regulate the boundary between them, the individual is confronting those very cultural forms, hitherto taken for granted, that provide the defensive structures and thus confronting his own primitive inner needs that these structures satisfy. In giving up an external definition of 'reality' and substituting his own, he is therefore giving up elements of certainty and security and substituting uncertainty and insecurity.

> Our argument is that the resultant disorder and chaos are the necessary risks and costs of undertaking change. Social change inescapably starts with self. (Lawrence and Miller, 1976)

Since we wrote that, I have puzzled a good deal as to how to make the content have real forms as part of living in industrialized societies.

In particular, I have been trying to come to grips with what meaning has to be placed on the phrase 'the cobweb of myths and mysteries'. What follows is a set of tentative working hypotheses about society and some thoughts on the possibilities of and constraints on the realization of the value of managing oneself in role.

Mass society

We have to acknowledge that the here and now of our lives is embedded in mass society. And the implications of this social fact must continually be identified and interpreted. There are, however, no really adequate theories, even fully elaborated descriptions that capture all the facets of mass society. Such major sociologists as Weber, Tonnies, Marx, and de Tocqueville, and Freud in his *Civilization and its Discontents*, have all attempted to capture and elucidate the phenomena of industrializing societies, charting their causes and effects. But in the final analysis we are left with *apperçus*, at most working hypotheses, or sketches, of mass society that will change over time because of the very nature of such a society. One such set of working hypotheses can be found in the work of a literary critic:

> By the mass society we mean a relatively comfortable, half-welfare and half-garrison society in which the population grows passive, indifferent and atomized; in which traditional loyalties, ties, and associations become lax or dissolve entirely; in which coherent publics based on definite interests and opinions gradually fall apart; and in which man becomes a consumer, himself mass-produced like the products, diversions and values that he absorbs. (Howe, 1971)

This is not the whole picture. Some live in a world that is felt to be increasingly shapeless and is an increasingly fluid experience. To understand our experiences we are continually pressed to a psychic exploration of a set of intangible boundaries: certainty and uncertainty, chaos and order, the tolerable from the intolerable, destruction and creativity. Rational culture, so prized for centuries, is in the process of dissolution (McLuhan and Nevitt, 1972). So the concepts that have shaped our perceptions are found increasingly redundant because our perceptions of our experience are bursting the frames of our well-tried conceptualizations that once gave full meaning to life.

But the overwhelming experience is of social passivity.

There is a wish, sometimes quite explicit and not so unconscious, that the State through its agencies will look after each individual. The governments of advanced industrial societies pride themselves on their ability to provide welfare services. Increasingly, however, it is expected that the State will always be able to find the resources to meet these demands. Such a primitive dependency arises when groups or institutions find it difficult to face the realities of their situation or feel that no solutions to their problems are possible. This is an outcome, or at least one effect, of what a colleague, Isabel Menzies, has called the 'I want' philosophy of society which is engendered by industrialized societies which convert citizens into consumers; public into mass. As she puts it, the 'I want' is

little related to the realistic possibility of getting what one wants or to considerations of the sacrifices the 'I' may require of others to get what he wants. This can be carried so far that people behave almost as though society's resources are unlimited. Political statements increasingly imply that all we need is more money: the resources it represents will somehow then magically become available. Money is treated almost as a thing in itself not as a symbol. This reflects a potentially psychotic and destructive social process, reflected in the rapidly diminishing real value of money. (Menzies, 1975)

There is a sense in which these unconscious processes of industrial societies are even more insidious. The 'I want' is related to the feeling of envy that others may also want and get. And so institutions are developed in society to ensure that there is an equitable distribution of resources thus further reinforcing dependency upon the State and its agencies.

The social passivity I am pointing to, then, is a strangely potent force. Equally, it is related to potentially psychotic and destructive forces. A socially passive mass spawns other crowdlike, unconscious social processes. The obverse of social passivity is the exaggerated social aggressiveness such as is demonstrated by urban guerilla groups or some striking students, for instance. To shock the passive, the aggression has to be inflated. The socially passive react in a more defended fashion against the destruction of the aggressive activists who, in turn, become more paranoid that they are not heard by the mass. So the violence has to be made even more monstrous.

Clearly, it is a social cartoon that I draw, but I want to hold firmly to the lineaments of destruction present in contemporary societies. Erich Fromm traces a connection between contemporary man's existential situation and destruction. The point is simple enough:

If man cannot create anything or move anybody, if he cannot break out of the prison of his total narcissism and isolation, he can escape the unbearable sense of vital impotence and nothingness only by affirming himself in the act of destruction of the life that he is unable to create. Great effort, patience and care are not required; for destruction, all that is necessary is strong arms, or a knife or a gun. (Fromm, 1977 edn)

Social passivity which is engendered, albeit unwittingly, by the State and its agencies, and is also engendered in industrial and other enterprises, means that individuals find it difficult to give meaning to their lives and become isolated units without a normal dependency on external objects. Individuals become preoccupied with themselves, unempathic, and hold an inflated self-concept of themselves. Furthermore, what is unacceptable to the self-image is repressed and projected onto external objects, which are then devalued. It is but a short step to destroying external objects. These are narcissistic characteristics.

Other writers have pointed to this kind of disconnection from the realities of life using similar terms. Friedenberg, developing themes of R. D. Laing, suggests that we are experiencing a psychic closing-off on the part of individuals, a 'psychological alienation which deprives people of the capacity to accept or even become aware of their own feelings' (Friedenberg, 1973).

This is familiar enough terrain. What is much more difficult to get a purchase on are the large-scale, unconscious social processes present in society. In the same essay Friedenberg makes the important point that in contemporary societies 'the wielders of power have a vested interest in keeping the sovereign people alienated, it exacerbates their paranoia, but it diminishes their insight and self-confidence, and hence their political effectiveness' (Friedenberg, 1973).

The experience of political ineffectiveness is one of the major effects of the social and individual processes I have been identifying. Friedenberg's hypothesis is tenable. There is a fatal split between man and the institutions of society. Raymond Williams has argued that this split, what he calls 'the crisis of the knowable community' (Williams, 1974 edn) can be traced to the 20 months between 1847 and 1848 and found in the major novels written in that period by Dickens and others. The novelists of that period experienced extraordinary changes in English society. Agreed social and moral codes began to disintegrate with the advent of industrialization. For the purposes of this argument the important point is William's hypothesis that this central process began to be apparent in society:

An increasing scepticism, disbelief, in the possibility of understanding society; a structurally similar certainty that relationships, knowable relationships, so far from comprising a community or society, are the positive experience that has to be *contrasted* with the ordinarily negative experience of the society as a whole (or of the society as opposed to the local and immediate community). An important split takes place between knowable relationships and an unknown, unknowable, overwhelming society. (Williams, 1974 edn)

So we are in a position where it is believed that society is unknowable, is a 'thing', is a reification. This is one central myth of contemporary industrial cultures, and one which structures the perceived and felt relatedness of the individual to society. It is, then, understandable why the mass becomes socially passive and psychologically numb and amenable to the power of the State and, by extension, to the power of any institution and enterprise of society.

Such a rupture of the felt relationship between the individual and society was not experienced at the same pace by others than the novelists to whom Williams refers. The dissociation was a more gradual process for the bulk of the population and there was resistance. E. P. Thompson has argued that the working-class community of the early nineteenth century was the product of a 'high degree of working class endeavour' (Thompson, 1968 edn). He has marshalled evidence to show that while the working class may have had their traditional roots of existence and essence wrested from a safe soil they were able to articulate a political consciousness, to form a picture of the organization of society out of their own experience. There was a radical culture held by skilled workers, together with a sense that Utopia could be realized. The early nineteenth century was, according to Thompson, the time of

the most popular culture England has known. It contained the massive diversity of skills, of the workers in metal, wood, textiles and ceramics without whose inherited 'mysteries' and superb ingenuity with primitive tools the inventions of the Industrial Revolution could scarcely have got further than the drawing board. From this culture of the craftsman and the self-taught there came scores of inventors, organizers, journalists and political theorists of impressive quality. (Thompson, 1968 edn)

Again and again in the last century such men resisted attempts to be made into 'tools' or 'implements'. Even 'when they knew their cause was lost . . . they reached out again, in the Thirties and Forties, and sought to achieve new and only imagined forms of social control' (Thompson, 1968 edn). But despite their heroic culture, with its dreams, visions, and utopian ideals, such men became what they feared the most: the proletariat; a dissociated aggregate of society; men and women converted from citizens to mass consumers. Now, a century later, we are in the midst of mass society, that 'half-welfare and half-garrison society in which the population grows passive, indifferent and atomized' (Howe, 1971).

In this dissociation of the knowable from the unknowable the social sciences have had their part to play. Indeed, the salient methodologies of the social sciences in a sense have legitimated the myth of the split between the individual and society. Practitioners of the social sciences, for the most part, have failed to use their imaginative capabilities. Subjectivity has been pushed out of scientific discourse. It may well be that this is because practitioners have been concerned about their own purity and have avoided situations and methodologies which might endanger their 'professionalism'. The danger for the social anthropologist has always been that he 'goes native' and ceases to be a 'professional'. More generally, the stance of some social scientists has been to maintain an I–It, instrumental, pseudo-professional relationship with their world of 'respondents'.

A useful way of thinking about the social sciences and which points to why social science practitioners may be failing to use their imagination has been advanced by John O'Neill who suggests that sociology is best thought of as a 'skin' trade. In this context, sociology is not unlike the skin trades such as haircutting or dentistry which, like the professions of priest or medical doctor, are concerned with the sacredness and profanity which surrounds the human body. Because of the ambivalence felt about this, skin trade practitioners literally have to surround themselves with activities which distance themselves from their clients. Metaphorical skin trade practitioners, such as social scientists, are also caught in the same ambivalence. Hence the movement to objectify the subject of research; to convert the person into a collection of variables, for example. As O'Neill puts it:

Much of the sociological apparatus functions, I suggest, to support a ritual of decontamination between the scientist and his subject. It is essential he view his subject only with professional eyes and that he resist the look in the eyes of the sick, the poor, and the aimless who turn his questions back on him. In this way the erotic symbiosis of talk is reduced to the interview schedule or attitude survey in which the client comes clean before the professional *voyeur*. (O'Neill, 1972)

My argument is that the social sciences ought to be a skin trade exploring the boundaries that are problematic—psychic, social, and political skins—because disorder is not to be kept at bay but entertained, understood, and worked with as a route to new forms of being which would include the political relatedness of the individual to society. Some research methodologies, however, because they protect the scientist from uncertainty, preclude this kind of knowing.

What Martin Buber has called the I–It relationship is often the organizing myth of the social sciences. The I–It relationship of the social scientist to his subject is often seen as being a proper scientific stance. But this is the inevitable outcome of the separation of the observer from the observed and rests on the presuppositions that there exists outside any one individual man a 'kingdom of order' in the sense that it is outside his will and desire. Hence, truth means the discovery of that preestablished order. The second presupposition is that man's 'cognitive apparatus does not materially affect the observation of this pre-established order' (Hampden-Turner, 1973). On these presuppositions are based social science methodologies such as behaviourism, functionalism, and operational research.

The question is whether the social sciences are to provide neatly ordered accounts of reality or whether the accounts are to reflect the complexity and the latent disorder. The behavioural sciences, for example, as Eugene Schwartz indicates, are a good instance of a particular formulation of the purpose of the social sciences:

The thrust of the behavioural sciences is to stamp out disorder because the sciences cannot deal with it; to create activities that are conducive to control and hence to prediction; to make the complex simple because otherwise it cannot be comprehended. More serious is that science declared it a *sine qua non* that it must be objective by eliminating all subjective values and judgements, although, as has been shown earlier, subjective judgements were the bases of the axioms upon which science itself was built. Science, it is claimed, is thus neither good nor bad, but neutral. But if science is ahuman in its neutrality by banishing all human qualities, is it not but a short step to become inhuman? (Schwartz, 1971)

All of these strictures can be applied to many social science practitioners. My major point is that such a conception of social science is not adequate for working with the complexity of reality. This is not an argument against measurement *per se* as, clearly, certain features of reality can be quantified. The issue is whether the quantification is an avoidance of complexity or not. For example, the social scientist, in trying to understand what takes place in groups of people, attempts to reduce human group life to variables and their correlations. Not only is the choice of variables frequently faulty—chosen, often, because of their measurability—but also such an approach only interprets the outward facts of the situation. The basis of the behaviour of the participants—that is, what they hold in their minds about the situation and themselves in relation to that situation—is not taken into account.

The kind of difficulty this gets us into has been identified by a colleague, Peter Barham, in an earlier paper on group relations training (Barham and Lawrence, 1974). He referred to Poulantzas, the political scientist, who wrote of the difficulty: 'in comprehending social classes and the State as objective structures and their relation as an objective system of regular connections, a structure and a system whose agents, "men", are in the words of Marx "bearers" of it—*träger*' (Poulantzas, 1969). Poulantzas went on to speak of the impression thus given that:

social classes of 'groups' are in some way reducible to inter-personal relations, and the State is reducible to inter-personal relations of the diverse 'groups' that constitute the State apparatus, and finally that the relations between social classes and the State itself as reducible to inter-personal relations of 'individuals' composing social groups and 'individuals' composing the State apparatus. (Poulantzas, 1969)

At this juncture I merely want to hold on to the view that this kind of impression is an inevitable outcome of the split between the knowable and unknowable community; the dissociation of objectivity from subjectivity; the division between modes of knowing. The healing of these splits, it is commonly believed, can only be brought about through 'solving' interpersonal relations; the mechanics of relating. The subjective society carried inside the individual is disregarded. But I am beginning to believe that it is the society 'in the mind', the internalized experiences, the introjected and projected experiences of that object we call 'society', that need to be identified. My hunch is that if the necessary language could be created to explore these experiences of the fatal split between what is perceived to be knowable and unknowable we would be some way towards making available for inspection the not so conscious social processes which I have been indicating, albeit in terms of a social cartoon.

It is to the lineaments of destruction, however, that I return. Mass society, I am suggesting, has more than its share of destructiveness. A major constraint on being able to identify and interpret this destructiveness rests in the very processes of an industrial society. Social passivity, psychological alienation, narcissism are all interrelated. This produces social impotence which produces passivity, etc., and a mindless destruction and violence. It would be too neat to see these in cause and effect terms. They happen; spasmodically erupting in confusing configurations.

What we can hypothesize, however, is that just as there is a fatal split between the knowable and unknowable of society, and the hows of knowing, so there is a fatal split between life and death. The presence of death is made absent, wished away in contemporary societies. In part this is understandable because the collective historical experience of people in the twentieth century has been of the arbitrariness of death and the realization that death can be manufactured like any other product. Wars, political purges, and exterminations and the rationality of the death machine of the concentration camp have caused a disjunction between the fact of life and the fact of death. The socially inherited, internalized rhythm of the sequence of life and death has been broken. Consequently, as Freud earlier identified in his 'Thoughts for the times on war and death' (1915), people become defended against the meaning of death as a process. The paradox is that the more people become defended against death, and the inevitability of their own death, the more it becomes possible for death to be manufactured and split off from life. Destruction and violence are thus split off from the fact of death and in such a nonemotional climate can be, at times, regnant.

But there are people who are identifying, exploring, and interpreting these frightening 'public issues', to use C. Wright Mills's (1970 edn) celebrated phrase. Almost predictably it is left to some poets, and not the majority of social scientists, to make some purchase on these near-intractable processes I have briefly indicated. Alvarez in his recent study of suicide describes the work of what he has called the Extremist poets—Robert Lowell, John Berryman, Ted Hughes, and Sylvia Plath—and suggests that they explore the experiences of the nihilism of contemporary, destructive societies. Since this cannot be controlled politically from the outside, he argues, the only way left is to try and control it artistically within the individual. This takes the individual, through the use of his feelings, to the friable boundary between the tolerable and the intolerable. And for Sylvia Plath this Extremist impulse became 'total and, literally, final' with her suicide as she explored 'the nexus of anger, guilt, rejection, love and destructiveness' (Alvarez, 1974) of her life.

Here, I think, Alvarez identifies the major problem if the kind of exploration indicated is to be embarked upon. Because the mass, and ourselves as part of that mass, are reluctant to start the journey, those who do are made, at best, scapegoats and, at worst, victims. The public issues are neatly converted into 'private troubles', again to use a telling phrase of C. Wright Mills's (1970 edn). The individual who explores his own subjective experiences runs the risk of being converted into the 'mad person', and then the remainder can hold the picture of being 'civilized' and 'contented'. The impotence is locked away.

Nevertheless, my postulate is that the social sciences have much the same task as the Extremist poets which is, as Alvarez ends his book, to force

its audience to recognise and accept imaginatively, in their nerve-ends, not the facts of life but the facts of death and violence: absurd, random, gratuitous, unjustified, and inescapably part of the society we have created. 'There is only one liberty,' wrote Camus in his *Notebooks*, 'to come to terms with death. After which everything is possible.' (Alvarez, 1974)

But I would want to turn around some of what Alvarez says. In particular, I want to suggest that the getting in touch with the nihilism of society is, in fact, possible through political management from within the individual. Social change, which implies an inspection of social realities, starts from the individual considering his or her authority for being in a role in institutions of a society.

The management of onself in role

My proposition is that this value has to be put into practice if we are to get in touch with, name, and interpret the kind of unconscious social processes in society to which I have been alluding. The realization of the value would be both a cause and an effect of this inspection process. This, it seems to me, is one way to create a shift in industrial societies in the direction of novel forms of living and existing in contemporary institutions. To put it tersely: the shift has to be 'from having to being', to use Fromm's (1976) phrase. This means, I suspect, a reorientation of the individual's understanding of his political relatedness to the institutions of his society; a reorientation from having/not having power and authority as some kind of social possession towards taking authority for the nature of one's being as a system interrelating with other systems, be they other people, families, enterprises, institutions, or society.

I have been trying to indicate that we are imprisoned in our institutions and in societies. W. R. Bion in a recent interview talked about institutional imprisonment but pointed to some basis for hope:

The trouble about all institutions—the Tavistock Institute and every one that we have— is that they are dead, but the people inside them aren't, and the people grow and something's going to happen. What usually happens is that the institutions (societies, nations, states and so forth) make laws. The original laws constitute a shell, and then new laws expand that shell. If it were a material prison, you could hope that the prison walls would be elastic in some sort of way. If organizations don't do that, they develop a hard shell, and then expansion can't occur because the organization has locked itself in. (Bion, 1976)

Institutions have locked themselves in both politically and psychically; and so have, perhaps, the majority of the people who serve them. Consequently, the realization of the promise of the value of management of oneself in role, or some variation on it, or a more radical alternative, while it remains always a possibility, always will be constrained. There are the constraints woven into the fabric mass society. These cannot be legislated away. No amount of rational planning will remove them or their causes but, paradoxically, will only reinforce them. So the starting-point is the individual in his or her roles in relation to the systems in which he or she lives and works.

This has always been a concern of the group relations training of this Tavistock Model. It has been, at times, an uncomfortable concern and has been to interpersonal skill work, or consultants have been invoked as millenarian leaders. Fortunately, there have always been sufficient participants in a conference who have held doggedly to the primary task. There are some now who are convinced that the value of management of oneself in role has to be pursued. So, for example, a recent venture has been a working conference entitled 'Authority and Social Innovation' which was sponsored by the Tavistock Group Relations Training Programme and La Fondation Internationale de l'Innovation Sociale based in Paris. More important has been the continued development of what can be called the 'living methodology' intrinsic to the work of this Tavistock Model. The methodology is concerned to focus on whole systems and their relatedness, and not be caught in the kind of reductionism that character-ises so much of what passes for social science. The methodology stands outside the scientific culture of society in these senses and also because the method starts from exploring what is experienced subjectively.

Evidence that the realization of this value is possible can be found outside conferences. Eric Miller in the previous essay shows this. More generally, however, it can be postulated that this value is one of the probable outcomes of conceptualizing enterprises as socio-technical systems with open boundaries.

The concept of socio-technical systems thinking is just over 20 years old and, since its first formulation in Trist and Bamforth's (1951) 'Some social and psychological consequences of the long-wall method of coal-getting', has proved to be a particularly useful heuristic tool for many Tavistock research workers and others. Essentially, the concept points to the interrelatedness of technical and socio-psychological factors in production enterprises. Other factors present are economic and political. The thrust of the socio-technical concept has been to call into question the salience of technology as determining social, political, and other relationships within enterprises. As a result, organizational choice becomes possible since it is possible to design forms of work organization that optimize the best fit among social, psychological, technical, political, and economic factors.

One consequence of a socio-technical approach to organizational design has been the emergence of the concept of semi-autonomous work groups. The corollary of this idea is that every individual who takes up a role in a work group, and by extension in an enterprise, is called upon to manage himself in his role. This is done in two ways: by managing himself in relation to his work tasks and activities, and by managing his relationships with other role-holders. And it is on the potentiality of and constraints on this notion that I focus in this essay.

To hold the view that individuals, enterprises, and indeed all institutions are systems with open boundaries is to begin a journey in organizational, political, social, and existential thinking which can cause a radical questioning of much of what is believed to be efficient organizational design. It can be postula-ted that if this journey were to be made it could lead to a reformulation of the nature of the relationship between the individual, through his or her role, and the work enterprise and, by extension, with society. Current ideas about bringing about compliance in enterprises would need to be overhauled so that the nature of the authority relationships between the enterprise, through its managerial representatives, and employees was redefined. My hypothesis is, however, that such a search for new meaning about that complex nexus can create such anxieties that people in enterprises very often revert to, or perseve-rate with, taken-for-granted modes of organizational design.

An example of the possibility of the value of self-management in role being realized was experienced by the writer and a colleague, Eric Miller, when they had the opportunity to act as consultants to the management of a factory which was being established on a green-field site. The task was to design jointly the plant and the organization. The chosen base for the organization was the semi-autonomous work group. In particular each task system responsible for the throughput was composed of workers who had authority to manage the transformation processes. A work group was defined as follows: 'a set of associates who jointly accept responsibility for managing operating activities, process control and correction to achieve agreed standards within a defined task boundary'.

The importance of the introduction of the term 'managing' in this context is not to be underestimated. In particular, it was being suggested that work groups were responsible for taking in imports across their task boundary, converting them into another state, and exporting them to the next system. This transformation process determined the primary task. Within work groups workers were to be free to allocate roles for the execution of the primary task. Management, therefore, was a collective responsibility of the work group.

Such an idea cannot be carried out unless there is a change in the external environment composed of other systems. Two changes were to be important in this context: the conversion of quality control from a traditional control function to one of support, and a similar reorientation of production management. In this instance the quality control management (one of the services) saw themselves as providing the means for work groups to monitor their process controls at the boundaries of their task system and during the conversion process. Under this arrangement it became quite possible for each work group as a system to consider refusing at the import boundary materials or products that they did not think were up to standard. The regulation of the import and export boundaries of each work group as a task system thus becomes crucial, not only because it is through the management of boundaries that each system relates to another as an open system, but also because it affirms that the work group's authority derives from their collective primary task.

The political implications of management within a work group seem clear enough: it is a collective responsibility concerned with transacting across the boundaries of the system and coordinating the activities and relationships of one role-holder with another in relation to the primary task of the system. Thus each role-holder is not only concerned with the management of himself in his role but is also having to hold the management of the work group 'in the mind'. 'In the mind', in this context, means that the individual in his role holds a *Gestalt* of the system as a whole with which he relates from his role, and that he can locate his work group as a system with the other systems of the enterprise. Consequently, decisions about the work and social life of the work group are located within that group, but have to be related to the realities of other work groups as systems with their primary tasks.

If the process of management is located within the semi-autonomous work group what is the function of those who are officially designated 'production managers'? Essentially, their role is to provide and regulate the conditions (materials, supplies, intelligence about the market, budget information, and technical expertise, for instance) for the work groups to manage themselves in their roles on the basis of the authority inherent in their primary tasks. On reflection, I believe that in addition they have an educational task which is not merely directed at obvious information-sharing but is directed at raising the political consciousness of themselves and their fellow workers. By this I mean exercising responsibility, authority, and leadership on behalf of the system as a whole, i.e. acting as an ego to the system. Since all enterprises exist in turbulent economic environments this function will become more important.

After three years the project ended because 'the management' felt that they had gone far enough. There are two possible explanations for this, apart from the stated one. 'The management' may well have found themselves bereft of a recognizable role. People change at different paces and the lowest common denominator tends to hold sway. Even though 'the management' had invested considerable enthusiasm and various kinds of energies for the success of the project which all said publicly they valued, anxieties had been expressed at various times by some managers that if this project continued there would be no job for them. The other reason probably lies with the workers. On what journey was this project to take them? While they could and did express a high degree of satisfaction with conditions in the new factory, it may be that the demands were too high. Only those who see themselves as having the status of manager tend to manage a career on their life-chances. My hypothesis is, however, that the project and its new work experiences put into disarray the taken-for-granted assumptions made by most workers about the relatedness between themselves and management both as a status and political aggregate and as a process.

But this is understandable. The project was always seen by the consultants as being an educational venture concerned with the politics of the involvement of the individual in his role in the enterprise. Without exception all participants in the project, irrespective of their roles, had shared perceptions and constructions of the accepted organization of enterprises which were based on their discrete, previous work experiences. They had all been inducted into one of the salient myths of organizations: management equals man-management.

Work in mass industrial societies is experienced as coercive. In part this is expected because it is seen as providing the financial means to live in a consumer society. (The reality, as I have been inspecting earlier in this essay, is that citizens have been converted into consumers.) The frustration of ego needs and the ability to exercise authority and autonomy in one's work role have been compensated for by consuming more social and other goods. (Having more, wanting more, and envy of those who have more, have replaced values about being.) When this has become intolerable, when the sense of social persecution and social depression has been allowed to be voiced, the result has been the 'go-slow', etc. The repressed feelings erupt in violent actions. Usually, however, the overconsumption has been channelled into the need to earn more which has sanctioned those who have traditional political power within an enterprise to continue to make work coercive and to continue to be able to define their role in terms of managing other people. They, in turn, have their shared myth that

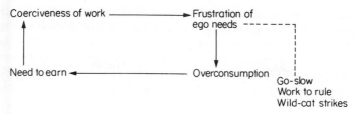

Figure 1

technology is value-free and neutral; that it determines the plant and social organization, and therefore the political relationships in the enterprise. And for the most part they are provided rationalizations by the motivation theory merchants who hold the view that men have to be made into *homunculi* otherwise there will be chaos as people pursue their self-interests. Figure 1 shows that it is a vicious cycle.

How can the cycle be converted into a virtuous one? An answer is beyond me at present. What I guess I know are some of the issues to be faced. The vicious cycle derives some of its energy from the basic assumption dependency (Bion, 1961) around which organizations are mobilized. The dependency and social passivity present in the larger society are taken across the boundary of enterprises by individuals as role-holders, and vice versa. Dependency of a basic assumption nature is preeminently available for study in enterprises. In education (Lawrence and Hakim-Goldsbrough, 1973; Lawrence and Robinson, 1975) and in industry (Lawrence et al., 1975) one keeps rediscovering, as a consultant, the social process of dependency. Often it makes the consultant feel depressed. This kind of experience I take, however, to be part of the role; he is available for projections. The experience of basic assumption dependency has its outcomes: 'the insidious costs of excessive dependency [are] erosion of self-esteem, chronic feelings of helplessness and depression' (Menninger, 1972). These are present very often in the consultant–client relationships and the consultant is available to receive these feelings from the client. These have to be contained and then made available through working hypotheses and interpretations, in order that the client has an opportunity to reintroject them on his or her authority. And there is a sense in which this essay has some of these qualities and an element of this task.

To acknowledge the helplessness, the social impotence, the loss of self-esteem, the social paranoia, the individual and social depression, would be to enter the disarray, chaos, and uncertainty that the breaking of excessive individual dependency, or its collective counterpart, social passivity, would incur. Alvarez (1974) has pointed to the psychic territory: the exploration of 'the nexus of anger, guilt, rejection, love and destructiveness'. To this can be added that other complex nexus: the bond, link, relatedness, relationship, or whatever 'it' is that joins or dissociates individuals through their roles to or from their groupings.

One constraint is that it is increasingly difficult for the individual to experience, let alone to name, these nexuses. Hypotheses to explain this difficulty have been offered. There is increasing narcissism; lack of questioning of taken-for-granted assumptions about authority; myths of political relatedness. Primarily, however, the constraint is anxiety against experiencing disarray. (In a mass society the freedom to experience anxiety is removed by the conventional belief that anxiety equals sickness and is to be wished away by means of tranquillizers.)

But anxiety, disarray, chaos, uncertainty are the seedbeds of creativity for renewed being. So I am postulating that we need to demystify assumptions about the social and political connectedness of individuals to society by putting them into doubt, making them uncertain; interpreting unconscious social processes; altering modes of knowing the social worlds of men and women.

Clearly, I am searching for ways of making real social hope. Despite the constraints, I come back to the proposition that managing oneself in role is a realizable value. It starts from the individual in his role in his enterprise questioning his responsibility and authority as a member of that enterprise. Hope cannot be placed in large-scale changes in society, in what passes for education in industrial societies, in consumer education, or in messianic movements. Social hope begins with men and women questioning cultural assumptions and taking authority for interpreting them, no matter where that search for truth leads. But that implies that they have made themselves sufficiently aware of the fact and process of death to make life worth the questioning.

References

Alvarez, A. (1974) *The Savage God*. Harmondsworth: Penguin Books.

Barham, P., and Lawrence, W. G. (1974) 'Some notes on Tavistock working conferences'. *Group Analysis*, **VII**, no. 2.

Bion, W. R. (1961) *Experiences in Groups*. London: Tavistock Publications.

Bion, W. R. (1976) 'Interview'. *Group and Organizational Studies*, **1**, no. 3.

Freud, S. (1915) 'Thoughts for the times on war and death'. Reprinted in J. Strachey (ed.) *The Standard Edition of the Complete Psychological Works of Sigmund Freud*. London: Hogarth Press and the Institute of Psychoanalysis, 1953, Vol. 14.

Freud, S. (1973) *Civilization and its Discontents*, trans. J. Riviere, ed. J. Strachey London: Hogarth Press.

Friedenberg, E. Z. (1973) *Laing*. Glasgow: Fontana/Collins.

Fromm, E. (1976) *To Have or to Be*. London: Cape.

Fromm, E. (1977 edn) *The Anatomy of Human Destructiveness*. Harmondsworth: Penguin Books.

Hampden-Turner, C. M. (1973) 'Radical man and the hidden moralities of social science'. *Interpersonal Development*, **2**, no. 4.

Howe, I. (1971) *Decline of the New*. London: Gollancz.

Lawrence, W. G., and Hakim-Goldsbrough, C. (1973) *The Schools Reception Centre of the Commonwealth Institute*. Tavistock Institute of Human Relations Document No. 871.

Lawrence, W. G., and Miller, E. J. (1976) 'Epilogue' In E. J. Miller (ed.) *Task and Organization*. London: Wiley.

Lawrence, W. G., and Robinson, P. (1975) *An Innovation and its Implementation: Issues of Evaluation*. Tavistock Institute of Human Relations Document No. 1069.

Lawrence, W. G., Barham, P., Jones, P., Mant, A., and Miller, E. J. (1975) *Towards Managerial Development for Tomorrow*. Tavistock Institute of Human Relations Document No. 1119.

McLuhan, M., and Nevitt, B. (1972) *Take Today; the Executive as Dropout*. New York: Harcourt Brace Jovanovich.

Menninger, R. (1972) 'The impact of group relations conferences on organizational growth'. *International Journal of Psychotherapy*, **22**.

Menzies, I. E. P. (1975) 'Thoughts on the maternal role in contemporary society'. *Journal of Child Psychotherapy*, **4**, no. 1.

Mills, C. Wright (1970 edn) *The Sociological Imagination*. Harmondsworth: Penguin Books.

O'Neill, J. (1972) *Sociology as a Skin Trade*. New York: Harper Torchbooks.

Poulantzas, N. (1969) 'Capitalism and the State'. *New Left Review*, No. 58.

Schawartz, E. (1971) *Overskill*. New York: Ballantine Books.

Thompson, E. P. (1968 edn) *The Making of the English Working Class*. Harmondsworth: Penguin Books.

Trist, E. L., and Bamforth, K. (1951) 'Some social and psychological consequences of the long-wall method of coal-getting'. *Human Relations*, **4**, pp. 3–38.

Williams, R. (1974 edn) *The English Novel from Dickens to Lawrence*. St Albans: Paladin.

Index

254